M000295717

THE CINEMATIC FOOTPRINT

THE CINEMATIC FOOTPRINT

Lights, Camera, Natural Resources

NADIA BOZAK

RUTGERS UNIVERSITY PRESS

NEW BRUNSWICK, NEW JERSEY, AND LONDON

LIBRARY
NORTHERN VIRGINIA COMMUNITY COLLEGE

Library of Congress Cataloging-in-Publication Data

Bozak, Nadia.

The cinematic footprint : lights, camera, natural resources / Nadia Bozak.

p.   cm.

Includes bibliographical references and index.

ISBN 978–0–8135–5138–8 (hardcover : alk. paper) — ISBN 978–0–8135–5139–5 (pbk. : alk. paper)

1. Motion picture industry—Environmental aspects.   2. Motion pictures—Production and direction—Environmental aspects.   I. Title.

PN1993.5.A1B69 2012

791.43'09—dc22

2011001087

A British Cataloging-in-Publication record for this book is available from the British Library.

Image of Allakariallak fishing (by Robert Flaherty) is reprinted by permission of the Cinémathèque québécoise.

Parts of this book are modified versions of previously published work.

Portions of chapter 2 appeared in "Firepower: Herzog's Pure Cinema and the Internal Combustion of War," in *Cineaction* no. 68 (2006).

Parts of chapter 4 appeared in "Four Cameras are Better than One: Division as Excess in *Mike Figgis' Time Code, Refractory: A Journal of Entertainment Media* vol. 14 (2008): available online at http://blogs.arts.unimelb.edu.au/refractory/catergory/browse-past-volumes/volume-14.

An alternate version of chapter 5 appeared in "Digital Neutrality: Agnès Varda, Kristan Horton and the Ecology of the Cinematic Imagination" in *Quarterly Review of Film and Video* 28, no. 3 (2011).

All are reprinted here with kind permission of the journals and their editors.

Copyright © 2012 by Nadia Bozak

All rights reserved

No part of this book may be reproduced or utilized in any form or by any means, electronic or mechanical, or by any information storage and retrieval system, without written permission from the publisher. Please contact Rutgers University Press, 100 Joyce Kilmer Avenue, Piscataway, NJ 08854–8099. The only exception to this prohibition is "fair use" as defined by U.S. copyright law.

Visit our Web site: http://rutgerspress.rutgers.edu

Manufactured in the United States of America

Typesetting: BookType

To Elizabeth Johnston, my pioneer grandmother.
May roots be respected and also transcended.

CONTENTS

Acknowledgments   ix

Introduction: 1

1   Energy   17

2   Resource   53

3   Extraction   88

4   Excess   121

5   Waste   155

Conclusion   189

Notes   205
Bibliography   223
Index   231

ACKNOWLEDGMENTS

I would like to express my gratitude to Linda Hutcheon, Charlie Keil, Thomas Lahusen, Peter Fitting, Eric Cazdyn, and Dudley Andrew for their support, insight, and guidance. Thank you to my brother Michael, Dad and Sara, my Uncle Don for that much-needed lift, and my dear friends Brian Beaton and Lila Graeme. Thank you to everyone at Rutgers University Press and especially to Anne Sanow and Leslie Mitchner for their encouragement and patience. Most of all I give thanks to my mother, an endless source of inspiration, wisdom, and comfort.

THE CINEMATIC FOOTPRINT

INTRODUCTION

This book is about the inextricable relationship between moving images and the natural resources that sustain them. The terms of this relationship between oil and cinema, the biosphere and the cinema's need for its energy, are contained in a photograph taken by Robert Flaherty in 1922 of an Inuk hunter Allakariallak, known now as "Nanook of the North." Let this book begin here, with the Inuk hunter and the movie camera, and the resource energy embedded therein (frontispiece). I could not have arrived at this image without the inspiration of Dudley Andrew's essay "Roots of the Nomadic." It is here that Andrew sees in Nanook a man directly tied to the seal he hunts, and in that seal a "mobile, subaqueous source of oil," whose caloric energy and economic value, Andrew states, would have burned in Nanook's lanterns and in his body and so given life to the film itself, energizing the very projector and screen where Flaherty's Arctic images premiered in New York in 1924.[1] "Roots of the Nomadic" was written some years before the present book was conceived of, and it was not read until some time after it was set in motion. That Andrew's reading of Nanook came before resource politics, ecology, and carbon footprints had so saturated the imagination testifies to two things: the essayist's perspicacity, first, and, second, that energy has always been discernable in cinema. Indeed, cinema is intricately woven into industrial culture and the energy economy that sustains it. The terms set by Andrew's essay and this image are uncommonly applicable to this book's structuring aspiration: to locate the energy in cinema. From there, an explicitly environmental line of inquiry can be broached, namely how cinema, thus energized, impacts upon Earth. This book asks how an awareness of movie making as an industry, one that is as plugged into "nature" and the resources it yields as any other, reconfigures our interpretive and practical approach to the cinematic image throughout film history, from its photographic beginnings to its digital present. This image of Nanook asks the questions at the heart of this book; and as it also supplies its "answer," it will be revisited in this book's conclusion. But as we make the journey to get there, I ask the reader to tuck Flaherty's photograph into memory and return to it as a visual point of reference—a reminder of this book's premise, as well as an ideal example of what will be called in the chapters that follow the "resource image."

Industrialization, mass-production, and the reproduced image are, as Walter Benjamin's famous essay maintained, mutually informing social determinants. Before "carbon-neutral" cinema (or Rupert Murdoch's mandate to "green" his media empire by 2010) made the connection between moving images and such things as fossil fuels and global warming so palpable, "The Work of Art in the Age of Mechanical Reproduction" set the terms necessary to intersect film-making technology and the biophysical world. Take, for example, Benjamin's evocation of poet and philosopher Paul Valéry, who wrote, and Benjamin quotes, "Just as water, gas, and electricity are brought into our homes from far off to satisfy our needs in response to a minimal effort, so we shall be supplied with visual or auditory images, which will appear and disappear with a simple movement of the hand."[2] Pumped in, piped out—water, natural gas, electricity, images, and sounds—where do these resources come from?

Arguing that mass production at once democratized the image and aestheticized politics, Benjamin's focus is on a work of art's reproduction and transmission and, specifically, the ways in which these processes dictate aesthetic parameters and reception, finally contributing to the political organization and ideological ordering of society at large. But before these dimensions are explicitly registered, we can push them back even further than the site of reproduction, transmission, or reception and ask by what processes are image-making mechanisms themselves generated? With processes requiring "a minimal effort," as it was and is still assumed, the ease of which is facilitated by energy resources such as gas and fuel and electricity which were in Valéry's 1930s being mainlined into most urban dwellings. What is immediately important here is that Benjamin foresaw that industry is embedded in the image itself, and, in Valéry's terms, accessing images at all means tapping into a complex system of resources—which is for most First World citizens today thoughtlessly simple: movies are accessed "on demand," in a steady flow, much as water, gas, and electricity. Now, though, the notion that natural resources are limitlessly available is quickly changing. The question that emerges, and with some urgency, is this: how might an end of oil affect not only the functioning of society and culture at large, and on a global level, but also, as a consequence, the way moving images are produced and received?

The image—cinematic, photographic, digital, or analog—is not only materially and economically inseparable from the biophysical environment, it is the environmental movement's primary pedagogical and propagandistic tool. Emphatic it is, then, that former U.S. vice president Al Gore was awarded the Nobel Peace Prize in recognition of his commitment to educating global citizens about the earth's mounting environmental imperilments. The prize, shared with the United Nation's Intergovernmental Panel on Climate Change, is the second award that Gore's environmental commitments have received—*An Inconvenient Truth*, the film based on his lecture tours, was recognized as Best Documentary Feature by the Academy Awards in 2006. The film's popularity has turned into a franchise of sorts, and confirms, as does the steady rise of environmental documentaries (many, such as *11th Hour*, replete with large budgets, Hollywood producers, and celebrity participation), that the image and digital technology (from DVDs to Internet forums to the operating logistics of Gore's PowerPoint slide show) is proving an auspicious way to educate and agitate—and ultimately spur into action—a global population that is inconceivably diverse. Because the decline of the biophysical world is seemingly all-inclusive, even equalizing, what better way to target and inform its citizens about what can be a complex scientific issue if not through visual media and the penetrating appeal of the moving image? Engaging the universal problem that is climate change requires a universal language. *An Inconvenient Truth* might ideally represent a significant moment of cultural dissemination wherein every citizen is targeted, inclusive of social strata or ethnicity, and is then mobilized to respond to, if not alter, the hastening conditions of global warming. Digital technology and its increased accessibility makes this ambition wholly possible—or at least in those specific realms where the image is, in Valéry's terms, as cheap and available as water or electricity.

An Inconvenient Truth's significance resides less in the nature of the film itself or the particulars of Gore's politics than in how it exemplifies digital technology, the cinematic image, and ecological politics (or rather the politics of global warming) are converging and coming to occupy a prominent place within the cultural mainstream. But of course environmentally motivated cinema and especially documentary has a long legacy outside of the sphere of dominant cinemas. "Alternative" and Indigenous enterprises such as Isuma Productions in Igloolik, Nunavut continue to exemplify how video imaging technologies (now digital video) and Internet distribution forward environmental concerns, and often in tandem with the preservation of Indigenous culture. Common to both dominant, alternative, and de-centered cinemas, however, is that the rise of digital technology in general and the digitization of cinema in particular finds parallel in the decline of natural realities; but that they are correlates and thus mutually inclusive is consistently overlooked. And yet what does digital technology, indeed all technology, represent if not the processes of industrialization that continue to perpetuate the myriad problems that come with global warming? Cinema and the image (digital and otherwise), like any other facet of our culture, simply cannot (as yet) unplug from the energy economy that is both the means and ends of current human existence. But, as the popularization and politicization of digitally rendered and often independently produced documentaries attests, the digital mode of expression and communication that is so far the pinnacle of industrialization might also play an integral role in challenging our culture's pernicious ecological habits. Indeed, Gore's film has been more than successful in its ability to reach, communicate with, and ultimately convince a sizable demographic of the importance of his message—and yet however sophisticated digital technology becomes, and however politically affecting as a result, it remains plugged into a turn-of-the-century system of energy generation that is so outdated it should long ago have been declared, like the commodities it has yielded, not just thoroughly inadequate and antiquated, but obsolete. Notably, the internal combustion engine has also not changed significantly since its standardization: as a result, the average car sold in the United States today yields under twenty miles to a gallon of gasoline, less than the ninety-nine-year-old Model T Ford did in its heyday.[3] So long as it remains in its current form, the cinema will be inextricably connected with these same unsustainable systems of resource consumption and energy production. Cinema is environmental; it is shot through with an ecological loop—open or closed, global and local. But it goes beyond the representation of nature or the environment in such eco-conscious films as *Earth* (Alistair Fothergill, 2007) or *An Inconvenient Truth*; cinema is, and has always been, environmentally determined and determining. As André Bazin recognized, the photograph comes from the earth and might be treated like "a phenomenon in nature, like a flower or a snowflake whose vegetable or earthly origins" might determine our interaction with them, as objects.[4] Once this fundamental relationship is recognized, cinema—all cinema—can be constituted as a product of and partner in a civilization that is not just industrialized but hydrocarbonized.

After oil refining, the production of motion pictures is Los Angeles's worst environmental offender. Such is the conclusion reached by UCLA's Institute of the Environment's "Southern California Environmental Report Card" for 2006 (each year's report focuses on a different industry). The report includes an assessment of the film and television industry's (FTI) direct and indirect contribution to environmental pollution in metropolitan Los Angeles, the state of California, and in the entire United States. Pollution generation, energy consumption, greenhouse gas emissions, and hazardous waste production are all considered. The environmental footprints of five other dominant industries (aerospace, apparel, hotel, petroleum refining, and semiconductor production) are weighed against that of the film and television sector. The report's intention was threefold: estimate the amount of air pollutants and greenhouse gases attributable to film and television activities; draw attention to examples of environmental "best practices" the industry has adopted; and assess the amount of attention paid to environmental issues in the industry's major trade publications. Finally, the report assigned the FTI a grade reflective of both its environmental achievements thus far and also the obstacles that this industry—termed a "complex enterprise"—still faces as it endeavors to produce and circulate moving images.[5] The grade assigned: C.[6]

The report's film and television section was derived from a much more extensive document: "Sustainability in the Motion Picture Industry," produced by UCLA in 2006 for California's Integrated Waste Management Board (CIWMB). The authors of the report, Charles Corbet and Richard Turco, acknowledge certain limitations within their methodology and caution that their findings are tentative. The geographical boundaries of the study, for example, were confined to a thirty-mile radius in metropolitan Los Angeles, the "most heavily filmed area in the world" where 75 percent of all film and television production takes place.[7] Nevertheless, Corbet and Turco conclude authoritatively that the motion picture and television industry's most glaring indulgence—if not abuse—is the amount of energy it uses. This as opposed to "visible" streams of environmental impact, such as solid or hazardous waste which have already received attention within the industry, evidenced by certain reduction and recycling initiatives duly noted in their report. Energy consumption, though, is mostly intangible and invisible, but is nonetheless significant when aggregated over the large numbers of individuals and firms who engage in profligate amounts of generator use, vehicle driving, and—in particular—idling during production. But what really motivated UCLA to commission the report was to expose the fact that film and television are industries and depend upon natural resources, and therefore impact the biophysical world. Embedded in every moving image is a complex set of environmental relations.

The UCLA report remains the go-to guide for carbon-neutral film initiatives and organizations in the United States; role models are those films noted in Corbet and Turco's "Best Practices" section. Ali Selim's *Sweet Land* (2005) is one such film. The independent production will bear a modest legacy on Earth, or so it intends. For while the film generated favorable criticism, its carbon footprint is negligible. Selim's post-production investment in a reforestation project in Germany and another distributing compact fluorescent lighting in Jamaica has offset "every mile driven by every vehicle, every gas receipt . . . every airline ticket, every actor who traveled, every pound of film," that went into making his film.[8] A more conventional example is Roland Emmerlich's *The Day After Tomorrow*, a film that grossed $186 million, had a budget of $125 million, and boasted one of the highest box-office sales of films released in the United States in 2004.[9] Because its plot engages the fallout of abrupt climate change, director and cowriter Emmerlich sought to ensure that production be consistent with the film's message by not itself contributing to global warming. Emmerlich contracted a carbon offsets provider to plant trees and invest in climate-friendly technology to counteract the CO_2 emissions generated by his film's production. The final bill: $229,000 to offset the 10,000 tons of CO_2 emissions generated by *The Day After Tomorrow*. The provider, The CarbonNeutral Company, claims to have coined and registered the term "carbon neutral" in 1998. Notably, the company granted *An Inconvenient Truth* its carbon neutral status in 2006. The emergent carbon economy, including offsets and carbon trading, is questionable on several levels; primary critiques include the difficultly of monitoring and regulating such intangible deliverables, while programs themselves merely allow industry and individuals (the viewers at home in the case of FTI) to absolve themselves of guilt or fulfill obligatory quotas instead of actually changing those detrimental practices directly responsible for resource depletion and environmental degradation.[10]

The evenhanded report does acknowledge the fraught politics of the carbon economy finding profitability in global warming, and goes on to cite industry case studies that actively demonstrate environmentally responsible behavior. The most interesting is ReUse People, a nonprofit organization that dismantles and recycles film sets. A typical big-budget movie will consume immense amounts of resources and produce, as a result, comparable waste. The two *Matrix* sequels, both released in 2003 (excessive in itself), were shot on three separate studio sets, as well as on the streets of Oakland and Alameda Point. One set was constructed out of 90 tons of material, wood, and polystyrene blocks; a second consisted of 300 tons of material, consisting of eight building facades; while an approximation of a freeway used more than 7,700 tons of concrete, 1,500 tons of steel, and 1,500 tons of wood.[11] A collaboration between Warner Bros., the Alameda County Waste Management Authority, and ReUse People managed to recycle 97.5 percent of all the set material. And yet, though positive as such, the report remains objective, if not neutral, and resists levying critique or suggesting further modifications. Indeed, UCLA'S report (and its CIWMB source) targets a contemporary dominant film industry and takes for granted that in order to render cinema an ecological practice, and ecology a cinematic one, we must heed those examples of sustainable filmmaking that are already—and often in spite of themselves—extant if not in our midst. Now, more than ever, cinema exceeds the conventional in situ Hollywood model. Globalization is not the only factor. As digital technology conflates the traditional roles of practitioner and the consumer, all dimensions of the moving-image industry are radically upended. Similarly, ecological consciousness is transforming the producer/consumer binary; industry is also a consumer (of resources) and the consumer is a producer (of carbon, pollutants, e-waste, and other forms of environmental residue). The report's most glaring omission is the role played by the consumers of film and television, those private individuals upon whom digital technology—advances in and cheapening of—confers increasing amounts of power and responsibility.

As Michel de Certeau has argued, the conventional association between consumption and "inertia" perpetuates an opposition between an elite set of producers and a passive mass of consumers. Taking the hermeneutics of reading as an example, de Certeau maintains that the everyday encounter with texts (either written or image-based) is anything but neutral. Rather, as each reader and each reading produces a text unique from its author's intentions, such acts of culture and information reception are inherently creative and—more importantly—active. This recognition liberates the so-called nonproducer and ultimately destabilizes the binary opposition between production and consumption, bestowing both agency and responsibility upon all of us—the heretofore inert consumer of words and images.[12] Ideally, digital technology's accessibility and network culture's broadening reach can, when harnessed, hasten the upending of social and political stratification. Though moving-image consumption is increasingly domesticated, consumers of images are not just individuals, they—we—are a collectivity, a mass. Add to this the fact that though digital technology might encourage social withdrawal, in its ideal form it is a tool of civic connectivity. As a point of comparison, while carbon offsetting is a potentially viable part of minimizing global warming, more can be accomplished by altering routine patterns of resource consumption—for example, by reducing reliance on cars and other forms of individuated mechanized transportation.[13] And is not the cinema also a form of mechanized mobility? If Susan Sontag's "ecology of the image" were updated for the twenty-first century's green economy, cinema—as a necessity and a privilege—would also need to be conserved, treated as a resource that is, at least in its dominant manifestation, unsustainable and potentially nonrenewable.

A carbon-neutral cinema formally and incontrovertibly points to a distinct set of relations between filmmaking and environmentalism, as well as between filmmaking and the biophysical world. Fossil fuels and natural resources drive the global economy and their availability and fluctuating prices determine the conditions of all our lives—that the moving image or any other culture industry is embroiled in the business of extracting and burning earth-bound energies should not be a surprise, and yet it is. As public consciousness is ever more alerted to (and by) the depth of the impact our behavior has upon land and air and water, our flesh and our breathing, connecting the dots between all human activity, industrial, social, or cultural, and our civilization's need for increasing amounts of natural resources to remain buoyant is becoming easier. Now, at this moment, the theory, history, and practice of making films can assume an explicit awareness of environment, that images, however intangible or immaterial they might heretofore appear to be, come bearing a physical and biophysical makeup, and leave behind a residue—a cinematic "footprint," as it were.[14]

That the cinema is connected to the earth is nothing new, and neither is making movies which for various reasons, economic or social, aesthetic or ideological, scrimp on budget and scale back on resources. If homemade, do-it-yourself, low- or no-budget fare is included in the mix, and encompasses transnational video and new media, most cinemas can be situated as ecological in that it is economical and low-impact by default. Such conservation is nothing radical or new, but simply a reformulation of the daily living requirements (rather than the lifestyle choices) of most global citizens. But as environmental politics saturates the imagination and populations become more self-aware (if not self-regulating) in their ecological behavior, cinema can be seen an ecological practice. Models and precedents exist, not only within the history of cinema but also in some of its current (perhaps less privileged) applications, as well as in other modes of expression such as painting, photography, philosophy, literature, and, indeed, in the very act of seeing. Reevaluating these modes and moments in the history, theory, and practice of peripheral cinemas demonstrates how cinema and the image have always been environmentally determined (and determining) and also how film, like life, can be more proactively or intentionally ecological.

But carbon-neutrality as a category, and resource consciousness more generally, *is* new to dominant, industrial filmmaking, its theory and history, which are only lately aware of the environmental relationships and dependencies that bind celluloid and videotape and laser discs to the earth. Situations of imminent crisis have a way of exposing the supply chain, and its network of essential and often imbalanced relationships between consumer and supplier, supplier and source. From big budget features such as Emmerlich's, or shoestring documentaries like *Saba and the Rhino's Secret* (Saba Douglas-Hamilton, 2006), however idealistic the carbon-neutral stamp, certifying a movie's practical ecology is significant in that it forces cinema's viewers, theorists, and practitioners alike to confront movie making as industry, a technology. Carbon-neutrality burdens moving images and our consumption of them with a set of environmental consequences that extend beyond the immediate realm of the theater or film shoot and into that of everyday living. But carbon-neutrality's intersection with cinema is as yet peripheral and even in its best intentions does not go far enough to implicate cinema as a facet of hydrocarbon culture, or posit that making movies and distributing and watching them will, like all industrial activity, be radically altered by rising energy prices. A vocal and vital selection of farsighted economists remind us that as energy supplies dwindle and oil prices rise, the economy slows, slumps, and falls into recession. So the cycle goes, rebuilding around a new supply only to crash again, until steady sources of alternate energy resources are developed and adapted and the energy economy retools itself around these fresh-faced inventions—solar, wind, nuclear, out-and-out primitivism—that is, nothing at all. In the meantime, we hydrocarbon citizens must scale back on the energy we do consume, and that means rationing, relying on backyard gardens and bicycles, web conferences instead of business travel, and thus (according to Jeff Rubin) making our worlds that much smaller.[15] And what of Netflix's ousting of Blockbuster—is the ascendancy of live-streaming over the more analog practice of in-hand DVD rental not a significant indicator of the shifting nature of the energy economy?

Consider that the electrification of the industrial world was not necessarily enabled by electricity's invention itself, but rather by the centralization of electricity supplies. When, beginning in the late 1870s in San Francisco, electrical power went commercial, the power and reach of generating stations extended out, drawing whole regions into the orbit of electrical and then hydroelectric service, and, ultimately, entrenching what would become a profound social and cultural dependency. As any blackout reminds us, the consequences of such intractable reliance upon a seemingly invisible form of energy are only fully understood upon system failure, when panic takes hold and a "paralysis" sets in.[16] Without electrical power and artificial light, the pillars of modernity—the factory, the city, the cinema—would not have developed as they have. In the case of the moving image, without electric power movie making would not have become an industry, and one that remains characterized by a dependence on the same centralized power supplies that facilitate almost all dimensions of industrial life. The question that needs to be asked, then, and for both theoretical and practical purposes, is the extent to which cinema, if denied what are our industrial culture's necessary resources, would be disabled (from fossil fuels to the electricity it generates, to the coltan and other ethically wrought geological materials packed into all and sundry electronic capacitors). Would cinema come to an end? Or is the moving image already one step ahead of the questions energy economists are asking?

During a panel discussion on carbon-neutral filmmaking at the 2007 Planet in Focus Film and Video Festival, a documentary filmmaker presented a direct and emotionally charged challenge to the participants and their assortment of efforts to make film production more sustainable. The documentarian argued, with some force, that an oil crisis was too imminent (his figure was thirteen years hence) and its fallout would be too catastrophic for the panacea of sustainable production practices to cope with. Indeed, with transportation and electricity suddenly unavailable, the filmmaker claimed, human culture will implode and the panelists' eco-conscious mandates will no longer matter. We need to do more, he said, to save cinema from disaster. After a stretch of silence, a lone response came from a freelance environmental advisor who asked, somewhat rhetorically and with certain resonance: given the calamitous terms thus outlined, would not filmmaking be the first thing to go? Indeed, will not a full-blown energy crisis or environmental disaster simply deem the cinema expendable? Though a clear answer was not forthcoming, it might have reasonably been a reluctant "yes," but only if the cinematic image is assumed to be a luxury and not a cultural necessity. This exchange between the documentary filmmaker and the carbon-neutrality advocate frames the problems that this book intends to address: if, indeed, film is a necessary medium, the question must be reformulated, and we should ask instead how film can avert its own disaster and learn to exist without resource dependence. How, then, can cinema separate itself from conventional means of energy and resources? Can film exist without film, its resource-bound support surfaces and infrastructures, and thereby provide a model for sustainable daily living? Eco-consciousness is saturating public life, informing political discourse and consumer spending, and invigorating marketing strategies with new tricks and tactics. As we amend our lives in accordance with real or perceived urgencies and emergencies, cultural theory and film theory in particular, somewhat cynically, lags behind. Environmental analytics exist, however, in philosophy, science, and political discourse, and once assumed and trained on film theory, history, and practice, just such an environmental lens exposes a selection of precedents and models that make an autonomous and sustainable cinema not just a possibility but a living, breathing reality.

Digital technology is of tremendous significance here, for it is at this moment, when cinema has as yet to be thoroughly digitized, that it can be configured into a self-sufficient and ecological mode of expression and communication. Can it make our lives more local, and thus our economy more environmentally sound? Or will digital technology merely contribute to the problem, further entrenching patterns of resource abuse and profligate rates of consumption which are, arguably, the root cause of environmental depreciation? But what if, when the crisis comes, cinema does not go blank? Would this mean that moving images have solved their own internal energy problems and the point is no longer relevant? At that stage, then, cinema could provide culture at large with a model for ecological practice and responsible environmental behavior. The problems that digital technology possesses (system failure, accelerated rates of innovation, consumption and resultant format migration, the potential disappearance of "born digital" information, a growing electronic waste epidemic) speaks to factors of sustainability and also suggests that it is fragile, inchoate, malleable. Digitization and environmental awareness are developing quickly, and they are often doing so in parallel. If these two defining marks of the new century were to intersect more deliberately, the end result—a digital consciousness and an energy revolution (as opposed to the skewed variants we have now, a digital revolution and an energy consciousness)—would mean something fundamental has changed.

Throughout the chapters that follow, some of the more invisible or indirect relationships between the image and the environment are considered. Ultimately, *The Cinematic Footprint: Lights, Camera, Natural Resources* posits that an ecological cinema is nothing new. Cinema has always demonstrated an awareness of its industrial self and therefore a connection to the environment, the realm from which it derives its power, raw materials and, often enough, subject matter. But because this biophysical layer is so inextricably embedded within film's basic means of production, distribution, and reception, its effects remain as overlooked as they are complex. This book theorizes the intimate and heretofore overlooked relations between the consumption of natural resources and film's ontological, aesthetic, and political dimensions. Because this book argues that cinematic history and theory can (and, indeed, ought to be) reappraised in light of the emerging ascendancy of environmental politics, all films, all cinema, could logically be included within my analytical parameters. Primary focus, however, is allotted to peripheral examples: documentary cinema, experimental films, Third and Fourth cinema, photography and installation art, as well as certain narrative features. For the most part, the texts I use here more do not overtly represent an environmental issue. Rather, they reflexively engage with and theorize themselves as films; thus addressing the technological and industrial dimensions of filmmaking, they in fact highlight the resource-derived, energy-driven essence of moving images. Of import here are films that reveal how specific formal or aesthetic choices (the duration of a take, the amount of natural light that is used, the stasis or mobility of the camera) reveal and critique the hydrocarbon ideology attached to resource consumption and abuse, and which is manifest in correlate aesthetics, something we might call the "hydrocarbon imagination."

This book is concerned with issues of production and representation and does not deal with the dimensions of cinematic reception or dissemination on a comprehensive level. Chapters are organized around certain conceptual and practical procedures that transform resources (light, film stock, labor) into moving image, from chemically derived celluloid to the binary-based and easily expended digital image, companion to the disposable (digital) camera. But while it composes a distinctly environmental trajectory of cinema, this book likewise historicizes, theorizes, and critiques these same developmental stages, and also challenges the Utopian and apocalyptic tensions that characterize environmental consciousness, urgencies, and emergencies, and its attendant politics. Interknit into the fabric of *The Cinematic Footprint* are the ecological dimensions inherent in the shift from a tangible celluloid-based cinema to that of digital filmmaking, which is still so erroneously assumed to be immaterial or at least less residual than hardcopy predecessors. An important goal of this book is to expose the energy requirements, economy of obsolescence, and, subsequently, lingering afterlife of digital technology concealed behind the crisp, clean infrastructure that supports binary-based images and information. "Going digital" is more than ever considered a default means of "going green" and is generally taken for granted as having sustainability built in. This book does not perform an empirical analysis of which mode is more or less wasteful, for the technology itself is inert. What is wasteful is how much we use it, how many images are produced and used. Of great import here is revealing the mythology behind the notion that digital images are immaterial; like analog formats, digital is industrial and each image consumed bears a material life. Images come from somewhere and are plugged into an energy economy that is becoming less of a phantasm. The point this book intends to make is that whichever the format, reducing the cinematic footprint, or any other deleterious ecological impact, needs to be done on the level of scale—limiting consumption and expenditure, however idealistic that may be. The tension that now pits cinema's material past against its ostensibly immaterial future corresponds with the sharp decline of natural reality; this parallel set of conditions fully evince the real and increasingly palpable overlap between the image and the environmental, embroiling both in a distinct set of politics. But that digital and environmental concerns are still emergent and not yet fully consolidated means that they are likewise fragile and malleable. Reconfiguring our priorities and using technology to Earth's advantage might take the shape of a digital consciousness and an environmental revolution (as opposed to a digital revolution and an environmental consciousness, or so the rhetoric is duly applied). *The Cinematic Footprint* is just such a reconfiguration of terms, and perhaps the first spark in a necessary debate about technology, cultural production, their shelf lives, and the residual effects of both.

Chapter 1, "Energy," argues that the cinematic image can be thought of as fossilized light, thus practically and metaphorically equating cinema with the geological dimensions of the naturally derived fuels (fossilized sunlight) that continue to enable industrial society and culture. This chapter engages Bazin's theory of the mummy complex and, specifically, the image as an unmediated inscription of reality or embalmed time. The films included here are ones that reveal the cinema's essences (energy, light, motion) through the pronounced absence of these same qualities. From Chris Marker's *La Jetée* and *Sans Soleil*, to Lev Kuleshov's experimental "films without film," these films are entropic, "sunless," perhaps rendered in situations of resource deprivation—scarcity rather than plenty—and so are the pillars of what might be considered a post-cinematic or resource-neutral filmmaking. The relationship between the natural resource, the image resource, and oil security is taken up in chapter 2, "Resource." While interrogating the way digital technology intersects with and represents oil procurement in Iraq and so-called secure oil in the Gulf of Mexico, this chapter likewise argues for the cinematic image as a material resource, one that is refined into a political tool and employed as ideological weaponry. The war over oil, for oil, finds a counterpart in its dominant mode of cinematic representation. Digital images of the Iraq conflict and, more recently, the gushing fuel deep in the Gulf of Mexico, show that the real objectives of oil greed is not the fuel itself, but what it facilitates, namely the privileges of industrial and post-industrial culture: the digital innovations that are its current apogeal achievement and thus the exponential speed and ubiquity of the digital image itself. Werner Herzog's *Lessons of Darkness* and Deborah Scranton's *War Tapes* illustrate some of the differences between analog and digital representations of oil war, while Samira Makhmalbaf's *Blackboards* reduces communication systems and means transportation down to its most rudimentary, corporeal essence, arguing for the possibility to survive without machines and be driven by something other than fossil fuels. Chapter 3, "Extraction," focuses on Jennifer Baichwal's *Manufactured Landscapes*, the photographer Edward Burtynsky, and the ways in which cinema and photography directly and indirectly formulate landscape as a both an aesthetic category and a physical reality, both representing and contributing to the decay of the environment. This chapter maps the relation between nineteenth-century photography's search for pristine natural vistas and digital cinema's increasing reliance upon computer generated or virtual spaces, both of which offer Utopian alternatives to an increasingly industrialized and uninhabitable world. The resultant paradox this chapter analyzes is how the image fabricates idealized perceptions of natural land-scapes while the means of its technological and industrial logistics actively erode them. Jia Zhang-ke's *Still Life* is brought in as a digital counterpoint to Baichwal's insistently analog format. Questions of electronic waste are taken up here, as is the discourse surrounding the representation of garbage and other disposables—from computer products to land itself, and, most recently, an oil-slicked Gulf of Mexico—Burtynsky's consistent choice of subject matter. Chapter 4, "Excess," theorizes the long take as an exhibi-tion of waste. Beginning with Georges Bataille's theory of economic excess, this chapter conceptualizes cinema in terms that are literally monumental, positing that Andy Warhol's exemplary use of the long take in his *Empire*—a "cinematic pyramid"—is a codified expression of industrial culture's access to and exploitation of time, space, and, significantly, material abundance. Meanwhile, this chapter argues, the ostensible democratization of digital cinema is manifested in the prevalence of the long take (the digital mode's shot of choice). James Benning's first digital film, *Ruhr*, is taken up in contrast to Warhol's portrait of industrial excess and Alexander Sokurov's *Russian Ark*, an example of the "digital Baroque," a literal, practical, and aesthetic rendering of the gluttony of image. "Waste," the subject of chapter 5, focuses on the residual life of accumulated and expended excess, and does so via a theoretical and practical concept described as "secondhand cinema." Beginning with Agnès Varda's *The Gleaners and I*, this chapter considers how cinema both creates waste (images, equipment, the residual effects of producing, distributing, and receiving film images) and also makes use of it. Digital cinema is weighed against analog so as to examine the tension cellu-loid preservation and the very possibility of digital's so-called ephemerality. Varda's work is set against representations of Hurricane Katrina—Spike Lee's *When the Levees Broke* and *Trouble the Water* by Carl Deal and Tia Lessin. The comparison foregrounds a biopolitics of disposability, and asks how the fate of the marginalized human subject and the unwanted image are directly linked to consumer culture's ideology of expendability and the paradoxical logic that renders intentionally impermanent objects out of durable, permanent materials. Zacharias Kunuk's *The Fast Runner* concludes this book. Kunuk's Nunavut-based video production company, I argue, points the way to the future of both cinema and oil security—and the direction is digital and the locale is the Far North. Kunuk's film is weighed against Robert Flaherty's *Nanook of the North* and the image evoked at the beginning of this introduction. The comparison does not concern the representation of Inuit so much the use of energy and the power of film and video as a means of cultural and planetary survival.

This book cannot be all things or cover all aspects of what could become an all-encompassing topic. If there is a guiding message here, it is that there is much work to be done. In order to deflect critique of what's missing, I'll say up front that this book does not address the concept of what is called "new media" in great depth. For example, video gaming, the medium that may, as film archivist Rick Prelinger has predicted, in fact overtake cinema, rendering it quaintly antiquated if not obsolete, is not taken up here. It should be engaged, but elsewhere, and perhaps when gaming has further consolidated its hold. The intention is to retain a cinematic focus, while at the same time addressing how cinema is converging with other interactive platforms, thus transforming the viewer into a user. Cinema is not "pure"; it now involves engagement with the Internet, for example, and other communications technology, a fact that will be addressed throughout this book. Separating out digital media, new media, communications, and moving-image technology is a slippery, if hazardous task, itself indicative of the twenty-first-century life of what is still, insistently, cinema. There is some convergence within this book, but effort is made to respect media specificity. And while much can be said about the enormous energy consumption of television, as well as of the staggering amount of e-waste generated by the great switchover from analog to digital broadcast standards (including upward of one hundred million obsolete analog TV receivers in the United States alone) substantial engagement with the televisual falls outside the present line of inquiry. This book's topic could conceivably address all cinema, as all cinema is hooked into the environment, its examples are drawn primarily from what is loosely regarded as the Second Cinema. These films interest me for they straddle dominate and peripheral realms, and thus draw from both "within" and "without" as they face the challenge of energy intensity, and likewise offer up solutions. Third or postcolonial cinema is touched on throughout as an ecological or sustainable cinema by default; but as the conclusion reveals, Fourth Cinema ought to occupy a more central position, as it points the way to cinema's and Earth's ecologically redemptive future.

This book does not attempt to rein in, frame, or otherwise contain ecology and cinema within a definitive narrative or theory. There is no true beginning here, nor middle or end, and to assign a definitive shape or arc to the problems and questions presented here would defeat the premise. Ecology, by its very definition, is unrestricted; it is impossible to say where nature stops and culture begins, or vice versa. We are now confronting the seeming infinitude of ways ecological degradation is rendering vulnerable every connection and dimension that holds together our daily lives and planetary future. Engaging with this topic entails writing and thinking in real time for indeed, the problems and questions taken up here seem to modify and broaden almost daily. This work accepts itself as malleable, subject to change and addendum, and so too must the reader. The ambition here is to set the conditions necessary to continue dialogue and debate. What does remain intractable, however, is the template this book provides for reimagining cinema and infusing its history, future, and present manifestations with the recognition that culture is environmentally determined and determining. As the 2010 British Petroleum oil spill disaster, the Iraq conflict, the Alberta Tar Sands, and now the momentous shift toward the Arctic's natural resources exemplify, oil is becoming ever more scarce and precious and its procurement increasingly more dangerous—sunk, as it is, far deeper into geopolitical strife, the earth, and the sea. And we and our images are all plugged into it, our imaginations fueled by it as well. The footprint is a fitting metaphor, encompassing the very paradoxical dimension at the heart of cinema—mobility and stasis, nomadism, and institution, the obsession with the ephemeral and the urge to preserve a physical legacy. What kind of cinematic footprint will we leave behind? And where will that impression be "felt," or "seen"? In the most filmed city on Earth, in the Arctic's taiga, or off the shore of the Louisiana Gulf coast—or everywhere, equally, and on-demand, for only $7.99 a month?

CHAPTER 1

ENERGY

Carbon-neutrality is achieved by balancing out a measured amount of released carbon with an equal amount that has been sequestered or offset, often by purchasing a requisite quantity of carbon credits. The widely used term is used primarily in the context of carbon dioxide releasing activities, often involving transportation, energy production, and industrial processes, such as the manufacturing of commodities. Low-carbon or carbon-neutral film initiatives elucidate that one such carbon-heavy industry is the making of moving images.[1]

Carbon-neutrality is indeed a rich term, loaded with discursive, if not poetic, possibility. When applied to filmmaking, as is increasingly the case, and then pushed to its literal and metaphorical limits, the implication is a cinema that does not leave a residue; a cinema, therefore, without a permanent infrastructure or, perhaps, any physicality at all. The carbon that proponents such as the Green Screens initiative—an environmental stewardship that oversees Canada's film and television industry—aim to neutralize is carbon dioxide, a greenhouse gas that traps solar energy as it is reflected off the surface of the earth and, thus hemmed in, warms the planet. Anthropogenic sources of carbon-dioxide emissions are, for example, deforestation and the burning of fossil fuels.[2] Taking the term carbon-neutrality literally is not overindulgent, for unpacking its rich rhetorical implications gets at the heart of some of the defining impulses our culture is currently negotiating: the rise of digital immateriality on the one hand, and the push for ecological neutrality on the other. Where these preoccupations converge is in a shared sense of the ephemeral: the ideology attached to both envisions an industrial culture, including its moving images, that leaves behind little or no evidence of its existence. Any film could be included here, for all cinema is, of course, literally composed of trapped light—what might be called fossilized sun. And yet certain exemplary films make overt attempts to conceptualize a cinema that functions "neutrally," "post-cinematically," without film, and other necessary resources and supplies. In order to interrogate carbon-neutrality and its correlate, the post-cinematic, we must first locate the heart of cinema, its fuel and perhaps even its spirit—the sun. The "fossil image" is the locus where geology, industrial civilization, and cinematic history intersect into an indelible fusion that is, like all matter and substance, traced back to the light (and energy) that comes from the sun.

Environmentalists, scientists, and natural historians continue to point out that the fossil fuel energy our civilization consumes, and at increasingly unsustainable rates, is finite. That fuel—which our engines combust, which forms our plastics, and which speeds crop growth—is a compressed energy derived from fossilized sunlight. As long as there is sun, the earth's fossil fuels could in fact be renewed, but the process of replacing what we have already reaped takes unimaginable amounts of time. So, rather than extract what is essentially sunlight from where it is hidden in sands, locked under the Arctic sea bed, a better way to manage that earth's power supply is to harvest it directly in the form of solar energy, much like the photographic or cinematographic camera—from the camera obscura to photochemical apparatuses to analog and digital video—all of which are in the business of sourcing the beneficence of the sun.[3]

As William J. Mitchell points out in his seminal study into the ways in which digital imaging technology is transforming the ethical, political, and aesthetic dimensions of how humans perceive the visible world, the basic physical distinctions between analog and digital modes of representation have fundamental cultural consequences. A digital photograph, Mitchell argues, is as different from a "traditional" photograph as both are from a painting.[4] What is essential here, however, is that both photographic modes are essentially configured around the sourcing of light. Heed needs to be paid to virtual reality, synthetic imaging, and the increased reliance upon Computer Generated Imagery (CGI) in motion pictures, but it still stands that images are powered by the sun in that all mediated vision is plugged into a larger fossil fuel economy.[5] So while Mitchell asks how digital imaging is "reconfiguring" how we negotiate phenomenological reality and thus conduct ourselves politically as we move through media-saturated landscapes, this book and this chapter asks how ecological awareness is reconfiguring Mitchell's reconfigured eye. The basic fact that fossil fuel is embedded in everything, no matter how ethereal or virtual, steps media theory back but also moves it forward. There is ecological difference between analog and digital forms of images, but those differences exist primarily in the physical infrastructure and residual lives of each. Getting at that difference begins with understanding how we might begin to see solar energy as the life source of our world and of the world of images.

The difference between digital and analogical images is that the former is a numerical *symbolization* of matter, while the latter is intaglio, a literal manipulation of matter; and that "matter" in both cases is the luminosity that radiates from the sun. David Rodowick reaches back to André Bazin to describe photographic image making as a sculpting of light as it falls upon the "hills and valleys"—the landscape, in other words—that compose raw celluloid stock and whose surface variations make images visible.[6] Digital data, however, lacks direct end-to-end interaction with light. What digitization is replacing is a chemical-based format: a pattern of silver salts interacts with the emulsion on photographic film and produces an analog transcription of the light that existed, right then and there, at the moment the photograph was taken.[7] In the case of analog video, light does not hit emulsion, but a sensor (such as a cathode ray tube), which then captures light's representation. Signals and transmissions make their way to magnetic tape, where the image is held, but is still an analog of that same indexical matter. Gone is the touchable impression of the referent, visible and tangible evidence of the phenomenal world: a fingerprint, a death mask, a footprint, a fossilization of light—the analogies abound testifying to the fascination industrial culture has with the very idea of the photographic image.[8] Digital imaging involves a conversion by a digital processor that translates received signals of light and movement into a binary code which is then reconverted back into an image. While this conversion introduces an extra step to the image-making process, digital is advantageous because by representing recorded images as numbers, reproduction is carried out with complete accuracy; nothing is lost, a copy is an exact replica and not the slightly degraded version an analog print would be. What comes with this fidelity and infinite reproduction is even further distance or separation between the image and its origin, screened picture and light source, the ontological ins and outs of which are the concern of media theorists and proponents of the auratic quality of analog formats.

The digital difference is not just in the image quality or delivery capabilities, but also in the machinery or support systems. While analog depends on a weighty infrastructure in order to turn light into latent image and then, after processing, into a strip of film, in fact, the only machine necessary to read the processed image is the human eye. Digital, however, because of conversion, renders the image infinitely less accessible, dependent as it is on sophisticated mechanics and engineering in order to produce the hardware needed to turn a data recording into legible images. Before sun makes the world visible, it makes it possible; it is the source of biophysical life, and as the substance of the moving images that document that life, it is also the fuel of that makes industry possible. Instead of inscribing patterns of luminosity on its celluloid support surface, and then through chemical processing, digital images, as Mitchell describes, are captured through a "transduction of radiant energy" into patterns of electrical current. But such image capture still uses sunshine indirectly, in the form of fossil fuel energy that that powers the operating systems which, taking over where the camera leaves off, manipulate data into images. After all, the digital camera is only part of the equation; the computer, its software and hardware both, must be factored in as well.

The Image World without Us

Instead of referring to the last 10,000 years as the Holocene or "recent epoch," the Anthropocene, or "human epoch," is a more accurate term to describe our planet's current interval of geological time.[9] The term clearly and precisely confronts the fact that the human ability to derive colossal amounts of power from fossil fuels is the principle determinant of how the biosphere has come to function—or, better to say, malfunction. Alan Weisman's *The World Without Us* boldly imagines a post-human Earth. Assuming this idea as a structuring device and narrative framework, Weisman explores the relationship between the earth and its sun without human interference. It is a powerful and resonant idea, bearing enormous implications. Weisman's narrative renders human culture distinctly fragile as our naturalized sense of permanence is replaced with the inevitability of termination. The significance attached to this semantic shift is Weisman's point of entry into an exploration of whether, or for how long, the Anthropocene would endure if humanity were suddenly and completely stamped out. If Earth was left alone, could it, Wiseman asks, thoroughly recover from our species' pernicious legacies? As he details the processes of reclamation that could potentially reverse humanity's ecological damage, the post-human perspective assumes a science-fictional tenor akin to the creation myths of Italo Calvino's *Cosmicomics* or Olaf Stapledon's *Starmaker*. Importantly, Weisman argues that our sturdiest and most durable infrastructures—bridges, military fences, and nuclear power stations—will in time erode and eventually decay. The grave concern Weisman alerts us to, however, is the danger posed by our more volatile infrastructures if humans are not present to monitor their decline. The pipelines of the Texas Oil Patch, for example, could over time succumb to pressurization and then combust; without a rescue mission or "top kill" procedure to extinguish it, the disaster would decimate flora and fauna and landscape perhaps irredeemably. Underlying the novelty of Weisman's post-human conceit and its ability to appeal to environmental anxieties is a profound philosophical, ethical, and political question. Is it possible to think about the environment altruistically, not for the benefit of future humanity, but for the future of the planet? Can we posit a nonanthropocentric environmentalism in which the planet's health, and not our own, is the primary motivation?

Transcending what might be thought of as an anthropocentric perspective or ideology outside the realm of science or fiction reverses the primacy of Cartesian philosophy and essentially undoes the intellectual and ideological foundations of Western civilization since the Enlightenment. Though Weisman's narrative is more concerned with imagining the earth without earthlings than with clarifying the terms of a new environmentalism, the implications of his contributions are indeed productive. Timothy Morton takes up the challenge as he attempts to think "an ecological state of human society" without the normative and culturally inscribed framework that is "nature."[10] But while cleaning the slate of the "ecological imaginary," loaded as it is with excess political and aesthetic baggage, Morton risks constantly replacing that which he strips away with constructs of his own. How, then, might we do away with devices and infrastructures of representation but still "represent"? How might one write without writing? Paint without painting? Render a film without a movie camera? Be a human but not think as one? Conceptualize the biophysical world without imposing something human upon it? Why should we even want to?

Engaging in this orphic conundrum is a human constant. Such is the challenge at the foundation of the art of storytelling, wherein an author attempts to capture the subjectivity of an "other," but with minimal interference from the author's own social, cultural, and political trappings. And so the last damnable, culturally determined perspective we might attempt to eschew is anthropocentricism; from dismantling the male gaze to denaturalizing the colonial imagination, the suggestion is that we must now think beyond our own sense of geological domination and biospheric entitlement. This is not a new impulse, but rather a return to a spiritual and philosophical mindset that was transformed by modernity. What modernity and its attendant humanism, rationalism, and habitual secularity ushered in was an end of infinity—a concept that determined how humans made sense of life on earth and, more importantly, of the earth itself. Human weakness in the face of what Zygmunt Bauman calls the "unperturbed solidity of the world" has determined human perceptions and experience since the beginning of recorded history.[11] Until the consolidation of modernity, life was understood as a confrontation between the transience of humans and the solidity of the earth, wherein the quest for longevity favored the phenomenal world, which was divinely equipped to outlive its inhabitants.[12] But when humans began inventing ways to harness and then dominate nature, "melting all that is solid," the belief in a greater infinity went with it; left in its wake was a modern condition of transience, or what Bauman terms "liquid modernity."[13] The end result is an overriding ideology of the ephemeral, faith in mere transience, and the conviction that nothing is thought to last forever. Planned technological obsolescence would seem the apotheosis of the transient postmodern condition Bauman describes. The difference now, however, is that because of industrial culture's overconsumption of just about everything, and the lingering toxicity of waste and pollution, the melting of all that is "solid" (refining fuels or harvesting forest and otherwise abusing biospheric life-support systems) undermines the same sense of human longevity it once bolstered—liquid life's residues are anything but transient.

Film theory has long negotiated the possibility and even inevitability of subtracting the human from cinema, a distinctly post-human impulse that in various ways envisions a post-human cinema which goes beyond the apparatus and the realm of knowable experience, foregrounding cinematic vision as its own energy source and engine, the prime mover of itself. Bazin's mythological utopia of cinematic realism and Paul Virilio's political dystopia of unadulterated cinematic vision can both be reduced to the same terms: the necessary disappearance of the sight prosthesis or the "hand of man" that mediates the image. According to Bazin's "myth of total cinema," the idea or essence of the cinematic precedes its invention; and that idea or essence is the means by which to satisfy the primordial desire to capture an authentic and unadulterated reflection of reality. Until it can be rendered without the intermediary, cinematic realism remains an ideal only, but one that is as old as humanity. Pure realism, as Bazin argued, is the goal and purpose of cinema and it exists as yet only in the imagination. An unattainable utopia, then, the cinema, as Bazin wrote in 1963, "has yet to be invented."[14] This paragon of a seamless, imperceptible satisfaction of humanity's urge to represent reality *realistically* is comparable to Virilio's conviction that human sight and imaging technology are on a path toward complete fusion, realized in the final eradication of the differences between eye and its prosthesis, the movie camera.[15] Cinema is, like Bazin imagined, the technological satisfaction of a primitive urge, a "primordial mixing of the human soul and the languages of the motor-soul," including philosophy, and, as for Bazin, pictorial and representational arts.[16] What connects these otherwise contradistinctive theorists, then, is the evocation of cinema as something primitive, essential; it is a component of the human condition rather than its result.

The Egyptian mummy, humankind's first statue, was a means of reproduction and preservation that took the initial step toward what would (or will) eventually be realized in the cinema, an art similarly premised on an embalming of time. Importantly, however, Bazin points out that the photographic or cinematographic image, modernity's manifestation of the "mummy complex," is no longer so anthropocentric but is concerned, rather, with creating an ideal reflection of the real world.[17] Indeed, the cinematic impulse is nothing new; its evolution has been long in coming. Film archivist Paolo Cherchi Usai traces the initial manifestation of the desire to inscribe living movement to the art of Chinese shadows, dating back to 180 B.C.[18] The emergence of digital technology and the so-called new media is accompanied by an ideology of newness and innovation, a widespread undercurrent perpetuated by media scholars as well marketing strategies within the technology industry itself. But by unearthing the technological continuity between our "new" medias and those "old" forms of the Victorians, say, or the Egyptians (as Bazin took for cinema's starting point) lays to waste what Charles Acland argues is an unfounded focus on newness and a belief that what is called new media represents a rupture with past technologies rather than a continuation. Archaeologies of film technology expose these roots, shattering the mythology of newness, and thus minimize the seemingly unprecedented urgencies that characterize our moment's obsession with erasure and impermanence, exemplified by the ostensible immateriality of digital images and information as well as the discursive richness that underwrites the pervasive rhetoric of the "carbon footprint." But though Acland and others who argue for a remediation principle underlying media innovation, ecological questions demand that materialist inquiries are pushed back even further when unearthing the complex social, cultural, and economic networks embedded in moving-image technology and take into account the fossil fuels that made it so.

Offsetting this overriding confusion between obsolescence and progress, Lev Manovich reminds us that new media is old media that has been digitized.[19] Dziga Vertov's cinema is an exemplar of how what is privileged as new technology in fact has long been extant—even on a theoretical level—for the Soviet's cinematic practice and theory represent a prescient distillation of human culture's representational impulses and visioning innovations, and is often cited as digital filmmaking's progenitor. The "mechanical eye," as Vertov wrote in 1923, for example, is "free of human immobility" and "limits of space and time"; the Soviet's words could be taken from any digital camera's marketing packaging.[20] Further, as the operator is absorbed by the camera at the conclusion of the filmmaker's monumental 1929 documentary *Man with a Movie Camera*, the cinematic apparatus exceeds its human dependency and acquires the status of the heroic. While the images the camera generates, meanwhile, become indistinguishable from the universe in which they were sourced, Vertov ambiguously insists, like Bazin and Virilio, that the future of cinema sees the camera and its accompanying apparatuses evolving into an ocular immateriality, the "kino-eye," which cannot be extracted from the reality it likewise creates and represents. For Vertov, like Bazin, cinema begins where the camera ends. The more obvious or overt the cinematic prosthesis, the more visible its infrastructure and its operative residues, the less ideally cinematic it becomes. Achieving a balance between what is represented and the means of representation, or between reality and the apparatus, suggests that same goals that drive carbon-neutrality and post-humanism: a residue-free, ecologically benign state of environmental symbiosis that exceeds the boundaries of physical materiality. The impulse toward realism and attendant diminution and eventual disappearance of cinematic infrastructure is strikingly reconfigured within the rhetoric of carbon-neutrality. Like the shift away from anthropocentricity, carbon-neutrality and the impulse toward a film-less film, a cinema without the camera, presents a state of equilibrium between energy captured and energy emitted. When matched with Virilio, Bazin, and Vertov, and placed within the broader trajectory of moving-image technology it is apparent that the so-called carbon-neutral cinema has always existed: a sustainable cinema which needs neither human operator nor refined fuel to exist but only, like the Chinese shadows of 2000 years ago, the consistent presence of sunlight or approximation thereof.

The Ephemeral Life of Film

The cinematic image is, like memory, inherently ephemeral, a quality determined by its basic chemical and storage structure, as well as audience demand for novelty. Statistics differ somewhat, but in general it is agreed that 80 percent of films from cinema's first three decades and 20–50 percent of all films produced have vanished.[21] Similarly, 95 percent of all artwork ever made is no longer in existence.[22] But this intractable feature does not preclude archivists, moving-picture makers, or consumers of ever-more powerful image retention technology from striving toward the unrealizable goal of memory preservation. Jean-Pierre Gorin comments that *La Jetée* (1962) and *Sans Soleil* (1982), by his elusive friend Chris Marker, are, like cinema itself, obsessed with the scientific procedure of "carbon dating." The suggestion that cinema could supersede memory and provide physical, tangible proof of when, where, and how an event took place is purely Bazinian: cinematic image as a mummification of time, a fossilization of place, and a document not of history proper, but of the human desire to ascertain history as it might have been. The cross-sectioned redwood tree that plays a prominent discursive role in the earlier *La Jetée* reappears in *Sans Soleil*. The sectioned tree, like cinema itself, is a way in which human culture attempts to stabilize memory, and so orient a sense of time and, therefore, of history. Innovation and technological evolution is the only difference between counting tree rings and watching or creating moving images as a way to map time; the means have altered, but the urge and the result remain the same. It is not just convenient that the analogy Gorin uses to explain a primary obsession of cinema (using compressed carbon to ascertain dates) infuses it within an environmental logic. Carbon is, after all, a naturally occurring chemical element and the basis of all planetary life. But a carbon-neutral cinema seems incongruous with what Gorin names as Marker's and cinema's most basic urge: to preserve time in material, tangible form so as to evoke and then revisit it. What carbon-neutral cinema suggests is that the production of the moving-image achieves an ecological balance: like the redwood tree, carbon-neutral practice absorbs as much carbon (dioxide) as it emits, thus eliminating any residue or carboniferous imprint. The suggestion is a cinema that will decompose, like the redwood tree, however slowly, and leave behind no residue or manifestation of carbon that could at some point in the future document or verify the occurrence of humankind and, therefore, of cinema itself.

But in its extremity carbon-neutral cinema is a film-less, incorporeal cinema: not cinema proper, but instead an ontological question. Does eliminating the traces of cinema entail erasing cinema itself? Without the umbilical cords of technology and the natural capital to support them, time is not kind the photographic or cinematographic image. Take for example the world's largest collection of photographs, owned by Corbis, a photograph licensing company. The archive is housed in a former limestone mine in Pennsylvania and buried within two hundred feet of geological layering; the climactic conditions therein guarantee the contents' integrity for 1,000 years. However, this anthropocentric initiative is in fact short-sighted, for it takes for granted the survival of the power generators that energize the dehumidifiers needed to create this ideal environment, as well as the supply of fossil fuels needed to run them.[23] Because of this precarious dependency, what is really being preserved for posterity is the preservation system itself, not the images. The Corbis mine will eventually be cleared of two kinds of resources, one natural, the other manufactured; the raw stone that has already been scooped out and, in time, the celluloid image. And while the celluloid image eventually submits to natural decomposition—nitrate stocks will, if properly preserved, survive for one hundred years—digital is limited by the fact that most commercial disks will last only two to five years. Another challenge to the digital image's endurance is readability, or continuous format migration; if digital images are not updated consistently each time a computer or file format becomes obsolete, they will be rendered inaccessible or mute. The longevity of home movies and news footage is particularly brief as this "born digital" imagery might never be consistently converted. If rates of innovation and obsolescence are not curbed, in only a generation we could find that the twentieth century's analog film records are still extant, while the digital record of the twenty-first has disappeared into unreadable formats.[24]

If our hydrocarbon culture suddenly ceased to exist or function, what would remain for posterity would be its infrastructure: cameras, generators, cranes, monitors, and other equipment. Its renderings, meanwhile, will fade away. Consider *Star Wars* archeology, a subculture within a subculture wherein devotees of the George Lucas series track down and then excavate the films' abandoned shooting locations. Artifacts unearthed from the deserts of Tunisia to those of California are bought and sold online; and because it is finite, authentic *Star Wars* detritus, wood, plastics, and Styrofoam enjoy an escalating price point.[25] But without such infrastructural residue, the film sets and heaps of oft-mentioned plastic water bottles accumulated by a $300 million dollar production like James Cameron's eco-flick *Avatar*, for example, or the electronic waste generated by technological investments in production, distribution, and consumption, a residue-free cinema would rub itself out of future history.[26]

Like *Star Wars* archaeologists, Marker perpetuates cinema's and the cinephile's obsession with getting at the past and fixing otherwise fleeting moments in time. *La Jetée*, however, does not suggest a belief in permanent documentation. Because Marker's film is composed of still images, he deprives it of movement and thus highlights cinema technology's illusory quality. Leo Enticknap opens his treatise on moving-image technology with the declaration that "images don't move on their own."[27] Rather, they are made to appear to move. Technology fools the human brain into thinking that what it sees on screen is are pictures moving continuously. *La Jetée* turns cinema itself into a fable, revealing it as a fabulous invention. But while the film indulges its foundational illusion, it also declines to espouse it. Because the dreamer of *La Jetée* cannot locate his own time or place within the rings of the felled redwood trunk, the film challenges the feasibility of retaining a permanent image—whether it is inscribed in memory or captured in the illusion of flickering light. Lost in the future, *La Jetée*'s dreamer returns to the past in order to reclaim an image that, we are told, has haunted him since childhood. The film can thus be read as a parable for the ephemeral nature of the image itself and the inherently unproductive enterprise of halting the decomposition of what are organic celluloid-based or paper-printed images. But the orphic inability to save what is an ephemeral art form is what inspires the desire to do the same. Utopia is never supposed to be attained; it is an ideal to strive towards and never quite realize. Likewise, if the past were reclaimed, it would lose its relevance as past. The idea of carbon-neutrality, similarly, introduces the conditions necessary to consider a cinema whose images are permanently lost to time and the decay induced by exposure to oxygen, just as the woman's face is inevitably lost to the dreamer despite the technological possibility of traveling through time in order to reclaim it. Marker's film argues that to salvage history is also to obliterate it. According to the same principle, leaving behind an intractable legacy upon the biophysical world is one way we are retaining a permanent record of our otherwise transient civilization. Like light upon celluloid, marks chiseled into stone, hydrocarbon civilization's relationship with the biophysical world is conceptualized as a footprint; an impression, or inscription, of humankind, one but that takes the earth itself as a support surface. In Tunisia, fiberglass remnants of *Return of the Jedi* are sold to tourists alongside Berber crafts, while nomadic tribes occupy what Lucas fans would recognize as a slave village.[28] Around the televisual world, plasma television sets are junked to make way for liquid crystal display (LCD) and then high definition (HD) screens; satellites are traded for digital personal video recorders (PVRs), thrown in for free when consumers make the switch to Internet television. What will survive us (but not our planet) are the image industry's durable machines, the plastic, metal, and glass that compose the cameras, monitors, and theaters of cinematic infrastructure. Weisman argues, however, that our ecological burden need not be permanent; likewise, neither does our cinematic heritage.

By semantics alone, carbon-neutral cinema insists upon a fundamental immateriality that at least superficially seems compatible with the imaging capabilities of digital technology, and in particular this lightweight format's need for only a minimal film crew or, thanks to computer generated imagery, direct interaction with the external world. Digital filmmaking does indeed accommodate low-budget independent projects, but it also suits mammoth productions like Cameron's blockbuster *Avatar*. Notably, the film's production company Twentieth Century Fox is part of Rupert Murdoch's massive News Corp. media conglomerate which as of late 2010 attested to having neutralized its carbon emissions. But a big-budget labor-intensive feature will remain energy-dense. Reducing the size of the image's footprint might then reside in the delivery system; however, the obsolescence of the DVD, like the videocassette before, does not dissolve the impact of production—and especially not Twentieth Century Fox's version of how a film is made. That is because the digital camera and the resulting image are only part of the package; the computer and other hardware components that perform the delivery must also be factored in if we are to fully understand just how heavy—and dirty and ethically questionable—the ostensibly crisp and clean and weightless digital image really is. But the technology itself is inert. Digital technology may have been harnessed, but where it goes is galloping off in all directions on behalf of making information—including images—endless and endlessly available; overconsumption is built into how quickly and efficiently moving images are produced, marketed, received, and often disposed of. Like any other industrial good, moving-image products are underwritten by a complex system of transnational economics. The rules of the game are profitability and competition and turnover—and, no matter our cynicism, we have all enjoyed the fruits of this, the dominant mainstream movie-making model. Movies have always been made to break rather than endure. In cinema's first decade, for example, audience demand for new movies grew so high that by 1905 films that had exhausted commercial interest were literally thrown out.[29] Part of cinematic culture is the propensity for rapid obsolescence, which is built into its commercial and technological fabric. Nowhere is this turnover trait more evident than in the composition of film itself—the stuff stored in canisters, spooled on reels—for the surface used to support the image will, ironically, perhaps tragically, eventually come to destroy it. Obviously there is tension here, a conflict if not a confusion between permanence and transience, wherein our cultural legacy will not be the "liquidity" of the image, but the solidity of its infrastructure. While Bauman argues for a modernity bent on the ephemeral, he does not consider the intransience of waste and the systems it has produced. Factoring in the toxicity of its residual effects, our transient "liquid" modernity is indeed solid, though not intentionally so. Pollutants that accompany throwaway disposable culture surely make us rivals to the ancients and premoderns who manifest themselves in extant structures, sculptures, and even mummies. For all the impermanence attached to systems of immaterial technologies, as long as carbon emissions exceed rates of carbon absorption (and the stratosphere continues to trap sunlight and the globe to warm), the liquid nature of modernity is a misconception.

Fossil Fuel, Fossil Image

Though the very foundation of mechanically reproduced images—the relationship between light (natural and artificial) and cinema technology—is not always obvious, the film industry's intractable need for sun and light is less so.

And the fact that it is the sun that provides the fossil fuels that power industry, and therefore culture, in the first place is an even more opaque relation. But when the sun is factored into both the history and material composition of the cinematic image it is possible to understand film as something intractably luminous, and therefore resource-based. Each film frame is a measure of our civilization's control of the sun, in the form of the fossilized sun or carbon that we have captured, refined, and duly exploited. The cinematic image literalizes in incontrovertible terms, how industry, the images of industrial culture, and the earth's natural ecology are, together and on their own terms, categorically derived from the power that emanates from the sun's rays.

Rather than a practitioner's name, *Sol fecit*, "the sun made it," was the signature typically inscribed upon the earliest photographs.[30] The convention is illustrative of how in its formative moments, photographic sensibility diminished rather than glorified anthropocentric assumptions, for it regarded the capturing of images not as a human or technological accomplishment but as a natural method of painting. The calotype or paper-negative processing invented by William Fox Talbot differed significantly from the more impractical daguerreotype which required an almost inter-minable exposure time before the silver plate within the camera obscura manifested an image. So, before the introduction of Talbot's processing innovation, all energy needed to record an image in silver had to be sourced the sun. But by adding gallic acid to his sensitizing solutions, Talbot found that the paper in his camera needed only a brief exposure time in order to yield a latent image which could then be developed and reproduced, allowing the inventor to make multiple prints from a single negative. Soon Talbot was rendering thousands of images, featuring nature, people, and architectural monuments, and became what is now called a "photographer." In 1844 he assembled his images into book form and released *The Pencil of Nature*, a collection whose title, like *Sol fecit*, acknowledges the essen-tial symbiosis between the image's reproduction of nature and a likewise dependence on the resources that it yields. Fittingly, however, *The Pencil of Nature* was also Talbot's undoing, for, as its primitive plates began to fade, his confidence in the feasibility of his own work also diminished.[31] What the calotype signifies, then, is not only the inherently ephemeral nature of the image, but also the way in which the cultural production of photography and then cinematography has industrialized the process of harvesting power from the sun. As the procedure became more refined and industrialized, it was also rendered anthropocentric. According to its conventional history, photography truly began only when chemical processing enabled Talbot to finally succeed in harvesting and then manipulating solar energy.

The history of the mechanically reproduced image is, like humanity's, the history of its exploitation of the sun. Sunlight, after all, is the source of the elemental carbon that is transformed into the energy that births organic life. The energy required to simply exist or to perform work, manual or mechanized, comes from the sun's core. Solar energy arrives to earth in the form of sunlight, whereupon photosynthetic plants process it into organic vegetation—the biomass that feeds animals and humans, energizing us with requisite calories. Geologists point to the relationship between the sun's energy and the human drive to innovate as that factor which has turned our geological time span into a narrative of how we have come to completely modify the biosphere in which we now live. Analogously, the history of the cinematic image and the photographic image from which it derives is equally determined by the relationship between the technology of the camera and the power of the sun. Of course the sun provides the light which inscribes the latent image upon the properly sensitized support surface, but it is also the source of the fuel that energizes the prime movers involved in producing, distributing, and then viewing the final product; this could include any number of projector motors, electrical generators, or lighting gear as well as any plugged-in components—monitors, laptops, DVD players, modems—used along the way. The sun is so intractably entrenched in industrial culture that narrating the entirety of its trajectory up to this moment is succinctly and easily accomplished by simply evoking the medium of film; opening a camera's aperture and randomly trapping and thus fossilizing a fragment of light is all that is necessary in order to gain a purchase on what has become the Anthropocene epoch.

What geologist Alfred Crosby calls our "biosphere domination" originated in learning how to access the solar energy that is concentrated in biomass.[32] The invention of fire and eventual burning of wood (a form of biomass) was the initial method by which humans procured the energy of the sun. But the energy concentration of such young biomass is low; yields become significantly higher when sources are densified—a process accomplished only by unimaginably long periods of time. Peat, coal, oil, and natural gas, those fuels that have enabled our civilization to transform the Holocene into the Anthropocene, are in fact intensely concentrated stews made up of billions of generations of expired plant and animals, life forms which, like all life on earth, were the product of sunlight. Having lived and died over eons, and having likewise absorbed the sun, these organisms were buried in the earth and then subjected to the conditions necessary to reduce them down to pure latent energy. Once extracted and refined, this matter is converted into what are our primary sources of "natural" energy. And it is oil, precious because it is higher in density than other fuels, that Crosby poetically terms "fossilized sunshine." The fossil fuels we extract and burn is compositionally residual plant matter in immense quantities, as well as other living organisms like phytoplankton, which live, die, and condense in deep oxygen-deficient spaces. Buried beneath the weight of oceans and ice, sand, and rock, time reduces this raw compost so thoroughly that its energy yields are such that a gallon of gasoline represents about ninety tons of plant matter, or forty acres of wheat.[33] The immensity of such figures translate into enormous social, cultural, political, economic, and environmental effects; the cinematic and photographic image correspond as an amazingly succinct visualization of the geological component of industrial culture.

The photographic camera works by capturing and ultimately controlling doses of light, which, when applied to the light-sensitive emulsion of raw film stock, are fixed or fossilized into the latent image. Taken a step further, processing too is also accomplished by controlled exposure to specific amounts of light. Photography and the cinematography it enabled are records of nothing less than light itself, proof that it existed in a certain place and at a precise moment in time. Drawing from photographic technology and the optical toy industry, the inventors we now call proto-cinematic innovators, including Jules-Étienne Marey, Eadweard Muybridge, and Thomas Edison, spent the late 1880s and the first years of the 1890s in varying degrees of concentration, researching, and experimenting with systems by which to transform a series of still photographs into a stream of seemingly continuous movement. By 1889 the ingredients necessary to mass-produce moving images had accumulated. These included a mechanical device that could stimulate the perception of unbroken movement; the chemical emulsions fast enough to make the images to feed through these devices; transparent film base that was strong and flexible enough to carry them.[34] After working though a series of procedural and technical problems, by 1891 Thomas Edison and his employees had begun making short films; in the summer of 1892, Edison's employees were operating what can be considered the first modern movie camera. By December, Edison's company had begun constructing a self-contained motion-picture studio, the Black Maria, completed in 1893. Covered in black tarpaper and roughshod in appearance, the structure rotated on its axis, following the path of the sun throughout the day, which, when available, entered through a retractable roof, and illuminated the performance stage located at one of its ends.[35] A photograph of the Black Maria taken on Edison's grounds in West Orange, New Jersey, in 1894 finds the studio's roof opened up in order to glean what it can of the sun, which the picture suggests to be in scarce supply. But what dominates the picture's background only adds to its energy density, as it were. Tucked just behind the Black Maria, and threatening to steal the movie studio's spotlight, is a factory. Complete with belching smokestack, and crowned with what appears to be a water tower or silo, the factory competes with the Black Maria just as surely as it reflects it; from compositionally putting into visual terms the relationship between cinema, industry, and the energy derived from the sun.

The cinema originated, at least in part, within the same imagination as the electric light bulb (1879); Edison's contribution of the electric power-generating station (1882) is also notable here. Underlying all this, however, is the huge drive for electrification that closed the nineteenth century and inaugurated the twentieth and to which Edison, among many others, contributed a significant part. But while Edison proved prolific and ingenious in terms of producing and then disseminating artificially produced light, he did not make the connection between light and the industrial potential of making moving images. In addition to major patent disputes that pitted independent American film producers against Thomas Edison and the Motion Picture Patents Company's (MPPC) aggressive attempt to monopolize the burgeoning industry, the pioneers of movie production—Edison's rivals if not enemies—migrated away from New York and New Jersey in search of lighting conditions better than what the cloudy east coast—Edison territory—could provide. At this point, filmmakers worked outdoors or in glassed-in studios (greenhouses), dependent on natural light. Factor in also that film stock at the time was comparably slower, requiring more solar power to saturate it, and the need for a consistent source of light is even more pronounced. So, while Edison's antagonism was indeed a real impetus to do business elsewhere, so was the economics of sunlight.[36] After the MPPC formed in 1908, companies chose to relocate production units to such sunny spots as the coasts of Florida and California, if only for winter months.[37] But snowbird firms like the Selig Polyscope Company eventually decided to make the move permanent. Eastern exiles found a perfect set of conditions on the California coast: plenty of sunshine, as well as a rich variety of landscapes to act as backdrops (mountains, ocean, desert, forest)—particularly attractive given the authenticity these vistas lent to the most dominant genre at the time, the Western. Local oil wealth sweetened the situation further, for it brought the burgeoning film industry potential investors.[38] By 1909 the New York Motion Picture Company was, like Selig, setting up permanently in and around Los Angeles and in the 1910s the city emerged as America's principle film hub.

Though the coastal climate was more favorable for the outdoor in situ movie shoot, with the introduction of powerful Kleig and Wohl arc lights in the mid to late teens, lighting technology developed to the point that movie makers had transcended the variability of the sun. East or west, geography and climate no longer determined a studio's success or failure. Greenhouse glass was quickly painted over, transforming the structures into dark studios that blocked the sun so that scenes could be illuminated by artificial lights. The open-air stages of the west coast—which, like the Black Maria, often rotated in accordance with the sun—similarly gave way to large enclosed studio complexes where interior and exteriors were engineered, and lighting was simulated and expertly manipulated. So, instead of bathing sets in sunlight and then blocking off the excess, American directors were able to eradicate the sunlight they once hungrily sought and create desired effects artificially. The abundant use of arc lighting in the late teens until the close of the studio system's silent period (when synchronized sound propelled studios to retool again) turned stage sets into complex webs of electric cables hanging from ceilings and snaking across floors, which were powered by overhead electrical runways.[39] Once fully implemented within the controlled environment of the studio, where electric sun was soaked up on richly photosensitive orthochromatic paper, the terms were set for cinema's industrialization. While the early primitive mode of movie making was characterized by the *sur le vif* spirit of the mobile Lumière cameraman who circulated freely outdoors, catching life on the street, with its conflicting planes of activity, it was now a far cry from its studio-modified version, aesthetically streamlined and internally lit. Studio movie making was static, limited by the need to be plugged in.

With its interior work spaces artificially illuminated so as to extend working hours and enhance levels of productivity, Hollywood studios came to resemble any other factory unit. Industrialized cinema of course derived an advantage from dependence on artificial light derivations; but replacing sunshine meant converting to energy supplied by another industry, namely that which produces and sells power. Electrification in Europe and North America announced the end of independent energy supplies; urban citizens now depended on centralized power sources generated by remote high-capacity stations. For example, a house connected to one of Edison's remote generators was no longer self-sufficiently generating its own sources of heat and light but instead was intractably plugged into an industrial energy producer.[40] Studio filmmaking, likewise, became harnessed to technological infrastructures of externally generated power, paradoxically rendering cinema less and not more self-sufficient. Compared to artificial forms, natural light is limitless; as Georges Bataille argues, the sun is the only resource that gives energy without demanding payback. "The origin and the essence of our wealth," Bataille writes, "are given in the radiation of the sun, which dispenses energy—wealth—without any return. The sun gives without ever receiving."[41] But solar power must first be sourced, converted, and mediated, bought and sold. It is also limited at any given time and place, more generous in California than in New Jersey, for example, and is thus not completely even in its yields. And yet, solar power retains a certain utopian dimension in that the source itself cannot as yet be withheld from the world or citizen at large. Though intermittent and by most insatiable standards relatively moderate in its energy yield, solar can still exist outside corporate or government-owned utilities.[42] From panels on privately owned rooftops to large-scale glass and photovoltaic (PV) structures and solar farms, solar power, as yet, functions best on an individual or low-scale level, meeting the relatively minimal demands of the private producer/consumer or a moderately sized geographical area. It is not difficult to see how filmmaking, like any other profit-driven industry, was compelled to transfer its need for light to a source that was consistent, stable, and accountable—and leave the Black Maria in obeisance of a temperamental sun.

The relationship between sun and cinema, light and the film environment, is especially apparent when cinema is juxtaposed against current environmental rhetoric, which ultimately fuses the fossil fuel with the fossil image, both manifestations, mummifications, of captured light. Dividing cinematic modes between the pre-industrial use of sunlight and its industrialization and electricification has both theoretical and practical value; this demarcation introduces historical precedents which, if refined and reintroduced, are perhaps more radical and effective than the purchase of carbon credits as a way to offset the waste produced by big-budget filmmaking. Early cinema, then, might be taken as an exemplar of a proto-solar cinema. Its productions, according to these terms, can be regarded as studies in natural light and textbooks for an "unplugged" cinema, filmmaking off the grid. The UCLA report or the Green Screen Green Practices Manual might be more serviceable to sustainable filmmaking were they to derive some "best practices" case studies from pre-industrial cinematic history rather than Warner Brothers, the production company behind the ostensibly carbon-neutral *Syriana*. The Black Maria, for instance, becomes a model for how natural sunlight is managed and manipulated and a showcase for how light is embedded in the very form and aesthetic of all films. "The future of the movies," said Abel Gance, "is a sun in each image."[43] The filmmaker is referring to his own *Napoleon* (1927) in which visual excess "stuffed the spectator's eye," and thus overpowered and felled him or her. In addition to being used rationally and economically as a way by which to extend the hours of the working day, light has long been employed as a means of conspicuous consumption.[44] The luminosity of Hollywood that so impressed audiences assumes ideological proportions, therefore attesting to the economic, technological, and cultural might of the American movie industry and its triumph over both the sun and other national film industries. What Gance's declaration attests to is the ideological power of the image to—like the sun—impress, dominate, and even blind the viewer with its potent splendor. But, taken literally and put in more practical, historical terms, Gance's words better serve as a metaphor for the way in which the cinema might yet minimize, rein in its seismic bloat, by returning to its elemental solar origins.

Shooting the Sun

Cinema, according to cinematographer John Alton, is "painting with light."[45] Indeed, there are numerous metaphors by which to articulate the intricate and complex relationship between the photographic/cinematographic image and the light that is its essence and its medium. Because film harnesses light as a tool, a medium, and an instrument in and of itself, this mode of expression and representation reflexively and inherently narrates the necessary relation between ways of seeing and the availability of illumination.

Archaeologies of moving-image technology pose a challenge to the conventional "key moment" approach to film history that has long tended to confine cinema's origins to a rather brief chain of events and a small group of central players (Edison, Muybridge, Marey, and culminating in the Lumière brothers, August and Louis). There are ingenious examples that topple the misguided perception that what we call "new" media is somehow self-actualizing and represents a rupture with the past rather than a developmental continuity. Lev Manovich cites one such moment: Konrad Zuse's 1936 rather do-it-yourself construction of what was essentially a digital computer, the binary code of which was punched into discarded 35mm film stock.[46] Where does cinema "begin"? In Paris in 1895? Or with the Chinese shadow puppets of 180 B.C.? Similarly, Thomas Elsaesser asks why Impressionism, with its obsessive drive to fix and record what is fleeting, is not as exemplary of a nascent cinematic imagination as Marey's chronophotography.[47] Wherever cinema begins, probing its more obscure roots locates the spirit that cinema—no matter the format—retains. Impressionism, to pursue Elsaesser's query, was caught up in a self-conscious and almost materialist preoccupation with the study of the very process of seeing rather definitive representation of a given subject. Claude Monet was in particular consumed by the study of sunlight and how it affected both the subject and the painter, altering his perspective and, as a result, his methods. The painter is defined by what is keenly cinematic: his attention to a single motif, but also that he painted that motif over and over, as serials. The fifteen paintings that composed *Haystacks* (1891) are particularly notable as they functioned for Monet as "neutral receptacles for light."[48] The intention behind *Haystacks* was the revelation of the infinite ways in which sun affects the subject at various times of the day and in different weather—visualizing, in other words, solar energy and its manifestation. And that the same image is serialized, reproduced in variations as cells in a filmstrip, is suggestively cinematic, especially as the work corresponds temporally with cinema's proto or scientific stages of development. Monet's serialized motifs highlights the impulse that prevailed in both the scientific and artistic domains of modernity, namely the desire to define what is indefinite and fix in place what is "fleeting and fugitive"—to capture movement, of light or bodies, within a frame.[49] Taking this further, Post-Impressionist Paul Cézanne's paintings are likewise spirited by the evaluation of light; many of his still lifes and landscapes from the period 1880–1906, for which he is most famous, foreground the relationship between sunlight and how it alters the surface quality of his subjects. More important, though, is the way the painter sees his subject; it is Cézanne's subjectivity or tendency for abstraction that separates his work from that of his contemporaries who were, in Bazin's terms, enslaved by a resemblance complex. Cézanne's paintings are distinct in part because rather than being about the representation of a given subject, each one is about a particular motif (the play of light on a leaf, the shadow on a mountain) and, importantly, the variable process of seeing the motif itself.[50] With this radical emphasis on process, Cézanne took his viewer behind the scenes, highlighting that it was not the final form or illusion that mattered but making comprehensible the way the artist had transcribed his vision. Before Cézanne, it was the artist's responsibility to find conclusiveness in what he or she saw. Suddenly, however, doubt itself became ingrained in a painting's subject matter; and it is this doubt, as Robert Hughes argues, that is an essential component of modernity itself. The pictorial representation no longer made a declaration—"this is what I see"—but asked a question—"is this what I see?"[51] The photograph and the cinema overtook the painter's urge to achieve accurate representation—"the ecstasy of absolute realism," as Roland Barthes described it—opening up the universe of abstraction and anticipating modern art from the stricture of mimesis.[52] The historical avant-garde picked up a new arsenal of tools and textures, materials and philosophical motivations, and rendered the artist much more than just a painter, sculptor, or photographer, but, often enough, a combination thereof. The shock of modernity at the turn of a new century came with a complex set of social and economic conditions that disrupted the very ability to studiously and accurately depict the world at large, because that world itself was suddenly rendered slippery, ill-defined, a site of rushing disputation; the sound, smell, and movements of city and its technology trumped even Monet's hitherto radical approach to the interplay of light and shadow, form and color. In its stead was an obsession with capturing the new century's mechanized forms of power: not sun but speed, not light on haystacks, but electricity, automobile's, "manmade" forms of energy.

In 1909 the Italian Futurist Giacomo Balla produced *Street Light.* The painting marks the transition from realism to abstraction and also exemplifies Balla's obsession with the analysis of the perception of movement produced by humans, sound, machines, and, here specifically, electrified light. The painting was inspired by one of the first electric streetlights installed in Rome where Balla lived and, as such, the painter was directly responding to the electrification of his city, his country, and his culture's imagination. What is notable about the painting's subject is how the lamp's vitality is contrasted with the faintness of the moon, which is depicted as a mere sliver.[53] *Street Light* clearly articulates the new polarities introduced by industrialization in general and electrification in particular. While the darkness of night recedes into the painting's outer limits, the encroaching rays of the lamp extend their powerful reach, and they do so actively, tentacles in motion. The moment of transition the painting pinpoints is historically complex and fleeting at best; Balla's study resonates because it recognizes as such within its own contradictory values. While the dynamism it achieves is almost cinematic (captured movement, or illusion thereof) its means are almost stubbornly painterly and somehow conservative; the naïve and almost primitive quality of the work directly conflicts with the progress and innovation implied by the subject. What differentiated cinema as a mode of representation is, of course, the mechanistic apparatus that not only removed the "hand of man" from the practice of image making but also tied the image and its producer to industrial processes. Balla's painting is a striking example of the transition to what was becoming modernity's specifically industrial imagination. Standing at the cusp of electrification and thus modernity's *literal* illumination and the transformation of vision within urban environments, Balla's painting points both ahead and is informed by a contradiction between its painterly part and photomechanical future. Balla, it seems was capturing his medium's very obsolescence.[54]

The Futurists were witness to what they considered the electrification of humanity itself, and set about not only documenting the process but also attempting to guide it toward political and social utopia. Fitting it is, then, that the first Futurist Manifesto commences with a testimony to the electric lights that allowed the artists to defy the dark of night and compose the guidelines by which they would both anticipate and document the rush towards the future. As Marinetti capably and feverishly describes it, "We had stayed up all night, my friends and I, under hanging mosque lamps with domes of filigreed brass, domes starred like our spirits, shining like them with the imprisoned radiance of electric hearts."[55] The electricity that enabled the Futurists' nocturnal labor would also be the subject of much of their art. *Street Light* was composed the same year as the first Manifesto. "Primitive" in its means, but industrial or modern in its imagination, painting's obsessive analytical detail is remarkable for the way it pinpoints the overlap of static painting and moving images as the means by which to produce pictures of light. Ultimately, what preoccupied early Futurist painting is the process of studying light through motion and studying motion through light. As painting and cinematic technology converged, the Futurists solved the problem of transcribing their society's velocity through a concept termed "photodynamism." The Futurists seized upon the chronophotographic apparatuses designed by Étienne-Jules Marey. But instead of the intended purpose, to "analytically decompose" the energy economy of the body, inscribing physical activity frame-by-frame, the Futurists used Marey's mechanisms to break down the movement and energy of electric light.[56] Such, then, is the basic distillation of the elements that produce the illusion of cinema: light, movement, and an industrial energy economy that fuses them together.

Just as Balla forges a connection between the gaslight of the past, the electrified future, and resultant effects on pictorial representation, Victor Erice's 1992 documentary *Dream of Light* is likewise obsessively invested in theorizing these same technological, cultural, and even geological relations. Erice's work, however, is further enriched and even burdened by the cinematic history that, for Balla, was only beginning. The narrative premise of Erice's remarkable film is simple: the documentation of a painter's attempt to depict how the sun transforms a quince tree growing in the courtyard of his Madrid studio. The film accurately informs the viewer of the passage of time—day turning into week, week into month—and so functions as something of a diary of both the painter's process as well as of the change of the season (and so the position of the sun). As fastidiously committed to detail as Balla's study of the light emitted by what now seems to be a simple the street lamp, Garcia (the painter) submits himself completely to sunlight's frustrating variability. His physical position is kept constant by a pair of nails hammered into the earth, just the right distance from the tree, and against which the painter buttresses his toes lest he shift his stance and, therefore, his perspective. What is more, each time Garcia moves his gaze from one point of the tree to another, he marks the spot directly, be it on leaf or fruit, with a tiny horizontal stroke of paint; by the end of his labor, he transforms the tree into a map of where his sight (and the sun's light) has traveled. There are in *Dream of Light* three paintings of the quince tree: one depicted on Garcia's canvas, another on Erice's celluloid, and a third within the tree itself, transformed as it is by sun, eye, lens, and Garcia's directly applied brush strokes.

The inflexibility Garcia imposes upon himself—legs as stable as a tripod, eyes as accurate as a lens—sets the metaphoric conditions for the film's final sequence. Against the voice-over of Garcia describing a dream, Erice (though we never see him) returns at night to the artist's courtyard and the quince tree, but the filmmaker replaces the painter with an autonomous movie camera; what is more, standing in for the sun are arc lamps and, thus, artificial light. Because the process of filmmaking itself corresponds so closely with Garcia's study of the sun and thus the tree, the two finally conflate into a single vision, united and likewise equalized by the dependence of both cinema and painting upon the availability of light. The dynamics of this relationship are literally and figuratively captured in Erice's film, particularly as Garcia's negotiations with the sun are fraught with conflict. Continually shrouded with cloud or else altering its position, the sun ultimately refuses to remain as accurate and consistent as Garcia himself, and so the painter gives up his effort, shutting the painting in his cellar. It is the camera, therefore, that finally achieves what the painter cannot, for the film we the viewers are watching is the only complete portrait. But what consolidates the power of camera over that of the painter is that it can record at night while Garcia is sleeping. Electricity, therefore, underwrites the cinematic image of the tree; an image forged in a light that is completely artificial and, for Garcia, inadequate. Thus, Erice's climatic scenario, makes overt reference to the final moments of Dziga Vertov's definitive *Man with a Movie Camera* in which an autonomous camera also supersedes the filmmaker and sets off into an undetermined future. Erice extends Vertov's discourse on the mechanization of representation, the industrialization of vision, and the resultant displacement of the artist. And he does so while preserving the same admirable measure of doubt or ambiguity that concludes the earlier Soviet film, wherein the viewer, like filmmaker, does not necessarily believe in the autonomous camera on screen and is therefore compelled to ask whether, and by what means, such a thing could be possible. With an air of reluctance, then, Erice's film argues that what has frustrated the painter Garcia all along is not only losing his contest with the sun, but also, and less explicitly, resigning himself to the camera that he is unable to imitate; along with fugitive light, what Garcia cannot stabilize is his own system of seeing. *Dream of Light* plays out the crisis of representation that Bazin pointed to as dividing abstraction and realism—an essential cultural shift that Balla's painting similarly articulates. But Erice's film resists simply extolling technological vision over that of the artist's eye, or favoring the "authenticity" of the human's unmediated vision. Instead, it is concerned with representing a desire to arrest what is fleeting and to give shape to transience.

And what is fleeting and fugitive to the cinematic image is light. Because the autonomous camera comes out at night, *Dream of Light* picks up where Vertov's earlier film *Man with a Movie Camera* left off: just before the sun has set. Erice, six decades later, elongates the waking and working day and further propagates the ascendancy of the camera: nocturnal capabilities reinforce its already considerable power. Operating seemingly on its own and in the darkness of night, what Erice's Vertovian epilogue makes clear is that the autonomy of *this* camera is false, generated as it is by the power of electricity, the prime mover of the unmanned apparatus and its attendant light source. Erice's simple film tells the complex story of pictorial art in the age of electrification, and at the denouement the image is subtracted of human hands, and it no longer must be saturated by the sun; the solar image is replaced by the electric one.

The Sunless Image

Though the capture, processing, and projection of the image depend on the availability of light, the technology of cinema relies equally upon the dark. In what Wolfgang Schivelbusch calls "light-based media" such as cinema, the very potency of artificial light to generate its own seeming reality is revealed, paradoxically, in darkness.[57] Celluloid stock's light sensitivity requires it to be sealed tightly away, protecting it from exposure; from the darkroom to the aperture to the projection booth, light and its power to alter if not ruin the filmstrip, raw or developed, is managed by the careful application of neutralizing darkness. For Bazin, by extension, the photographic process is one of "molding," the taking of a death-mask impression.[58] First, however, light must be sequestered, then manipulated; the transformation of what is fugitive into what is frozen, chemically fixed: light fossilized, in other words. But when the process itself, the trap that is darkness, overpowers the light source, dimming or even depriving cinema of its essential ingredient, the material basis of cinema, a light-based media, is made readily, self-reflexively, apparent. And what this reflexivity reveals is cinema's fragility and its inherent limitations, not only to infinitely retain memories or impressions but also to function without industrial society to sustain it. Just as Victor Erice discursively saturates his film with light so as to underscore the essential relationship between representation and the manipulation of illumination, the same can be accomplished by withholding light sources and thus foregrounding how the constant availability of this cinematic ingredient has become naturalized as part of viewing expectations. Noël Burch's denaturalization of what are an accepted set of cinematic conventions signals film as language artificially derived, ideologically marked by the historical, cultural, and political moment from which it arose. The way dominant cinemas operate is not organic or latent, but patterned according to what has become an "institutional mode of representation." In order to produce this category, Burch contrasts what has become naturalized film language against the pure, uncut version that was early cinema's as yet undefined expression: the "primitive mode of representation."[59] What Burch finds in filmmaking pre-1909, before editing continuity was established or lighting systems were industrialized, is an unregulated mode of making moving pictures and thus a way by which to counter the perception that film form is neutral, and specifically for Burch, somehow devoid of dominant (capitalist) ideology. By contrasting our "evolved" viewing conditions against what were embryonic ones, Burch reveals that what is natural or organic about film's formal state is anything but. Nothing about cinema is solid, then; every dimension of the cinematic institution is formulated and illusory therefore, vulnerable to challenge and change. Burch's evocation of primitivism operates as a force of resistance against that which is entrenched and solid, and so picks up some of Gilles Deleuze and Felix Guattari's vision of the nomadic "war machine."[60] The concept loosely describes those invisible undercurrents and disruptions that move amorphously along the periphery of dominant culture, whose centralized and static institutions are always trying to absorb them. Dudley Andrew makes an important interjection when he argues that this metaphorical struggle between the rhizomatic nomad and arborescent state apparatus (fluidity versus rootedness, primitive versus institution) described in *A Thousand Plateaus* can be readily applied to cultural production and cinematic economies that fall outside of U.S. and European models.[61] Importantly, though, the nomad does not break apart institutions so much as it resists them; the nomad—like the primitive that Burch evokes—is predefined rather than undefined; its only framework is that it remain unframed, unnamed, and, by nature never constituted. Burch's project locates the nomad in early cinematic practice. With linguistics as a starting point, he argues that cinema, like language, can be situated as a sociohistorical construct. Further, all cinema, consciously or otherwise, is always about, first, cinema itself and, second, the conditions that produced it; cinema cannot but be about the terms and limits of its own materiality, that which makes it solid—or appear as such. Chris Marker's *La Jetée* and Michael Haneke's *Time of the Wolf* can both be situated within a similar methodological framework for this pair of films: first, as a critique of the naturalized presence and stability of light in cinema and, second, by imposing upon themselves a distinctly primitive formal system. Both directors evoke the illusory, fragile character of cinema by thinning out its very resources: light and movement. What remains after cinema is thus distilled as an aesthetic that relies less upon light and more upon dark—a "sunless" cinema, in other words.

Michael Haneke's *Time of the Wolf* (2003) envisions the post-industrial world suddenly become post-apocalyptic. An unnamed conflict immobilizes contemporary Europe, depriving it of resources, electricity and water specifically, and forcing citizens of all classes and races to resort to basic and desperate means by which to endure. As the bourgeois family at the centre of the narrative travels cross country by bike and foot, following a set of train tracks which it hopes will lead eventually to a place of safety, it is forced to negotiate new codes of survival and, with them, new social positions. The discursive values attached to the train rails and the illusive and impassive locomotive loom over the film, but ultimately are matched by the constrictive imposition of darkness that is *Time of the Wolf's* truly dominant metaphor and structuring device. The darkness the film exudes is particularly potent because it is produced and explored for all its political nuance by the form of the film, thus drawing self-conscious attention to the presence of the cinematic apparatus itself. As this formerly privileged world reverts back to rudimentary sources of light, heat, and energy, Haneke's evocation of primitivism is manifested not only in the social conduct of this world's resource-poor citizens, but also in its means of light. Haneke's decision to espouse the low-light conditions his characters endure literally obscures them from each other and from the viewer; the filmmaker therefore challenges his spectator, forcing him or her to likewise experience the alienation and discomfort induced when the privilege of artificial light is removed. Haneke equates the audience with the bourgeois society his work so thoroughly undermines, and he does so by turning the cinema against the viewer just as the world has turned against his otherwise advantaged characters. Entitlement to natural resources and their conveniences is radically denaturalized in *Time of the Wolf*, but so is entitlement to the cinema as a source of enlightenment (literally, metaphorically) and also, therefore, of comfort. Without the ability to make out and so orient the action occurring within the darkened scenes, the medium itself becomes as fragile, sensitive, and limited as the world it depicts. All systems in *Time of the Wolf* are subject to breakdown and failure, including that of the cinema itself. Here is our privileged world without its natural mechanisms of power and structure, and here is our light-based media, deprived of its electrical supply. The viewer is as destabilized as the oblique and unyielding representation of this darkened primitive world. But Haneke's darkness is neither inexpert nor unwieldy. It obscures his subjects, but does so as deliberately as carefully filtered light might otherwise reveal them. Rather than revert to the raw or amateur qualities associated with a handheld camera in order to balance the form of the film with its uncertain and even chaotic narrative content, Haneke employs what is an uncompromisingly solid, if not severe, cinematic infrastructure and so maintains his signature control and restraint.

The film's penultimate image is of an immense bonfire burning in the night, laid out across the wayward train tracks, in an attempt to force the locomotive to stop when (and if) it should once again thunder past. The semiotic values here are productive indeed, granting the primitive light source the impossible task of stopping the elusive, fugitive train and enabling what it so lucidly embodies—the deliverance of civilization. But the final sequence, however, is a radical and even shocking contrast to the one that precedes it. Shot from the perspective of a train in motion, the images travel from right to left and depict the steady flow of uninterrupted forest, bathed in the full light of day. The source of the point of view is withheld, as is the train's origin or destination. It seems that the train is an abstraction, and, as such, it belongs less to the narrative of the film than to its political and aesthetic discourse. In purely narrative terms Haneke's suggestion might be the return to civilization, however hopeful or ominous this might be. The train also foregrounds Haneke's deliberate attempt to denaturalize the privileged viewing conditions that "institutional" (from Burch) or "state" (Deleuze) viewership takes for granted. In terms of cinematic history, the presence of the train is surely evocative. The first cinematic images presented to a public audience were of a train, the illusion of which, though comparatively "primitive" to Haneke's, had a powerful physical affect on the audience. But as Akira Mizuta Lippit argues, the fear was displaced from the train to the image itself, the power and energy embedded therein. However contested the mythology surrounding that initial screening of the Lumières' *The Arrival of a Train at La Ciotat* (1895), what remains is that the audience collided with cinema itself, and was in Lippit's Freudian terms "swallowed" whole by an unseen energy—the very illusion of cinema bearing down upon and consolidating an industrializing visual economy.[62] Because the forces of cinema are so indelibly connected with the image of the locomotive and its associations of industry, engineering, transportation, and the consumptive terms of the engine, the sense is that Haneke's final images return cinema to its earliest primitive moments, further wrenching away the viewer's assumptions and comforts. Haneke invents his own system of cinematic primitivism whose formal codes and aesthetic decisions dismantle the cinematic apparatus as an entitlement and a zone of bourgeois repose. By destabilizing the expectations of cinematic viewing conditions, the question Haneke ultimately posits is how altered production conditions—either willed by a filmmaker's own choice or imposed by economics, war, or other monumental trauma—forces

the viewer to respond differently to, and even question, the inherited terms of
the cinematic image.

Chris Marker's *La Jetée* (1962) is in even more radical terms an evocation
of cinematic primitivism and a challenge to the natural illusions upon which
viewing expectations depend. Marker made do with resources available to
him: the film was shot on a silent film camera and the sound recorded
on an antiquated audio cassette recorder. One of the film's first images is
of what we are told is a "frozen sun." Light is held in limbo, and so is the
energy it provides. This frozen sun has direct bearing on the form of the
film itself, for it is, so famously, composed of still images. As Bazin argued,
what cinema is exists in its ideal form in the imagination: there is no need
for a camera in order for there to be cinema, in other words, and so there
is no need for light or, by extension, for movement. The sense of motion
that cinema provides is just that—a sense, or an illusion. Thirty years after
being told that a movie cannot be constructed with still images, Marker
revisited his childhood conviction that cinema needed only imagination and
what was "within reach" and made *La Jeteé*.[63] Marker renders his film out
of an approximation, a memory of moving pictures; there is a suggestion
of motion, but the pictures do not "move" themselves. As Enticknap puts
it, "There is no such thing as a moving image."[64] Two processes are necessary in order to create the illusion of motion. The first is the ability of the
camera to record a sequence of images (frames) at a rate fast enough that
the difference between two distinct frames cannot be detected by the viewer
when they are projected at the same speed. The second is that the transition
between each frame has to be achieved invisibly, that is without a "flicker"
or perceptible variation in light level when it is reproduced by a display
apparatus. "Persistence of vision" was long thought to explain both these
processes, but theorists often now regard this inclusive category as flawed.
The two-part theory of "critical flicker fusion" and "apparent motion" is the
most widely accepted account of how the eye is tricked into turning broken,
rapidly changing frames into the illusion of continuity and movement.[65]
Whether or these terms succeed in explaining the illusion accomplished by
cinema technology, they themselves are richly suggestive and theoretically
provocative. Vision is indeed persistent, as Marker's film puts forth; for
the cinematic imagination, despite an absence of the apparatus necessary
to render a conventional, moving film, is still able to construct a work of
cinema. Film, according to *La Jetée*, does not need "film" to transcribe it, but
only the willingness to believe in the illusion it supplies. Foregrounding illusion as the film image's true support surface insists that cinema is materially
fragile and, at the same time, ethereally durable.

Where Haneke constructs a Europe in the midst of a resource scarcity that results from and produces some form of conflict, Marker's Cold War–era film envisions a post-apocalyptic planet Earth. The narrative originates underground, beneath the radioactive streets of Paris, and thus the black and white film is characterized by heavy shrouds of darkness that are punctuated by beams of light from powerful, single-source lamps. The film's lack of motion suggests that it comes from a time and place deprived of the means necessary to create the moving picture's most conventional illusion. The cinema of the future, then, is neo-primitive and thus resembles the cinema of the past. The film forces the viewer to use the imagination to invent cinema again, to find the idea that preceded the essence (or the apparatus) that has come to establish a set of what might be abnormally prescriptive cinematic expectations. Just as the film's protagonist, the dreamer who is sent into time in search of food, medicine, and sources of energy, is chosen because of his obsession with an image from the past, so too is the viewer forced to re-create the cinema itself, the correlate of the viewer's lost image, trying to remember the roles and rules that make the cinema what it is or was. As a series of photographic images, *La Jetée* is the fossilization of light; but it is also a fossilization of cinema itself. What remains of the film's diegetic future (post-apocalyptic Paris, the dreamer's present) is an artifact, the static residues of some other "illusory" mode of cinema that is no longer possible to render in this resource-deprived, subterranean, and darkened world. The artifacts of the still images are accumulated and displayed in the museum that is *La Jetée*; such a self-reflexive gesture connects the film we are watching with the consistent references to things petrified (the redwood tree), stuffed (the animals in the natural history museum), chiseled from rock and stone (the statues the dreamer sees in the Parisian past and also which litter the halls of the galleries that compose the underground world), or frozen, like the sun. The proliferation of these forms or representations of life that are, like the film, rendered static, constantly reinforce the idea that in order to supply them with their former energy, the imaginative power of memory must be harnessed and even manipulated, not unlike the fugitive essence of cinema, its light. And like Haneke, Marker's film operates according to a primitive formal system and aesthetic that forces the viewer to think about cinema both before its language was defined or mode of representation naturalized. But, like Haneke, *La Jetée* also imagines the future of a cinema deprived of that which facilitates its illusion; certainty is replaced by palpable doubt, thus reinstating the terms of perception inaugurated by Cézanne's studies of the variability of human sight and natural light.

Sans Soleil, made in 1982, twenty years after *La Jetée*, is in more ways than one a companion to Marker's earlier film. The link that connects them within the present framework of a primitive, post-cinematic filmmaking is the way in which the later film also posits that film can be rendered without film, and specifically, without the presence of a light source, namely the sun. Commencing as it does with several seconds of black leader, the film can be located within the same inert luminosity that emanated from *La Jetée*'s frozen sun. Building upon what is the film's more obvious gesture of obscuration, *Sans Soleil* subtly and consistently eschews the direct sourcing of light by gleaning extant images from television, video games, and other films that are woven into a complex narrative fabric. One of the films that *Sans Soleil* embeds within its own porous framework is *La Jetée*. Its presence is explicitly visual, suggestively metaphoric, as well as obliquely referential. Perhaps the most resonant gesture Marker makes toward his earlier film occurs when *Sans Soleil*'s itinerant cameraman Sandor Krasna describes his plan for an imaginary film, one that fits the description of *La Jetée*, but which he tells his reader (and viewer) he "will not make." And yet he is making it, for he is continually "collecting [its] sets," "inventing [its] twists" and "putting in his favorite creatures." "Sunless," as the diegetic film is called, exists in Krasna's mind. The imaginary film is the idea that precedes the cinematic apparatus; the impulse to capture a reality that Bazin maintains has always obsessed humanity, and whose first material rendering Cherchi Usai posits is as old and as basic as the blocked passage of light that generates a shadow. This is *Sans Soleil*, a truly "sun-less" cinema, and a means of making films without its essential ingredients, light and thus motion; without, also, the active presence of the filmmaker/protagonist who disappears behind his images into his letters and who is also absorbed by the voice of the woman who reads them. But as Marker harnesses Krasna, and Krasna likewise harnesses Marker, the result is a means by which to generate film without the use of a camera; along with the use of existing images, Marker's primary medium is reflexivity, referentiality, and the capabilities of the pure, raw imagination. And if all film is derived first of all from the imagination, the idea and the urge to represent a picture of reality, it does not need the sun and it does not need a camera.

While the original footage was shot on a silent film camera and the sound recorded on a non-sync portable tape player, colorized portions were manipulated using a video synthesizer. These are used at several instances throughout, but the most prominent occurs at the end of the film. "The Zone" we enter is the realm of video artist Hayao Yamaneko, the "maniac who busies himself with electronic graffiti" (and who is Marker himself). The journey's final leg is spent beyond "film" proper, but fast-forwarded into cinema's electromagnetic future. In terms of the technology itself, video synchronization has the capacity to produce visual material without input from a camera—film without film, in essence. While video patterning can manipulate live television feeds or other extant images, the process can also be used to create a range of original imagery using purely electronic manipulations; abstractions and patterns move in real time, as they are created, then are made visible when the output video signal is displayed on TV monitors or computer screens. Exploiting video synchronization, Yamaneko produces pictures "less deceptive" than those aired on television because they are overt fabrications that do not pretend to be true. So what of Krasna's images, the film just witnessed? How real are these? When a sequence of images sourced from earlier moments are subjected to Yamaneko's manipulative video effects their glimpses of Krasna's travels melt into puddles of throbbing color, decomposing into the unreal real of video. These moments are intercut with close-ups of the practitioner's fingers moving along the video console, selecting switches and pulling plugs, and otherwise producing a new cinematic register whose language finally "touches" Krasna. Yamaneko summons up and effectively freezes the face of a woman glimpsed earlier at a market in Praia, stretching it beyond the limitations of its original blink of film frame. Here is where the journey ends, at the video console, the film-factory in other words, and the realm of video, where we bear witness to the next iteration between the conflation of time and human memory.

Timothy Corrigan has argued that videotape technology, beginning in particular with the portapak's swift rise to popularity in the 1960s, was shot through with a discernable aesthetic and ideology that pinpointed it as peripheral and marginal, the medium of choice for artistic expression and social justice activism.[66] Compared to celluloid methods of image making, video was accessible and inexpensive, user-friendly, production-rapid, and less labor intensive, and so enabled the marginal, de-centered, and here-tofore voiceless groups—women, Indigenous, people of color, gays and lesbians—to speak. The digital camera's thorough penetration of a massive commercial market embodies the same emancipatory possibilities for de-centered groups and concerns, but its widespread appropriation also renders it the lingua franca of mainstream image and information industries. Digital filmmaking's universal acceptance and ever-sharpening applicability mini-mizes its potential recognition of radical marginality that analog video bore. The path for the digital revolution (for so it is called) was laid by the VCR which, when introduced to the domestic market in the late 1970s and 1980s, radically redefined the heretofore clear separation between producer and consumer, author and audience. The ability to control and manipulate a text simply by stopping or rewinding at will empowered viewers by granting them a tangible means of image ownership. The VCR signaled the end of an ineffable cinema and ushered in a fragmented one, a change that was both liberating and constricting in its possibilities and thus thoroughly postmodern in its sentiment (or lack thereof). Like the Icelandic village buried under a volcano's ash at the end of *Sans Soleil*, or the moss of time that melts Krasna's images, videotape technology, like the digital variation that would supersede it, dissolved global space and toppled the dividing lines between public and private: "a cinema without walls," as Corrigan calls it.[67] The cinema that *Sans Soleil* hints at is video-based, without boundary; a cinema that never sleeps, therefore, and over which the sun never sets. Krasna predicts that Yameneko's version of poetry will become universal, made by everyone: the Zone itself will melt, and become absorbed into the status quo of the center. Like the nomad who moves away from the state's striating currents, the video artist will be compelled to flee again, in search of another refuge in which to speak his imaginary truth; either that or he will disappear into a sunless, film-less reality that was his own making. Like Vertov's cameraman hero, Marker's Krasna (and his kindred spirit Yameneko) assumes the self-referential role of the filmmaker whose movie apparatus is the means by which he negotiates a changing world and, along the way, creates one of his own. But because of the parameters the film sets, creating a film instinctively rather than directly or actively, Krasna is cast as the evolutionary outcome of Vertov's man with a movie camera—engendered here as the man without a movie camera. In both cases, the result is the satisfaction of the myth that Bazin posited—a total cinema, a medium that bears no seams between itself, its user, or the external world.

As Georges Méliès understood it, cinema was not the seventh art but "the art that combines all of the others."[68] Just as other modes of representation have decomposed into cinema, cinematic history is nothing less than the narrative of its own disappearance, wherein a total "synergy" between eye and motor, operator and apparatus, finally abolishes their differences.[69] Virilio has consistently argued that the movie apparatus becomes the prosthesis for a perfect, unadulterated vision; after dispensing with the crane, dolly, or tripod, and then the operator, it becomes indistinguishable from the images it produces. Having then assumed a form that is both indistinct and imperceptible, allowing it to survey without interruption or interference, the camera achieves its total autonomy and finally disappears. The focus here is on the disappearance of the camera; but that vision technology has become so perfected that it is rendered imperceptible is only one dimension of what is growing into a precarious social and ecological condition. To remain a powerful theoretical category, "disappearance" must account for the current height of cinematic technology, the digital camera and its attendant parts, software and hardware included. The digital camera might become more imperceptible, but its disappearance is undermined by the nagging facts of disposability. The dystopian evolution that Virilio charts, shrinking the camera into an invisibility, ends not in indefectible triumph but in failure; because the camera (no matter how sleek or small) is composed of such durable materials, decomposition—and, therefore, disappearance—is fundamentally precluded. Thus the invisible or disappearing camera that Virilio, like Bazin and Vertov, has argued for, is replaced with a disposable camera; out of sight, perhaps, but still physically present. Disposability might be recognized as a failure, but it is one that continues to work, or it will until economies built on technological obsolescence and the attendant entitlement to freely discard are held accountable for the residue left behind—or are suffocated by them. Digital technology has "disappeared" the differences between imaging modes, frames and screens, image and information, and has also drastically shortened the temporal increment between the latest innovation and the most recently outmoded. The disposable camera is the falsely disappearing one; in order to impede or at least denaturalize what has become the ease with which the material of cinema is subtracted from established theory, history, and viewing conditions, instruction can be taken from the primitive aesthetics of Haneke and Marker, comparably dominant alongside the shoestring videomaking of postcolonial and Third Cinemas and Fourth Cinemas discussed elsewhere in this book. Though strategies, formal practices, and sociopolitical contexts diverge, the intention and the result of these filmmakers and their works is what matters in the present framework; making cinema less obvious, depriving it of its illusory values which leave it unassailable, intractable, and incapable of change. By "disappearing" the camera and the broader cinematic apparatus, Haneke and Marker render it more, not less, conspicuous. Such is the paradox the "sunless cinema" both exploits and perpetuates. La Jetée is particularly notable, for its system bears an intentional flaw. As Marker inserts a single quiver of movement (blinking eyes, what might be thought of as the primordial editing device) into an otherwise static film, the filmmaker not only offers the hope that cinema can in fact revivify the past, but also, more importantly, he inscribes an essential element of doubt into his own position. The viewer is therefore compelled to question not La Jetée so much as to confront the elemental flicker—the blink—that is at the root of both human and cinematic perceptions.

Luminous Data/Digital Light

If it were to be formally marked, the ascendancy of the digital cinema, and the raw or amateur aesthetic still commonly attached to it, might be said to have been initiated by the Dogme95 collective. Lead by director Lars von Trier, the group took advantage of his presence at the 1995 conference held in Paris honoring cinema's centennial year to publicly declare the beginning of a radical new anti-cinema that would, via the possibilities of the digital camera, eradicate the "cosmeticised" illusion that one hundred years of filmmaking had achieved. The goal of the collective was not only to wrench the camera away from the exclusivity and privilege of the auteur, but to politicize cinema by making it both universal and its presence more conspicuous and intrusive. According to the group's "Vow of Chastity," "Today a technological storm is raging, the result of which will be the ultimate democratisation of the cinema. For the first time, anyone can make movies."[70] To make certifiable Dogme movies, however, a filmmaker had to, among other things, use only a hand-held (digital) camera, dispense with any optical tricks, and employ only available means of sound, set, and lighting. Though the movement was officially declared defunct in 2002, under claims it had grown into a predicable "genre formula," filmmakers can still take the chastity vow and obtain official Dogme certification (there are at present a total of 219 officially recognized Dogme films in existence).

Von Trier's call for cinematic chastity is superficial, and a sign of decadence in itself. It is easy to impose strictures upon the self rather than have limitations imposed externally, in the form of economic, political, or social obstacles—poverty, censorship, war. Shoestring cinema exists, has existed, continues to exist. It does not need a manifesto, only the fate of falling outside the mainstream, industrial variant that von Trier, despite his flamboyant austerity, surely represents. The "Second Cinema" or European art cinema of which von Trier, like Haneke and Marker, are a part might manage to exist outside the "fortress" (as Godard called it) of institutional models, but if such filmmakers make claim to exile, it is self-imposed. The so-called Third Cinema (the postcolonial, Third World or "accented" cinema, according to Hamid Naficy) or Fourth Cinema (encompassing Indigenous populations), as well as de-centered groups within the First World (of which there are many) need not take a vow of chastity or deliberately strip away the lush veneer that von Trier excoriates in order to be pure, for budgetary and logistic limitations have already been thrust upon them; "cinematic hunger" is what drives these filmmakers in the first place.[71]

Digital is generally regarded as a democratizing technology. Though the camera itself (and accoutrements) are inert, its low price point and user practicality continue to facilitate a "culture of access," for traditionally voiceless groups (not to be confused with the "culture of excess" discussed elsewhere in this book).[72] Corrigan notes that video formats have since the 1960s enabled filmmakers to render history immediate and public, refusing the rigid temporality and textures of dominant narrative systems.[73] While Dudley Andrew connects the dots between the freedom ushered in by the emblematic VCR and the robust cinematic practice in West Africa, frontline, Igloolik-based video-maker Zacharias Kunuk has similarly shown how analog and now digital video gives voice to Inuit populations by making it possible to make movies without the lavish budgets von Trier must actively turn down and scorn. But a decade and a half after the manifesto, Dogme95 takes on a new relevance, for it is in these production strictures that carbon-neutral cinema seems to have already found a model. Though an ideology of democratized access-culture defines the two initiatives, it is for reasons of literal rather than aesthetic purity that carbon-neutral cinema commonly touts digital—delivery systems in particular—as the future of environmentally benign filmmaking. Of course the radical difference between digital and analog is in the immediacy and spread of digital's delivery system. While Internet-based dissemination is extolled as the cost effective and energy-saving mode for delivering and accessing content within the home, digital delivery and projection is likewise being embraced by brick-and-mortar theatres who adapt to the format for "green" reasons, now inseparable from economic ones. HDNetworks, for example, is a pioneering network that delivers large high-definition file downloads to theaters around the globe. In 2009 the company signed a sizeable deal with Emerging Pictures as part of the theater chain's "100% green" data delivery platform. Emerging Pictures, the largest such HD network in the United States (sixty-five commercial theaters throughout North America and with plans for global expansion), considers digital the most environmentally benign, if not carbon-neutral, platform for delivering content; the method avoids petroleum-based 35mm prints as well as the carbon emissions incurred from shipping heavy film canisters. It is also highly economical. But as yet Emerging Pictures' product is not going to reach a large audience, because it does not include mainstream commercial fare among its offerings, which currently consist of independent films and HD broadcasts of live opera and theater events—the Second Cinema, in other words.

Will carbon-neutral be the Fifth Cinema, after the Indigenous Fourth Cinema? Practitioners of these "minor" cinemas need not situate themselves underground or render themselves purposefully primitive; these cinemas are often already Dogme-ready, and many are already carbon-neutral. So what does it take to neutralize cinema and green the silver screen? Models and methods are as far away, or as close, as Chris Marker and Zacharias Kunuk; their ecological vanguards achieved out of circumstance rather than by design.

CHAPTER 2

RESOURCE

Set during the Iran–Iraq war (1980–1988), Samira Makhmalbaf's *Blackboards* (2000) uses a basic and obvious metaphoric logic to forge connections between war, nomadic culture, and communications breakdown, and likewise anticipates some of the questions that carbon-neutral cinema and the resource image call out. The narrative follows three itinerant Kurdish teachers carrying large blackboards on their backs, wandering hills and villages along the warring border in search of students. The film reduces such vital cultural and social institutions as education, communications, even literacy, down to their essence and, juxtaposed against air raids, bomber jets, and groups of displaced Kurds struggling to find refuge, asks whether or not the teachers and their blackboards are necessary to Kurdish survival or extraneous to it. As the teachers are featured hiding under their cumbersome writing instruments as jet fighters rage above, the viewer recognizes that Makhmalbaf trades in elementary symbols—but so do the teachers; chalk and graphite, knowledge accumulated and remembered, offered up in exchange for the most basic provisions. The film was shot on handheld cameras and features nonactors; while the production does not appear unpolished or rough, the filmmaker's formal choices complement the crisis conditions endured by the refugees. The handheld camera and the backbreaking blackboard converge in Makhmalbaf's film, ultimately daring the viewer to make the connection between the necessity of mobility and communications systems in times of emergency and war. That cinema is a system of mobile communication is taken for granted; the ability to communicate, and thus to express, to protest, is one for which lives are risked. While environmental ideologies promote the need for a sustainable cinema, for filmmakers enduring conditions of scarcity or crisis, the terms ought to be reserved: not a sustainable cinema, but a cinema that sustains. Making movies is a basic cultural necessity, a resource necessary to maintain language and promote tradition—and so to stay alive, literally and culturally, in the face of imperial aggression, more often than not motivated by the thirst for resources.

Paul Virilio's seminal *War and Cinema* both narrates and theorizes the patterns of development that have merged war and cinema into a single techno-ideological regime of surveillance and, by extension, cultural management. But Virilio's intention is not just to prove how entrenched war is in cinema, or cinema in war; rather, the theorist of speed provides the tools with which to regard war and cinema as two symbiotically related entities that modify each other in accordance with the political needs and technological capabilities of a given historical moment. While the two operations bear political, ideological, and historical differences, a key feature that separates the 1991 war with Iraq (Gulf War I) and the 2003–2010 conflict (Gulf War II) is the digitization of the latter's media coverage and, even more so, its representation in digital documentaries and random, user-generated. and putatively open Internet forums such as YouTube. Added to this, however, is the specificity of the war itself, the essential root of its cause, and how the conflict over natural resources, in this case fossil fuels, underpins the materiality (if not the very ontology) of cinema, the chemically and now digitally produced image.

By extending its presence beyond Iraq into Iran, and from there to the central Asian republics and eventually to the oil riches contained in the Caspian Basin, the United States could come to control the globe's oil supply and thus ward off political competition from other economic heavyweights dependent on fuel imports, including Europe, Japan, China, and Southeast Asia.[1] It is essential to recognize that industrial militaries are motorized and technologized, and thus require fossil fuel energy. Gulf Wars I and II were oil wars twice over: battles fought both with and for fuel resources. But because the weaponry and ideology of war are inextricably linked to the means and ends of cinematic vision, what emerged from Gulf War II was a conflation between the categories of "resource" and "image." The resource image renders visible the subordination of nature as the root of industrial culture and is found in such displays of power as the moving image as a technology, as well as in what those images display: war, mobility, ecological incursion. It is here in the resource image that oil politics and attendant environmental contingencies become a discursive cultural category, the energy resource as a strategic way to locate and critique the means and ends of cinematic representation and of industrial culture itself. Virilio argues that war's victories are not counted so much in geographic, economic, or other material conquests, but in "appropriating the 'immateriality' of perceptual fields."[2] This subtle move calls attention to how vision and the image are not merely conceptual counterparts to material resources; they are themselves resources, and for strategic value alone outweigh the typical spoils of warfare. Virilio's inquiry and his process of theorization provide the groundwork necessary to formulate the resource image as a distinct discursive category, which then enables a specifically resource-conscious history of war's impact on the development of the cinematic image. Ever more overt is how environmental is war. In Iraq, for example, not only did battle itself impinge upon Iraqi terrain and infect the operative ecology of that country and indeed the globe, but the war's oil stakes were directly linked to supporting coalition countries' consumptive lifestyles both in the field and on the home front and, attendant to that, perpetuating full-scale environmental crisis. What is made legible via the representation of Iraq's years of devastation and continued horror is the convergence between war and image making and, as a necessary extension, the environmental impacts of both.

Taken together, Werner Herzog's *Lessons of Darkness* (1992) and Deborah Scranton's *War Tapes* (2006) capture the differences between how celluloid cinema and digital video behave toward and interact with the specifics of resource-driven war. The more overt points of contact between these films include the ways in which each engages environmental decay, the looming energy crisis, as well as challenges to the cultures of mobility from which each filmmaker so plainly springs. But what renders these documents of resource war truly fit for comparison is not their similar traits but rather their inherent differences—the most obvious of which is their technologies of representation: Herzog's analog film as opposed to Scranton's digital project. What is more, these films as a pair foreground how the already convergent technological histories of cinema and warfare are being reframed by the dominant lens of environmental politics. It is necessary to burden cinema and the image with a specific set of environmental concerns; digital video (DV) especially so, since its aesthetic values and technological capabilities are increasingly taken for granted as an immaterial form of communication and therefore "green" by default. But digital complements the environmental just as readily as it counters it. The conflict resides in DV's ability to facilitate political activism, while at the same time perpetuating the cycles of consumption and waste that are anathema to political and social equality and environmental stability. What happens when separating out and then reformulating the basic discursive units of a digitally imaged resource war is this: not only do digitization and militarization become increasingly inseparable, both aesthetically and ideologically, but environmental rhetoric surrounding resource procurement and consumption emerge as the heretofore obscured dimension that links war and cinema, both of which are moved by fossil fuel energy. Though Iraqi-generated images are included when possible, examples taken here are coalition-sided documentaries. Filmmaking in Iraqi does exist outside of sensational insurgent videos that make it onto YouTube, but after decades of political suppression, years of international sanctions, and then the emotional and physical devastation of war, the Iraqi film community is just beginning to find its footing. Recurrent electricity shortages, lack of basic cinematic infrastructure, and patchy education resources dog the efforts of practitioners, and yet they persevere. Filmmakers Mohamed al-Daradji and Oday Rasheed, for example, are gaining exposure at international film festivals, and were slated to open Iraq's first center of film production in Baghdad by the close of 2010. Their work, though as yet unavailable outside of Europe and Asia, will be included here as far as it is possible. Of course emerging Iraqi filmmakers present a vital and necessary contrast to Herzog and Scranton's perspectives, but the heretofore absence of Iraqi cinema speaks loudly in its own right, not only to the unbalanced representation of that country's invasion but also to the impact of resource scarcity on cinema during periods of devastation and crisis.

War Zones and Image Rations

Virilio's understanding of the mutuality between cinematic and military development takes for granted that film resources are readily available and so is focused on privileged cinema, the cinema of excess rather than the under-privileged cinema that emerges from zones like Iraq where scarcity rather than surfeit is the economic dominant. *War and Cinema*, then, is characterized by a centricity that ignores how the war-torn filmmaker manages when dispossessed of a steady or reliable means of producing images. As the narrative of early Soviet cinematic history reminds us, deprivation does not preclude cinematic production or innovation. Indeed, the integral Soviet-derived editing practices that provide an essential basis for both narrative and non-narrative cinema as we know it are rooted in a civil war economy impoverished of both basic life provisions as well as the resources necessary to make films. Thus, the cinematic experiments performed by the filmmakers and theoreticians of early Soviet cinema ("filming without film," in particular) speak to how the unilateral representations of Iraq and now Afghanistan are as much about politics as about material scarcity. By sheer contrast is the glut of Iraq war images that accumulated on television and Internet news sources, YouTube, and, more rarely, in theaters, thus signaling how unsustainable was the war and the level of energy it consumed.

During Russia's unstable post-revolutionary period of War Communism (1918–1920), the country's fledgling cinema industry experienced a prolonged spell of pronounced resource scarcity. What became or was becoming the USSR did not manufacture either raw stock or film equipment and so, with production companies having either fled the country or else hoarding whatever supplies remained, this phase of filmmaking was defined by consistent resource shortages. But in a sprawling and mostly illiterate country, the cinema was not an expendable indulgence but rather recognized as a vital instrument of propaganda and education, and so production and dissemination of moving images continued by whatever means possible. Notably, the discovery of numerous tsarist films in 1919 provided the country with a limited supply source and enabled the subsequent nationalization of the film industry. But low levels of production did not reflect in the ingenuity and enthusiasm of the newsreels and Agit-films that Dziga Vertov and Lev Kuleshov, later pillars of the montage movement, were generating out of whatever raw stock and recyclable bits they could muster. Paradoxical though it might seem, the most successful phase of early Soviet cinema overlapped with the lowest point of that society's well-being, marked with years of civil war, blockades, and famine.[3] This exceptional conflation of enthusiasm and impoverishment is exemplified by what has become a legendary moment in film history. When, in 1919, a copy of Griffith's *Intolerance* was smuggled past the anti-Soviet blockade, the film was embraced as a living textbook for a group of deprived and industrious Russian filmmakers who screened the images with obsessive repetition, cutting, and reediting sequences to thus discover and manipulate Griffith's techniques. An even more stunning example of cinematic thrift is Kuleshov's famous "film-without-film" experiments. The director of the newly inaugurated Moscow Film School instructed his students by cutting and re-editing extant films and also staging cinematic skits and montage sequences using curtained "frames" so as to simulate producing and viewing images. Additionally, the Soviet film practice was rounded out by the rigor of thinking through and writing about the politics of the image itself; regarded now as film theory, Kuleshov's or Eisenstein's philosophical accounts of cinematic form and practice are surely an instance of film-without-film.

The war economy and ideological fervor that forced cinema to survive in the absence of source materials is manifested in an editing style and a cinematic aesthetic that is economical and thus laconic.[4] In view of the relationship between the aesthetics of a film and the availability of necessary supplies, Eisenstein's characteristic repetition of a single shot defines how cinema has long been informed by an awareness of the image as a valuable, potentially *finite* resource. Kuleshov's experiments were likewise invested in image economy; the filmmaker discovered that a single cut could and must function simultaneously on three levels—narrative, emotional, and intellectual—thus inscribing the space between shots with as much discursive and aesthetic value as possible.[5] The political imperative to use the image to build a new society is the primary motivation behind this incredibly influential and even robust period of cinematic practice. But when resources and their scarcity are introduced as an evaluative framework it is not difficult to regard early Soviet filmmaking as a model for resource consciousness, forced as it was to defer to principles of recycling and reuse as well as an ideology of lack rather than one of excess. When crisis strikes, citizens, photographers, and filmmakers alike all reach for their cameras. But though the Soviets break the rule, prolonged periods of warfare typically freeze production. A more recent example is Oday Rasheed's *Underexposure* (2005), the first feature film shot in Iraq after the fall of Saddam Hussein. The production conditions make the film remarkable, harkening back as they do to the ingenuity of the early Soviets. While fellow Iraqi filmmakers spent the war years in Europe, Rasheed remained at home, and managed to work there too. His film was shot on expired 35mm stock salvaged from Saddam's archives and then purchased on the black market; the project itself was financed by local fundraising and selling off the crew's possessions. The stock, then, would have been as precious to Rasheed as the Griffith print to the Soviets, for after the Iraqi invasion of Kuwait and subsequent international sanctions, Iraq's film resources—stock, camera, and other necessary infrastructure—dried up profoundly. Add to that a government ban on film labs and processing chemicals, enacted in fear that biological weapons and not films would be the outcome. *Underexposure* is notable for nothing if not that it is the first feature film out of Iraq in fifteen years.[6] The cinematic rationing that the Iraqis and the early Soviets endured speaks to how filmmaking manages when dispossessed of the very energy and industrial materials over which conflict occurs. In terms of an environmental cinema ("green" or carbon-neutral), that is, the initiative to mitigate filmmaking's environmental footprint, it is not unreasonable to suggest that such organized efforts as Green Screen look to extant examples of cinema made in extreme political conditions for a model. The shoestring or no-string production in 1920s Russia and Iraq at the beginning of this century fights for life, to have any kind of impact or footprint at all, and is, therefore, sustainable by default.

The imagination does not need to stretch to conceptualize the resource-dependant networks which configure cinema and make the moving image mobile: from vehicles to lights to the gas-powered generators used on location, to shipping film reels or manufacturing the Netflix-compatible television set. The cinematic image, digitized or celluloid-based, is a manufactured or "unnatural" resource in and of itself. Like any other constructed resource, it is underwritten by other external resources—fossil fuel, for example, as well as the resource-based processes by which technologies industries manufacture imaging equipment. It is impossible to separate out the manufacture of technology from the so-called natural world that supplies the necessary building materials. Our network culture's "technological literacy," as Giles Slade calls it, must extend beyond interaction with electronic equipment and include a consumer-oriented understanding of the material politics compressed in the technological devices that lend so many contemporary lives unparalleled convenience.[7] The global demand for coltan (colombo-tantalum ore), for example, the essential ingredient in the tantalum capacitors used in laptops, cell phones, personal organizers, and other ubiquitous devices, has helped perpetuate the brutal civil war in the Democratic Republic of Congo where 80 percent of the world's coltan is mined. The "blood" that spoiled the glint of diamonds is also splashed across most consumers' cell phones. The 2010 gold and copper mine collapse in Chile that left thirty-three miners trapped in the depths of the earth foregrounds the risks taken by those human resources who are in the employ of an industry infamous for dangerous work conditions and exploitative labor policy. Such are the social, political, and material realities embedded in the products and physical components that enable global visual culture. The images (and other forms of what is broadly understood as information or digital content) that a simple mineral like coltan, once mined and refined, helps to record and then convey are not as ethereal as we might imagine; as such, the relationship between the consumer and the digitized image (the focus here) is not neutral, and images are themselves not weightless. This, of course, is precisely because that incorporeal mass that is the digital environment is in fact loaded with the complexities and burdens of social, environmental, and cultural politics, all of which need to be factored into the conventional historical trajectories, cultural shifts, and ontological conundrums pursued by media scholars. While Lisa Parks's and Charles Acland's inquiries into the residual life of technology so accurately argue against the cult of the new that is blinding technologies scholarship to the economic realities and marketing motives underpinning the false perception that our culture is in the throes of true innovation (rather than just serial replacement), the resources politics embedded in technology (and the images transmitted therein) also need inclusion. From mine shaft to end-user, Congo (the bloody coltan capital) to Ghana (the "digital dumping ground," as a 2009 PBS documentary of the same name calls it), the digital image is shot through with dirty geopolitics and environmental toxicity. Similarly, Slade's important inquiry into the history of planned obsolescence within technology industries and its connection to the global crisis of electronic waste, while critical, does not take cultural production into consideration. What the technology itself produces—photographs and e-mails, for example—must also be included within the larger problem of resource extraction and e-waste pollution. The material politics—including human injustice and environmental negligence—that Slade argues is embedded in the plastic and metals of contemporary mediation tools is equally applicable to the cultural and personal information these devices are intended to manufacture and convey. So, though technology has rendered information almost weightless, its production and transference is accomplished only by means of a mechanized infrastructure that remains as material and tangible as ever. While David Rodowick argues that digital media introduces a new regime of communication which breaks down any remaining differences between "plastic" and linguistic representation, the same rhetoric (plastics and decomposition) can and ought to be taken liter-ally, thus shifting digital/analog debates to include the essential questions of consumer politics, transnational economics, and the ostensibly shared global environment—questions that ingrain a broad spectrum of ethics into each digitized image or text we encounter daily (or reencounter, but of course in a bold "new" form).[8] The transformation of the concept of materiality is central to understanding the differences between the digital and analog arts, the former as abstract data, the later as workable matter.[9] But it is also vital to understand the continuum, one that is registered within the density and energy-intensity of making and transmitting moving images of any kind. It is because of the mythology of immateriality associated with the digital that cinema continues to eschew its increasingly topical associations as a "constructed" or "manufactured" resource—a material substance, in other words. So it remains that the overtly physical form of celluloid cinema (with its polyester-based, petroleum-derived film stock, cumbersome canisters, darkrooms, and, often enough, public theaters) more firmly and directly situ-ates the cinema, both in terms of the image itself and its technology, within the category of the resource. But because the digital yields a different set of medium-specific problems and complexities, it must be pulled down from the ether of the incorporeal and affixed with the ontological, environmental, and cultural designations appropriate for all resource-derived commodities.

But whether contemplating either digital or celluloid cinema, an essen-tial question remains: if the impoverished economy of war and subsequent rationing of film resources are the circumstances that ultimately structured Soviet montage and much of the editing practice that came after, what will the digitally imaged war in Iraq do to inscribe that medium's as yet inchoate and malleable aesthetics and practices? Or has the war—so readily available via Internet forums and the horrific shots soldiers so carelessly snap and then circulate—already shaped the ideologies and aesthetic values associated with the digital medium? Additionally, how might wartime models of cinematic scarcity inform carbon-neutral or sustainable filmmaking practices? At the root of a comparison between the early Soviets and digital imaging during the Iraq war is not only the shared conditions of a war economy, but also that the cinematic media specific to each moment were in a relatively early stage of dissemination and development, a fact directly related to either the availability of resources or lack thereof. The sheer abundance of digital videos and photographs intended to exploit or explore the Iraq war embodies a critical mass of protest, or what Megan Boler considers a "viral front" of antiwar sentiment. Boler reminds us that form and content are as inextricable as producer and consumer; but that does not always mean that viral communications, digital forms of dissent that operated within the matrix of dominant media environments, are politically disabled or their subversions rendered impotent by virtue of their placement with a dominant mode of representation.[10] At the same time, however, what this incredible deluge of unmanaged user-generated political engagement represents is a privileged consumer-culture ideology of overabundance, surfeit, and excess. The so-called "culture of access" enabled by digital technology has a flipside: a culture of excess. A dialectic tension thus emerges from the unfortunate and unavoidable irony that sees dissident or viral cinema's good intentions infected by this mode's inherent capacity for profuse excess, defined by the ability to record, transmit, and download seemingly without limitation. The swollen category of anti-establishment, counter-coalition DV dissidence is rendered a further example of what practitioners were attempting to dismantle: the ideology of consumption, waste, and disposability (of life, of landscape) and even the surfeit of technological speed itself that is both the means and ends of the resource war that undid Iraq. The "aesthetics of honesty" that Charles Musser attaches to the antiwar documentaries that responded to the Iraq invasion overlooks the fact that the democratization of digital video and photography that empowered the amateur filmmaker/ photographer heralded a grand visual exploitation of Iraq, visible in the images of Abu Ghrahib and the violent displays uploaded onto YouTube.[11] The dialectic between the image's ability to both challenge and consolidate dominant ideology or power structures, to give voice to the suffering of the Iraqi and also to exploit him or her, needs to be accounted for. The urgency of the situation and the stress of the circumstances were part of what accounts for the unpolished production values that characterize the films and videos Musser is considering; the conditions of both war and an emerging set of technological circumstances produces an aesthetic which requires the viewer to likewise adjust his or her cinematic expectations. Iraq-war documentary features, many digitally rendered, make prominent use direct cinema (or cinema verité) stylistics. Indeed, perhaps the most salient feature of both DV and direct cinema is the long take, a formal choice characterized by a seemingly random, roaming camera and accidental, ambulatory aesthetic, and which is now ever-more easily facilitated by digital's lightweight equipment and abundant capacity for uninterrupted recording. On an ideological level the long take produces a distinct set of problems, especially when the resource-based economics of DV excess are juxtaposed with the Soviet model of celluloid conservation and image rationing. What is ultimately at stake in situating the direct cinema style of antiwar documentaries alongside the Soviet example of cinematic scarcity is the inherent conflict of interest between form, content, and intent, wherein the pairing foregrounds and then complicates some of the utopian dimensions attributed to the political possibilities of digital video. Read as a signal of material excess and an ideology of material decadence, DV's long-take capacities (the camera effectively left to idle) represent, if not perpetuate, habits of waste and overconsumption. There is, then, something insidious about these very strategies, for when employed to represent and also ideally resist the war's hubris, they often entrench rather than subvert the patterns of overconsumption that are at the heart of the desperate turn of geopolitical oil interests, of which the invasion of Iraq was a crowning example. Jon Alpert and Matthew O'Neill's 2006 HBO documentary series *Baghdad ER*, for example, exemplifies how rough production values tend to absolve the filmmaker of the obligation to control the camera and thus engage directly with the politics of war. The text is completely open; devoid of narration, the only words spoken are those of the medics, physicians, and soldiers whose chaos and pain unfold before us without the obvious interference of authorial or editorial intrusion. This seemingly detached post-ideological approach renders the camera and the operator seemingly—dangerously—"invisible" or neutral, just as it did the adherents of direct cinema. But this neutrality is a silence and like all deliberate silence it speaks loudly, in this case testifying to a lack of political literacy and an inability to even attempt to map out the causes or consequences of the war itself.

The politics of disposability are a further dimension that informs the aesthetic of the Iraq war documentary and random open-access upload. Understood as a measurement of both waste and technological development, disposal marks the end-point of a trajectory of technological innovation and, ostensibly, perfection. Consumer culture's design and production ideology dictates that the final stage of a product's developmental evolution is marked not by its longevity or endurance, but rather by when it is rendered gloriously expendable and can thus seemingly disappear. Mass production and what Vance Packard called the "waste-maker" society depends on the expedient and endless circuitry of consumption wherein the affordable commodity wears out, is thrown out, and is then duly replaced by its identical equivalent.[12] Such is the ecology and the economy of planned obsolescence. The earliest phase of intentionally rendering products obsolete occurred in 1913, with the introduction of the electric starter in the automobile engine, the upshot of which was the outmoding of all the cars that came before it.[13] Technological obsolescence, then, is the outcome of innovation; creativity is matched by destruction and perfection, and likewise is measured by how well a product anticipates its own end. The defining assumptions and behaviors of digital culture are legible not only in the expendability of its technology, but also, necessarily, in the formal practices and principles of the disposable digital image. According to the inevitability of what is called "bit-rot," the digital image is, like all digital media, ephemeral—deterioration will occur in as few as five years and as many as fifteen. As ideologies of obsolescence drive the technologies industry it would seem counterintuitive to replace ephemerality with a long-term preservation solution. Hard storage mediums (celluloid or print) are relatively long-lasting when compared to digital's precarious rates of retention. Unless, that is, it is maintained. Continual format migration can offset decay, but it costs time, money, and hardware. The persistent illusion that digital is a long-lasting if not eternal means of preservation is attributable to the fact that digital copies are exact replicas of an original, without the downgrade that occurs with each analog print.[14] The problem that scholars and archivists recognize is that the speed of technological obsolescence renders digital holdings inaccessible. Information scientist Howard Besser expresses some palpable frustration and lament when he writes that while we can still engage with three-thousand-year-old cave paintings, we cannot "decipher any of the contents of an electronic file on an 8-inch floppy disk from only 20 years ago."[15] In tech-time fifteen years seems an eternity. Surely the bit-rot contingency will have been ironed out by then. Or perhaps not. The economics of obsolescence drive the tech industry; ephemerality is the name of the game—not longevity.

Daniel Rombes maintains that all films can be considered disposable; intended meaning and integrity is lost and so films (and photographs) are rendered expendable and valueless as they are fated to become fragmented, clips and bits atomized across the infinity of cyberspace.[16] What, then, of DV-inscribed conflicts such as Iraq? Susan Sontag insists that the glut of images introduced by technological innovation must come with an ethics of viewing, such that the suffering Other put on display is not rendered essentially disposable.[17] Does the instantaneity and abundance of digital imaging lessen the image's ability to sear our consciousness and perhaps prompt action—even if on the level of simply remembering? That so much of its coverage is "born digital" means that the technology that makes the war accessible also dictates that the media documents that would otherwise serve as historical records may in fact prove ephemeral. How thoroughly disposable, then, may digital technology render contemporary war? The scarcity of images that informed the early Soviet cinema's civil war years could be outmatched by digital's limited retention rates; an image scarcity, then, could come not during the conflict, but after, when these specific images and their supporting formats have disappeared. So it is that hidden within digital's image glut is its opposite: the potential for deprivation and a total, utter lack.

The Pipeline: Image as Resource

When Internet delivery began to supplant print, radio, and televisual forums, CNN took initiative and began offering live and on-demand coverage of international and national news via broadband Internet connections—but because it was commercial-free, it was available only with a subscription. CNN called the service, now discontinued, its "Pipeline." Though only a few years before the time of this writing, it is difficult remember a time when one paid to access what seems such a cheap commodity as news information. The Pipeline was opened in 2005, at the height of the war in Iraq war, when it seemed that there was something to constantly justify the service's uninterrupted liveness. The service consisted of four feeds, each called a pipe, one of which was the conventional news service, while three others broadcast live "raw" video of weather, international, and national news. In 2007, however, CNN rerouted the pipes to its commercially sponsored website where all video content would be made available for free. The transition was perhaps a response to the emergence of YouTube, which, along with major television networks, was granting free and open access to online video—as was not the case when the Pipeline was launched.

Pipeline has two accepted definitions: first, as a conduit for the transportation of petroleum or natural gas and, second, as a channel of news and information. The metaphorical value here is significant. Not only does the term describe news and information as resources, it also ironically aligns CNN's live images of Iraqi horrors—the dominant source of the service's content—with the same petroleum politics that were the rationale for the U.S. invasion. The rhetoric of oil distribution infrastructure unintentionally but richly fostered new possibility for how the image of war was conceptualized: before it is refined by editors and technicians, cut and presented according to editorial and advertising criteria, and finally pumped down the pipeline and into the marketplace of Internet broadcasting, the image must be extracted from the rawness of the world at large. By equating the process of retrieving, refining, and then disseminating news and information with the transportation of petroleum, CNN's VIP subscription site exemplified how resource consciousness has seeped into the conceptual and aesthetic terrain of image culture. Pipeline was truly a semiotic gem, marking as it did the last decadent laugh of the Bush administration, and also the weakening of U.S. economic and geopolitical domination. Caught in its fossil fuel framework, the Pipeline conflated such seemingly disparate items as the energy debate and the crisis in American car manufacturing, as well as features on pollution, global warming, and, of course, resource warfare in Iraq. Whatever its coverage, the Pipeline never ceased to encapsulate what this book calls the resource image; every last one of its gratuitous dimensions magnified how petroleum resources cannot be separated from a single facet of industrial culture, including the images and information that it produces. In the summer of 2010 the politics of oil exploded, literally and imagistically. The Deepwater Horizon disaster was followed by pipeline explosions in Michigan and then Illinois, events punctuated by vitriolic ad campaigns targeted at the well-managed ecological disaster in Alberta's Athabasca tar sands energy development, the images of which introduced a new set of energy politics: namely, the increasing danger that comes with securing "friendly" sources of oil. The resource image thus assumed new focus, and it came in the form of pictures gleaned from submersible cameras capturing the action live as oil gushed into the waters of the Louisiana Gulf Coast.

Then the war in Iraq ended. The military will instead grant Afghanistan's reconstruction more concentrated attention. And so it should; as George Monbiot reported in the *Guardian*, if U.S. energy giants want to control the movement of oil riches from the Caspian Sea to markets in Europe and North America, the route to pursue are pipeline networks through Afghanistan. The reconstruction is counterterrorist and it is equally colonialist; energy-hungry, in other words. As Chalmers Johnson argues, the nature of contemporary warfare continues to shift; the total war that characterized the Cold War period has been replaced by the even more entrenched and insidious form of U.S. imperial expansion which he calls an "empire of bases." The multitude of U.S. military bases abroad, some 725 acknowledged by the Defense Department, are positioned in areas accessed during World War II and the Cold War but extended in scope once the Soviet

Union collapsed and its former oil-rich territories opened up for imperial expansion.[18] This particular brand of political culture is premised on the business of rationalizing and maintaining active and deactivated military and thus perpetuating its vast networks of what has become the nebulously termed military-industrial complex. The empire of bases exists to support an inactive or seemingly dormant state of permanent war designed to drain foreign territories of their resources. The United States is after all the globe's largest consumer of energy. Justifying its foreign presence under the guise of humanitarian initiatives or disarming rogue states, chief among the real, predatory goals of post–Cold War military, is to consume the product it is structured around securing.[19] Emptying its energy reserves in order to refill them, the means and ends of oil war are the same. The resource-based conflict and imperial incursion is thus engaged in an endogamous and self-defeating circuitry that is determined by the same petroleum it must consume in order to operate.

Indeed, as political geographer Phillipe LeBillon argues, war in the post-Cold War period is characterized by a political ecology that is intricately tied to the geography and political economy of natural resources.[20] What Cleo Paskal terms "global warring" concisely intersects weather calamity with fossil fuel security, which are together shifting the balance of geopolitical power and turning citizens of even heretofore impervious Western nations into environmental refugees.[21] However, it should be pointed out that resources are not immanent; they do not exist, they become as such, created as they are from historical processes of social construction. Through semiotic production and manipulation, societies manufacture the values that transform rocks into gems, cows into beef, or raw crude into energizing fuel. Diamonds, for instance, exemplify how cutting processes and other stages of refinement as well as the power of marketing transform a worthless material into something else, a precious commodity with economic and symbolic value. From this, it is not difficult to see how hydrocarbon culture's desire to further innovate (replace) its means of mechanization and mobility is produced by industry marketing. But the satisfaction of this desire has gone beyond transforming fossil fuel into a resource, rendering oil's energy density invaluable. What is "natural" about petroleum reserves does not extend beyond the basic fact that it exists in nature; industrial culture, however, is defined by and thrives upon the manufacture of "unnatural" resources. LeBillon, for example, points to how Japan, a country relatively poor in naturally occurring resources has built a globally expansive economy through technological innovation and the manufacture of consumer goods; these are artificial resources, in other words, but resources all the same.[22]

The image and the determinants of its technology are the manufactured resources of industrialized culture. Thinking about the image as a resource both practically and metaphorically alters how cinematic representations of the chaos in Iraq, violence in Afghanistan, or pure toxicity spilling into the Gulf Coast waters are received. Affixing the designation resource image to the war documentary or live-feed news item undermines and even demystifies the naturalized, normalized categories that resource wars both produce and keep separate. According to the "political ecology of war," the availability of resources determines a nation's likelihood for conflict.[23] Engagement in conflict is, of course, sustained by resources (fuel, food, soldiers), which in turn determine how extensively the environment will be tapped and ultimately drained, thus necessitating or inviting further conflict. War, in other words, has a two-fold dependency on resources—their abundance facilitates belligerent greed-driven conflict, while their scarcity rationalizes need-driven aggression. In industrialized warfare, petroleum resources physically mobilize forces, manufacture and then transport arms, and render weaponry operative, as well as keep the lights on and, perhaps more indirectly, keep the troops feed. Warfare conducted by so-called post-industrial nations obviously still requires the availability of naturally occurring resources; indeed, just such an exigency was both the means and ends of the U.S. war in Iraq. Both Jean Baudrillard and Virilio have suggested that Gulf War I was the war that saw the image explicitly weaponized and employed as a tool of strategic surveillance, missile guidance, and propaganda, and to the point that the TV, computer, or movie screen became an alternate battlefield.[24] The coalition side of the war was facilitated by means of image-based technology which allowed its forces to fight virtually—that is, from afar—and also enabled news broadcasters, CNN most famously, to manipulate and exploit their images within the zone of ideological warfare. Winning a war, CNN's urgent live broadcasts proved, meant controlling public perception through visual representation. Indeed, Virilio's opus of criticism is largely founded on the idea that weapons are equally tools of destruction and perception. From convenience foods to cameras, to communications tools such as the Internet, civil society's most innocuous features are often appropriated from military usage. The form and content of cinematic production is no exception; our moving images are inherently militarized. What distinguished the images of the first war in the Gulf (Operation Desert Storm) was the rapidity with which they were disseminated, a feature that directly corresponded with the conflict's brief duration. The war was undetectable and invisible—the war "that did not take place" as Baudrillard similarly assessed it.[25] What is different now, however, as Henry Giroux points out, is that access to digital resources characterize both sides of the conflict. In a war of images, video technology is also the terrorist's primary tool whose "regime of spectacle" Giroux posits is not tainted with consumer society's oversaturated image economy because of the sway of its political intentions.[26] That the violent nature of insurgent videos is concordant with so-called Western tastes grants them potency and value in the "war on terror's" image economy and thus demands that they be equated with and not separated from, say, the images broadcast by CNN. Indeed, there is no essentialist claim to ownership where the "unnatural" resource of imaging is concerned: when both sides are thus armed they are equally advantaged and disadvantaged by the culture of access (and excess) that comes with digital technology.

Ten Cameras Are Better than None: The Absent Filmmaker

Werner Herzog's 1992 documentary *Lessons of Darkness* is structured around the Kuwaiti oil fires that signaled the conclusion of Gulf War I. The film enjoys a singular, if not notorious, reputation both for its intrepid subject matter as well as its unconventional and ultimately genre-bending strategies of documentation. Herzog's dictum of the "ecstatic truth" conflates nonfiction and fiction, real-world with the imaginary, in order to capture a sense of veracity that is only obtainable when the bounds of representational accuracy are exceeded. *Lessons of Darkness* behaves as a science-fictional repositioning of the 1991 oil war wherein the operations of Desert Shield and Desert Storm are kept anonymous and instead are rendered a future intergalactic event. It is a heady work, one in which Herzog evokes and then abuses an impressive arsenal of documentary rhetoric and conventions; the intention is to wrest the events of Iraq's withdraw from Kuwait away from the discursive dominance of CNN and challenge the oversaturated sensibilities of its viewership. The film determines to turn warfare back into an unspeakable monument to horror and despair. *Lessons of Darkness*'s technological means are conservative, and stubbornly so; Herzog's sententious document polarizes itself against the digitizing video-game aesthetic that characterized 1991's war in Kuwait and thus remains almost archaic in its decision to avoid what was then the emergent new media technology utilized by both the U.S. military and the media to create a spectacular onslaught of urgency, present-tense liveness, and maximum efficiency.

While Herzog's analog film had few competitors and came at the close of the 1991 war, Deborah Scranton's *War Tapes* (2006) is but one of a robust genre of documentaries, many digitally rendered, continuing to emerge from the war zone of Iraq. Despite the title's anachronistic reference to tape recording, an earlier mode of video technology, Scranton's contribution to the representation of the globe's second grandiose resource war embraces the digital technology that is the common currency of journalists, documentary filmmakers, snipers, and suicide bombers, as well as the U.S. soldiers who harness it to both correspond with the home front and survey the enemy. And with these multiple, often conflicting user groups comes the attendant conflation of production and reception forums and the defining erosion of the distinctions between news broadcast, professional documentary, insurgent video, and YouTube upload.

The juxtaposition of the analog Herzog and the digital Scranton exposes how ideological dimensions implicated in these shifts is manifested in each mode's technological capabilities—including the limitations of a single camera versus the multicamera strategies of digital verité—and its ability to manufacture pictures of war. On behalf of articulating the newly emerging temporality of deferred destruction that characterized 1991's Gulf conflict, *Lessons of Darkness* takes for it subject the wasted terrain and suffering ecosystem of an unnamed planet. The film is premised upon exploiting the First Gulf War's heavy-handed abstraction, wherein the desert is washed out by deliberately spilled oil, petroleum fields are turned into infernos, and human life forms are rendered nothing less than extraterrestrial beings. The seeming purity and cleanliness of the war that was not a war, with its minimum of U.S. casualties and end to hand-to-hand combat, is hyperbolized by Herzog's science-fictional documentary as it strategically removes the soldier from the war and transforms the casualty of combat from the human being to the natural environment. Scranton's *War Tapes*, however, like the war she is representing, operates in stark opposition to the putative nonevent that was Operation Desert Storm and reinstates the soldier into the zones of battle and cinema alike.

It was with the permission of the U.S. military that Scranton equipped ten GIs with digital video equipment before their unit shipped out for a one-year tour of duty in Baghdad. Shifting camera power from the expert (documentarian) to the amateur (foot soldier), Scranton's film is premised on expediting the disappearance and indeed obsolescence of the actual or firsthand filmmaker herself. Using e-mail and text messaging in order to provide advice and technical assistance, Scranton was able to collect eight hundred hours of footage during the course of the year; these were electronically transmitted from Iraq to Scranton, who then edited them into the resultant *War Tapes*. The film has been called a "virtual embed" and "participatory journalism," wherein the soldier is transformed into a variant of the journalist, particularly as some of the footage shot for Scranton was later acquired by CNN. Because of the unprecedented danger of the war zone, combat journalists were scarce and in their stead news media used the digital film and photos captured by Iraqi stringers and U.S. soldiers. The paucity of journalists in Iraq was hardly noticeable. Digital video and photography enabled the outsourcing of image extraction to amateurs—Iraqi citizens and U.S. soldiers—and added to that was a significant number of independent documentary filmmakers. The result is a sheer abundance of images both representing and dismantling seven years of resource war.

Because of the ubiquity of the digital camera, Scranton's group of soldiers was already more than familiar with how to use the camcorders she provided. Scranton thus shot the war virtually, by technological proxy, but digital imaging and recording devices do not abstract the war so much as they abstract the filmmaker, who attempts to confine her film's focus to U.S. basic infantry and the tedium of soldiering. In exchange for the stark desert environment that characterized the 1991 conflict, Iraq was a predominantly urban war and it was a ground war, war fought with hands and on foot—its reality is characterized by a distinct sloppiness instead of the First Gulf War's detached virtual precision. Scranton's soldiers occupy the entirety of the screen, and their collective physical presence dominates the competing spaces of back and middle ground; likewise, the messy, amateur associations of the Iraq war are manifested in the aesthetic logic of its digital representation. Scranton's film exemplifies how the image-currency of Iraq's war economy was not only inherently digital but that it was also amateur, instinctive, and largely unguided. The disorder of Iraq and the unpolished rawness of its cinema challenge the precision, cleanliness, mystifying complexity so often associated with digital technology. The velocity that characterized Gulf War I's image-weapons complemented its quick duration and is now even more definitively located in the very medium that turned Iraq into the DV war. In addition to DV's quick-release capacity, the progressive scanning camera's sixty frames per second inscription rate records images at twice celluloid's twenty-four frames per second rate. But the precision of the technology belies the base, corporeal dirt of what was Iraq's interminable occupation just as readily as it attempts to capture it.

As far as camera work is concerned—that is, the actual, literal labor of capturing footage—Scranton and Herzog's films have in common, at least in part, the filmmaker's absence. Scheduling urgencies and entrance visas dictated that much of the aerial, helicopter portions of *Lessons of Darkness* were executed before Herzog's arrival in Kuwait, and so his voice-over was later dubbed in to create the impression of the filmmaker's omniscience and omnivoyance. But while *Lessons of Darkness* exploits the director's authorial presence, the legitimacy implied by Scranton's physical detachment is the very premise of her enterprise. With Scranton's strategic withdraw from the firsthand, footage-gathering stage of filmmaking, *War Tapes* can be read as a challenge to the conflict's failed and much criticized promotion of embedded journalism and the degree to which it erodes the chances of producing critical insights rather than sanitized, sanctioned views of military operations. Scranton's film is both evenhanded and inherently critical of the war in Iraq. Through the careful editing of soldier monologues, what emerges is a critique of the conflict's privatization and what seem lavish living conditions enjoyed by the employees of U.S. contractors, particularly when compared to the underpaid and ill-equipped troops who are charged with extracting her images. But exposing the shameful reliance on private contracting via the soldiers' videos, the director unintentionally builds a self-reflexive irony into the virtuality of her enterprise. Indeed, while preserving her safety and claims to objectivity, what Scranton herself is doing, consciously or otherwise, is outsourcing the labor of wartime documentary filmmaking, rendering it privatized, commodified, not to mention militarized; she thus inadvertently demonstrates how digital technology enables the possibility of contracting out the work of the film crew, not only to private industry, but to the military and citizens themselves. The film is thus hinged upon the implicit and explicit portrayal of competing systems of labor: the lavishly paid private contractor is pitted against the slavishly exploited GI and, by extension, the absent filmmaker is situated in opposition to the unpaid soldier-journalist. Indeed, in a revealing post-tour interview, one of the ten soldiers cynically acknowledges the business opportunities military conflict creates: not only do Haliburton and other private conglomerates profit from providing and maintaining the infrastructure of warfare and the extraction and transportation of petroleum resources, but so does the soldier, by earning his wage and education credits. And so does Scranton, he cynically insists, by means of the film he imagines she will profit from. And Scranton's film does betray its own best intentions. Because of its production logistics, it can be situated not apart from but symptomatic of the oil war's shifting discursive categories including, for example, the privatization of the military, the militarization and digitization of journalism, the outsourcing of filmmaking and news gathering, and the conflation between the resource and the image. The film is remarkable because more than other Iraq war documentaries, its ten-camera strategy makes explicit digital technology's capacity for excess, glut, resource abuse, and the inevitable waste thus generated. Scranton's film represents an assumption about resource availability and entitlement—not always directly, in terms of the war's procurement of natural resources, but indirectly, through the ideology of resource excess and access that the digitally equipped soldier/filmmaker harnesses and transforms into a distinct aesthetic which characterizes digital cinema on the battlefield and beyond.

Werner Herzog, by contrast, favors the stalwart rigidity afforded by analog formats. Freeze-frames, zooms, or studio shoots are also anathema, and whenever possible the filmmaker relies on a stationary camera. Herzog "holds onto his images with vulturous patience" and avoids both "flashy tricks" and "excess of cuts."[27] Rather than adapt to what has become the industry standard of approaching a scene or shot with multiple cameras, Herzog has acquired a reputation for stubbornly relying upon a single camera to capture a staged scene or live event. A lone camera reduces the amount of footage an editor has to work with; such limited resources can result in having to accommodate or even include inconsistencies or imperfections. Obviously there are generational and cultural reasons for Herzog's stubborn aesthetic of conservation. As he postulates in his own *Little Dieter Needs to Fly* (1997) and *My Best Fiend* (1999), Herzog's psyche is informed by the poverty of postwar Germany and so possesses a resource consciousness likely unknown to those who have not experienced a war economy's scarcity. In direct contrast to the limitations of the comparatively cumbersome and expensive celluloid-based cinema, Scranton's digital embed easily sources from ten cameras and ten separate operators to gain ostensibly privileged access to the war in Iraq. The resultant film is only ninety minutes long; thus, we might wonder not only what happened to the other 710 hours but also whether ten cameras provided any greater sense of clarity or insight than three or four, or one, might have done. Of course, because the footage accumulated by these ten cameras is ostensibly immaterial it is not conceptualized as overtly wasteful, unlike the physical discards that would have been generated by its analog counterpart. And yet the symbolic logic of Scranton's substitution of ten cameras for her single self still destabilizes digital's mythologies of thrift and economy. Replete as the film is with overt implications of glut and patterns of overconsumption, the most insidious example is self-reflexive and resides in how she herself engages in the same consumer-cultural behavior and aesthetic of overabundance—the very foundation of the oil war that she and her soldiers are representing and often critiquing.

As Virilio noted some months after the 1991 war, a "golden rule" common to both war and post-industrial economies is that success on the battlefield or controlling market share depends on the ability to innovate.[28] And so cinematic representation must reinvent itself, or seem to do as such, and not only in terms of accommodating the benefits of new technology but also in terms of its ability to use that same technology to criticize and theorize, self-reflexively or otherwise, the very systems and structures from whence it comes.

One remediating approach to technology argues that what is new does not represent a clean rupture with what came before but, often enough, a replication of it, contemplating the expressive and archival possibilities that digital presents often enough perpetuates the production of desire for its speed and crispness.[29] There is a connection between form and content, the digital image and the war it is representing. While technology itself might be inert, where it came from—the drive to innovate—and the energy it consumes is not free or neutral, and neither is how we commandeer the technology when we hold it in our hands.[30] The ability to overuse, waste, and dispose of a technology, whether that happens in accordance with the ten-camera aesthetic or the single-use shot, signal the kind of cultural behavior that contributes to the inextricably linked environmental crisis, the resource conflict, and the strife that continues in Iraq.

The Absent Story: Information as Resource

Harper's reported in 2007 that the previous year the "weight, in ounces, of all the information that passed through the Internet" was a mere 0.00004. The conveyance of information is industrial and now post-industrial warfare's most potent means of combat; visual or linguistic, information is facilitated by technology's systems of rapid transference and has assumed a velocity so fierce and encompassing it has merged with the very speed of its conduction. But is information really weightless? Social, political, and economic dimensions surely grant it substance, as does its technological burdens.

Just as communications technology and weaponry are engaged in a race for ubiquity and immediacy, the power of information is "like a bomb's destruction," contained in how quickly it is disseminated.[31] When information is absorbed by its delivery system, the information source itself is subject to disappearance, and so is its referent. Virilio's aesthetics of disappearance and politics of speed privilege the idea that technological capabilities will only accelerate further and will therefore continue to render information increasingly immaterial; these convictions do not acknowledge the very real and hazardous material manifestations of our culture's electrified and digitized systems of communication and information production. In other words, while media theorists argue for a symbiosis between speed and technology, a more accurate materialist assessment of the velocity that characterizes post-industrial culture would have to include fuel and energy within the theoretical and political networks of its geography. The energy war in Iraq was a battle fought over nothing less than the right to generate speed, remain mobile, and keep motors running.

Digital media, the rhetoric goes, promise ever more pure, effortless, and purportedly energy-efficient means of paperless mass communication, while at the same time ruling out how its technological innovations contribute to a crisis of techno-trash, electronic waste, and, by extension, global environmental decay. However, "the entire edifice of new communications technology," Jonathan Sterne writes, "is a giant trash heap waiting to happen." Immateriality, invisibility, disappearance—these are privileged categories, part of the "hubris of computing and the peculiar shape of digital capitalism" which is defined by a self-perpetuating and self-defeating decadence that reflects not only the ideology of screen culture's technology but much of the theorizing that has accompanied it.[32] The ascendancy of digital cinema is matched by the rise of environmental politics (and, of course, ecological decline) and together represent a curiously conflictive moment in contemporary culture wherein digital immateriality ("pure," efficient, and ephemeral) and environmental materiality (the pernicious residues of technological obsolescence, disposability, and waste) are at once converging and also canceling each other out. Ecologizing the image, situating it within a network of unnatural and natural resources, means that the immaterial or built environment contained within images is causally linked to the material, global environment upon which "disappearing" post-industrialized cultures depend—and, by extension, destroy.

Walter Benjamin's essay "The Storyteller" captures something of the idea that information is not unlike a manufactured resource; largely expendable, it is characterized by the same principle of planned obsolescence that informs technological innovation and perpetuates systems of disposability and waste accumulation. "The value of information," Benjamin writes, "does not survive the moment in which it was new. It lives only at that moment; it has to surrender to it completely and explain itself to it without losing any time."[33] But as opposed to time-sensitive information, a story does not "expend itself. It preserves and concentrates its strength and is capable of releasing it even after a long time." Industrialized warfare erodes the capacity to tell stories; after World War I, Benjamin notes, the men who returned from war had "grown silent"; they were not "richer—but poorer in communicable experience."[34] Benjamin's essay anticipates network culture's challenge to narrative (from its formal linearity to the diminished linguistic literacy of techno-centric citizens), while also suggesting the reciprocity between military innovations and the evolution of communication technologies. Likewise, Benjamin's description of information as expendable and the story as durable is prescient, for it thinks through the ecological ontology that underwrites the digital documentaries, news reports, and YouTube uploads that are herein termed resource images: expendable, intended to be consumed, burned up in the very act of viewing. The trash heap of history is made, at least in part, literal, assuming the formlessness of accumulated information and the creative waste of digital imagery.

The value of information, as Benjamin argues, is that it does not outlast itself; if the documentation of events becomes dependent on digital forms that are not responsibly migrated to durable support surfaces, the memory of the event itself is fundamentally compromised. Understood in terms of the limited shelf-life of digital dissidence as well as Benjamin's informational expendability, *War Tapes* and its colleagues represent not only a specific subset or even genre of Iraq war cinema but a new category of conflict representation in general—the disposable war documentary. The very possibility of this conception is reflective of the war itself, and not only as the Iraq war was premised on the further extraction and consumption of fuel resources—that is, the search for the next momentary energy fix. There is also an attendant critical cynicism evidenced in media and governmental rhetoric that continues to degrade the war as something lesser, not a war at all. Iraq has euphemistically been popularized as a "conflict," an "occupation," a "mission," or an "operation." It is fitting that a war that is a part of an imperialistic presence is equated with a technology in possession of an almost infinite capacity for shooting and storage. Though batteries have limited energy and must be replaced or recharged, a DV camera's storage space does not deplete nearly as rapidly as does a reel of celluloid film stock. It is a technological innovation that corresponds to total war, pure war, war that is spatially and temporally continuous, as well as to Chalmers Johnson's thesis on the empire of bases, also conceived of as a state of total war—diffused, thinly spread, inherently insidious. While Gulf War I was decreed to be invisible, post-human, and, apart from the enemy, almost without casualty, the war in Iraq was characterized by a sluggish tempo and after seven interminable years, an anticlimactic finish. Its violence, though, is still, for the moment, visible, and fully accessible in all its excess.

Ecologized War: The Meteorological Image

"Homeland Security is strengthening our northern and southern borders. Unfortunately, the biggest threat we face may come from the east." So read Protecting America's full-page ad in *New Yorker* magazine in 2007, at the height of the conflict in Iraq and the memory of Hurricane Katrina crisis painfully fresh. What the ad's richly layered implications and metaphors exemplify is a crisis in the representation of the temporal and spatial shifts of post-industrial war's environmental manifestations. Interconnecting resource war, the built environment of the screen image, and the biophysical world that sustains war and culture alike, the ad foregrounds colliding categories of ambient warfare, digitized and militarized time and space, and resultant manifestations in what can be called the "meteorological image."

The real eastern threat to American security is not, as we might imagine, Middle Eastern terrorism, but meteorological imbalance. The ad's fine print explains (and scientists have proven) that the Atlantic Ocean is heating up, resulting in a record number of increasingly devastating hurricanes. "We can't afford to leave ourselves exposed like this any longer," the message warns Americans. Trading on the metaphorical value of a thinly veiled foreign category of weather-related threat, the rhetorical choices both exemplify and literalize what Mike Davis calls the "ecology of fear." Writing in 1998, Davis described how the "cultural immune system" of disaster-prone California is equipped to deal with localized environmental traumas such as forest fire, earthquakes, and floods, but categorically ignores the equally inevitable occurrence of tornadoes and hurricanes; these latter weather events, Davis argues, are considered "exotic" or alien, and therefore accepting their existence on home turf demands a radically altered environmental perspective. The terrorist menace now seems to have filled in the blank of this nascent meteorological other, lending new relevance to Davis's prescient assertion that environmental perceptions are ideologically determined. Just as Davis's arguments situate California's precarious environmental conditions within the larger framework of race and class politics, global warming is a telling barometer of social and political relations, both globally and locally. The ecology of fear exceeds Davis's immediate time and place and exposes some of the discursive overlaps between the anxious anticipation of environmental disaster and the panic generated by the war on terror. Oil security and ecological disaster (anthropogenic and "natural') are increasingly spilling over, muddying each other's waters, and revealing themselves as flip sides of the same volatile coin. Categories of fear shift such that the environment assumes the role of the homeland's chief menace, the invisible intruder that will not be deterred by fences or defeated by conventional weaponry. According to the imagination of the advertisement, weather events or meteorological threats are not localized but generalized, bred somewhere vaguely understood as "offshore." They remain irrational and indiscriminate; rooted in nothing, they arrive bearing no discernible episteme, just an inert and innate sense of ill will. The current sense of meteorological hazard in the U.S. is both personified and reduced to the very basic essence of "east." The twenty-first century's tropical storm is thus cast as the terrorist other—disguised, however, not as an immigrant at the border, but as brutal winds, torrential floods, and sweeping tidal waves.

This new warfare is environmental, and as such it assumes a temporality that is continuous; its leaking physicality exceeds borders and thus cannot be contained (or detained, imprisoned, or questioned). What makes the Protecting America spread remarkable is that the image chosen to represent the menace gathering strength in the east is as small as it is ambiguous. But the innocuous image introduces a larger problem: the inability to represent the space and time of the chronic rather than acute manifestations of environmental collapse. How, then, to visually frame an invisible threat? How also to make a film about a war that was not a war?

The geopolitical oil empire has repurposed the terms of the "cold" war of the Soviet era, rendering war an "occupation" in the case of Iraq or an ideological battle against such amorphous categories as terror. All told, the presence of war, however vague, is defined by and inscribed in the ambient nature of its news broadcasts and in particular digital representations. But as the continuing relevance of Herzog's *Lessons of Darkness* testifies, 1991's transition to an ecological warfare means that pure war is not clean war; blood and gore must now be reconsidered as dirt and pollution. The devastation wrought by eco-war is prolonged and invisible; its residual effects are mostly chronic rather than acute, deferred until the next decade, lifetime, or generation rather than made immediately palpable. Operation Desert Storm implicitly framed itself as a component of the environment. A storm is natural, indiscriminate; its devastation can only be fully measured in terms of the unforeseen aftermaths of its effects. Because *Lessons of Darkness* is science fictional, it refuses to submit to the context of 1991 politics and the aesthetics of its warfare. Herzog exploits the spectacle of Kuwait's oil spills and burning wells on behalf of exploding the idea of war, both in itself and specifically this new speed-of-light war of nonaggressive aggression and bloodless, bodiless victims. By insisting on a futuristic environmental war, a war waged against the no-man's-landscape, Herzog's film essentially anticipates and then thinks through the consequences of Gulf War I before they were manifest. The documentary posits that post-industrial war is defined by a principle of deference, wherein the casualties, environmental as well as human, surface later, after the conflict has been forgotten, and thus take on a burden of invisibility. Beyond the virtuality of the coalition's electronic warfare there loomed the real repercussions of Iraqi aggression: destroying the enemy's land and natural resources. Iraqi soldiers withdrawing from Kuwait systematically polluted the region; nearly five hundred oil-producing wells were set on fire, the resultant slicks from which spread for over 40,000 square kilometers. *Lessons of Darkness* visualizes what Virilio described as the future of this war, "pure" (sterile, bloodless, trans-human) in the sense that the casualties were as yet undetected.

Because it is specifically connected to oil production, and so to the entirety of a nation's industry and economy, intentionally ravaging an enemy's fuel industry and supplies renders petroleum a malevolent and dangerous force precisely because the outgrowth of the effects are incalculable. Israel's 2006 bombing of Beirut's power plants and petroleum tanks are exemplary. The massive oil spillage devastated Lebanon's Mediterranean shore and ecosystem so extensively that the manifestations spread as far as Turkey and Greece. Surely the BP spill in 2010 could spawn conspiracy theories had not the British oil giant not accepted blame, however reluctantly.

Indeed, the effects of 1991 are still with us; deterred manifestations, for example, now include post-traumatic stress disorder and Gulf War syndrome. Like chronic environmental effects, war injury is rendered invisible, an embodied illness rather than a visible wound. As a way to manage the cinematic representation of unseen injury, it seems that the prolonged release of narrative films about 1991 reflects the fact that the war's 760 direct casualties had by May 2002 taken an additional 8,306, with 159,705 more reported injured or ill from exposures suffered during the operations; from there the figures will only continue to grow.[35] The intangible, immaterial nature of digital media corresponds to emerging categories of invisible injury, exemplified by Jonathan Demme's recent adaptation of *The Manchurian Candidate* (2004) as well as John Maybury's *The Jacket* (2005), both premised on the psychological injuries of Gulf War I, finally manifested after ten years. In Demme's adaptation of the 1962 political thriller the hero's dilemma remains the inability to provide physical evidence that his body has been infected and thus injured. And because it is a remake of a Cold War text, the film also suggests that the temporal and spatial continuum of pure, total war remains relevant; defined by its own logic, the conception sprawls into the present moment and, as an implicit warning, beyond it as well. Indeed, in terms of cinematic or literary representations, there are relatively few examples of Gulf War I; no doubt the "nonevent" of the war-that-was-not-a-war corresponds to the slim interest cultural practitioners have given it. A few examples, though, have emerged relatively recently: in addition to the films of Demme and Maybury, David O. Russell's *Three Kings* (1999) and Sam Mendes's *Jarhead* (2005) are notable examples. This belated response is not only attributable to how the Iraq War might have inspired 1991's conflict with fresh topicality, but can also be seen as an extension of Gulf War I's futuristic reconfigurations. If the Vietnam War was the TV war and the First Gulf War was CNN's video-game war-that-was-not-a-war, the war in Iraq was the DV war. And because DV cinema is generated so quickly and cheaply, with production and dissemination times kept absolutely minimal, Iraq war images feverishly accumulated.

While representations of the First Gulf War were largely confined to and defined by CNN's urgent live-feed ticker-tape broadcasts, Gulf War II lacked the same broadcasting limitations. Internet access and digital video lent Iraq a breadth rather than a depth, extending coverage and representations over any number of times, places, and screening surfaces.

As opposed to the touchless, trans-human precision of the First Gulf War's smart bombs and pilotless aircraft, Gulf War II saw an almost regressive transference from remote-controlled aerial-based sighting devices to hand-held cameras; detached causality-free attacks meanwhile were replaced with hand-to-hand combat undertaken by foot soldiers, barely organized into ground-force patrol units. Unmanned Predators fly over Taliban strongholds in Iraq, Pakistan, and Afghanistan, their video operators located in the safety of an army base in the desert north of Las Vegas. Despite the sophistication of such detached measures, conflict in the Middle East is shifting away from big-ticket fighter jets and remote space-age satellites and is primarily fought on the ground. While oil facilitated the "speed of light" war, and just as much as energy interests and petro-dollars were its cause, the battle has shifted to a war *for* speed and *for* light. Forays into volatile political zones and deep-sea drilling continue to remind us that oil is becoming more dangerous to access. In what seems an increasingly overt twist of decadence, the final section of *Lessons of Darkness* features extinguished oil fires, indulgently reignited in order to derive pleasure from the display of waste and therefore wealth. The consumptive appetite and combative gratuitousness captured in Herzog's critique of the First Gulf War could now be read as a prognosis for how the return to terrestrial warfare and the ambulatory soldier is ultimately attributable to the disappearance of oil. An air force, as Harvey points out, is useless without jet fuel.[36] Herzog's portrait of a decadent planet thus marks the beginning of the fall from the air to the earth, from wings to feet, from overhead shots to hand-held close-ups and from aerial strikes to hand-to-hand combat. The disappearance of oil renders this war logistically unsustainable and so inscribes it with a palpable desperation, one that is inseparable from how it is increasingly fought bare-bones, with hands and feet.

The war in Iraq and then Afghanistan has become what Zygmunt Bauman might call a "perceptual liquidity": environmentally dissipated, it surrounds, sprawls, and is defined by a permanence that renders it ultimately a reliable consistency. As it feeds live round-the-clock coverage of the nebulous images of the Deep Water Horizon oil gusher or grainy aerial views of the collateral damage incurred by the latest drone attacks, the digital medium itself—its capacity to penetrate space, spread itself across time—finds perfect ideological and aesthetic correlate the ecological (and economic) fallout of resource war, or, more euphemistically, "oil security." Unlike the distinct, individual cells of an analog filmstrip that organize moving images in a linear fashion, and in contrast to the strip itself which can be read with the human eye, digital operates according to random access, a different technological logic. Detached, off site, percolating under the surface of things, the digital "shape," as Gilles Deleuze and Felix Guattari might privilege it, is rhizomatic in essence as opposed to arborescent celluloid.[37] Timothy Murray is one among a contingent of theorists including David Rodowick who cue off from Deleuzian frameworks to think through the nonlinear geography and seeming infinitudes of digital media. The same terms Murray pulls from Deleuze's notion of "the fold" and juxtaposes against artworks rendered in binary code—terms such as elasticity, fluidity, labyrinthine continuousness—do equally well to describe the sprawl of the oil slick.[38] Taken further, the rhizomatic analogies theorists lavish upon the digital medium, wherein the digital universe functions as a living organism, texts sprout from other texts, in an unpredictable and anti-historical fashion, also describes the inability to contain a ecological disaster or even to cognitively imagine who or what is responsible. Digital art's fluidity and nonlinearity, as Murray describes them, have environmental and political manifestations, therefore, exemplified by the BP spill as well as in the amorphous nature of the multinational corporation whose cross-border transglobal networks defy space, time, and accountability. In response to the spill in the Gulf, incensed citizens around the global pledged to boycott BP oil. But the gesture was naïve and fruitless, for not only does BP own only a small percentage of the filling stations that bear its Helios logo; the fuel the company drills is not transported directly to the gas pump but is first sold off to wholesalers and then refineries, its final destination decided by the contingencies of buying and selling, and then of shipping to a given market. BP oil could be anywhere, it has no identity. Add to that the fact that few if any oil companies are free of negative associations, making it difficult to boycott a single supplier without incurred hypocrisy. If it is all a sprawl, a slick without seeming epicenter, beginning, or end, how, then, do we conceptualize this convergent set of conditions, the fluidity that underwrites ecology, digital media, and geopolitical oil interests? The rhizome, as Patricia Zimmerman has pointed out, is contradictory in nature, embodying both the shape of global capitalist markets and the possibilities of politicized social and cultural networking.[39] How, then, do citizens begin to pose questions, decide what to buy or what to boycott? Where do we direct our protest? From within the digital dichotomy, or outside it?

Ambience: Digitized, Militarized, Ecologized

Live from the battlefield or from the depths of the Gulf Coast seabed, the resource image has breached the boundaries of specificity on multiple fronts and gone ambient. Taking a site-specific approach to television and screen culture, Anna McCarthy uses ambience as a way to theorize the various roles TV performs in specifically nondomestic environments. The term can be utilized to describe how a lack of specific or acceptable sites of perception diffuses the war to the point it absorbs and is absorbed by the cultural and sensory environment. Ambience, then, applies not only to mediation devices, but also the actual flow, dissemination, and reception of information itself. Understood as that which surrounds, McCarthy approaches media in terms that are distinctly environmental; television, for example, comes burdened with associations of pollution and contamination, especially when imported to nondomestic viewing sites.[40] In addition to the equations between ecology and digitization articulated by Bill Nichols, McCarthy's terms likewise set a precedent for understanding visual media within an environmental discourse.[41] As Internet streaming becomes the dominant means of delivering moving-image content, services such as Netflix complicate McCarthy's stance for the multiplicity of its offerings and availability disorganizes expectations of site and medium specificity, upending television and cinema as places, spaces, and forums and eroding the distinction between screen and environment, and further consolidating the broad heterogeneity of the "screen." Digital's essential capacity for ambience is achieved by a spatial and temporal fluidity that transcends both physical geographies and media categories and, with each new shape and capability it assumes, continues to eschew the limitations of production, dissemination, or reception.

Nicholas Mirzoeff's reading of the Iraq conflict adapts and reformulates Hannah Arendt's "banality of the image" in order to argue for the naturalization of this war through the abundance of its specifically digital representation. Important to note, however, is that Mirzoeff's idea of banality is not reserved for the frequency of the war image, but applies to the nature of what is put on display. In Scranton's film, for example, war is a job, routine labor, and daily performances of a mundane and sometimes predictable set of tasks. Indeed, the numerous documentaries on Gulf War II are theatres not only of violence and danger, but also of the frivolous tedium of armed conflict; the occupier patrols the streets, manages the population, and slogs through the requirements of the working day. The Gulf War I that was not-a-war was also characterized by tedium, at least as *Jarhead* represents it, but this was veiled by CNN's urgent live-feed imagery as well as the spectacular technological showcase that was the U.S. military's aesthetic and strategic framework. Thus, the issue is no longer that the viewing public is inured to the grandiosity of the first Gulf War's firepower, as Herzog feared, but that there is "no longer anything spectacular about this updated society of the spectacle."[42] Herein lies the cynical essence of the ambient war, as America's side of the conflict was rendered a steady grind rather than an unthinkable crisis. While Mirzoeff argues that pervasive anonymity of the war's images is directly attributable to the media saturation, he acknowledges only a partial account of how digital excess renders war a naturalized feature of the media environment. Mirozeff contends that more images were produced in Iraq but with less impact than at any other time in human history. But by simply blaming profit-driven media outlets and audience passivity for this climate of oversaturation, theorists and critics fail to acknowledge how the "culture of access" correlates to a "culture of excess"; digital technology's vast storage capabilities presupposes the availability and thus banality of the Iraq war's flood of visual representation. As in Iraq, and as in the BP "Spillcam," the resource image's ubiquity is tedious. The overriding ideology of resource gluttony and overabundance that undergirds oil interests, its warfare, and security can be located in the camera itself—a product of a frontier-style cultural drive to gain more spatial breadth and depth—not just in the images its practitioners generate and we, the viewer, consume. We see war grow newly "mundane" in large part because the far more selective, expensive and cumbersome constraints of celluloid film-making would simply not provide the necessary conditions for cultivating the same level of habituation.

Even a cursory trawl through YouTube's growing galleries of shorts from the war zones in Iraq or Afghanistan testifies to the manufacturing of images that have become not a spectacle but an expectation, a performative duty in which the camera-equipped soldier readily engages. As Scranton's film depicts, occupying forces, in Iraq and now Afghanistan, supply their troops with home-front leisure activities (including making movies) and indulge consumer culture habits as a necessary dimension of militarizing the day-to-day. The Humvees tour the roads of war and the streets at home, the car bomb is manufactured with items purchased at the local hardware store, and digital technology is used as a device to both track the enemy and to capture scenes of domestic life: Virilio's basic thesis about the militarization of sight continues to resonate. Dissident (digital) documentaries of Iraq or the War on Terror are defined by an exigent and necessary need to make the war visually available and expose to criticism its tragic ineptitude, but at the same time DV's capacity to expose also neutralizes the urgency that the efficiency and ubiquity of its technology is equipped to convey. The ubiquity of digital video—screen culture's dominant means and ends of representation, mediation, and continuous presence—is the ideal companion to resource war and the oil security of offshore drilling: non-site-specific, diffused, split between screens, more ambient, and therefore total.

The Visual Combustion of War

At the ostensible conclusion of the First Gulf War, CNN's real-time coverage made a constant spectacle of the near apocalyptic fires ravaging as many as five hundred Kuwaiti oil fields. Set by retreating Iraqi soldiers, this final, last-ditch attack waged against the enemy's resource-based economy was a grandiose demonstration that turned ecological damage into a functioning metaphor and a visual weapon. Virilio has argued that war has always been imagistic, deceptively perceptive: the spectacle of war is itself a form of weapon. The power of the oil inferno was psychic, economic, and environmental. While the coalition forces relied on a touchless, informational war that was automated electronically and from afar, Iraq engaged in the spectacle of resource burning. Assuming a stance as reserved as Desert Storm's military strategy, Herzog's film reformulates the destructive fires, rendering them an ambiguous weapon that refuses to side with either of the war's participants, challenging the film's audience to remember the power of the fires that burned Kuwait, wasted the world's oil, and polluted its atmosphere. Internalizing the war's point of view, Herzog decidedly merges with his subject matter in order to undermine it. *Lessons of Darkness*, for example, makes extensive use of helicopter traveling shots, thus ingesting the mechanics and mechanisms of that war's aerial preoccupations. Like an automobile engine, or like the burning wells we see on screen, Herzog views war through the lens of war; burning it with its own flames, until it combusts—driving itself forward at the very moment it also is destroyed. The idea is not to engage with the enemy or the object of critique, but to consume it, become it, alter and then invert it. Herzog testifies that a new war demands a new mode of theoretical engagement. How then might criticism of the current conflicts—in Afghanistan, Pakistan, on generically branded "terror"—espouse or detract from the means and ends, strategies and tactics, of the war itself? The Iraq war, of course, was consistently prodded and attacked, successfully or otherwise, by dissident digital videos like Scranton's as well as viral videos taken by both U.S. soldiers and Iraqi counterforces. Mauro Andrizzi's documentary *Iraqi Short Films* (2009) was, like *War Tapes*, made off-site; no footage is original but rather is sourced from the YouTube videos uploaded by both Iraqi insurgent and America troops, cut into a feature. Because it was screened in theaters, Andrizzi inserts the contingency of context and sites of reception into the digitization of the Iraq war, thus radically questioning our cultural tolerance for war as it appears online as opposed to the space of the cinema where we are held captive. As Giroux has pointed out, the violent image, typified by independent circulation on user-generated websites, is supplanting print or broadcast news forums as a source of information; likewise, as the direct cinema tendencies of the documentaries that flowed from Iraq relentlessly testify to the unwillingness to engage with the political fundamentals of conflict beyond opening the aperture and then uploading the results. The potential for digital video to be politically disruptive, a challenge to the hegemony of established media networks, does not guarantee translation into informed, sustained critique beyond the representation of horror and violence, especially when viewed online, when we are "users" and thus in control of the images. How, then, to dismantle the new politics of war, resource abuse, and ecology without succumbing to their same ideological dimensions?

Like Deleuze and Guattari's evocation of the nomad's war machine, an assemblage characterized by flux and mobility, Virilio contends that the capacity to wage war entails the ability to constantly move. Situating post-industrial resource conflict as the maintenance of our culture's speed and light posits that war itself is oil; it is fuel; it is flying and driving, motion and mobility at whatever measure of speed, as long as it is increasing. *Lessons of Darkness*'s fifth section is thus read as subtle portrait of cinema as told in a sky reflected in a lake of spilled oil. Transitory and illusory, the oil-portrait reveals that the essence of cinema is mobility, and therefore depends, like industrial society, its culture, and its warfare, on a disappearing nonrenewable resource. The oil-reflection, as cinema's self-reflection, demands reflection on a cognitive level. If cinema is derived from war and war is dependent on the shrinking oil resources that it fights for, the futurism of Herzog's vision implies a reevaluation of cinema—and not just as a renegotiation of the status of the image, but reconsidered as an industry and a technology. Herzog's portrait of the burning, spilling, exploding, and leaching of petroleum aestheticizes the self-sacrificial, self-reflective, and rhetorically internalized practice of internal combustion. Demonstrating on a visual level the cultural logic of resource consumption, combustion, and, ultimately, two-sided, mutually-assured destruction, the film manages to make literal and metaphorical both the means and the ends of where industrialization has taken the globe, its environment, and its humanity. So it is that the image of the oil war prefigures a coming climate of deprivation and scarcity that would befall Iraq—and its film industry—from its years of sanctions in the 1990s to the U.S. pullout in 2010. No images more lucidly condensed the intricately tangled dimensions of cinema, resource availability and ecological incursion than those of Iraq's wars.

Like the presence of transnational rigs siphoning fuel from the Gulf Coast or any other resource-driven incursion, the invasion of Iraq was characterized by a sense of entitlement to the natural resources necessary to maintain industrial civilization's systems of speed and physical mobility and by extension the increasing velocity of perceptive, psychic, and cognitive mobility as well. Internal combustion and oil resources have facilitated the advance of physical mobility, the industrial infrastructure, and processes upon which image production depends, as well as the very perception of movement, the defining feature of internal combustion culture. Not only is mobility the essence of war, but taking out the enemy is accomplished through the manipulation of his perception, on a visual level, through the (moving) image; such is the essence of war and cinema. The image's value is ideological. Mobility, movement, and *cine* itself, with all its mythological, metaphorical, and perceptual attendants and associations, is the supremely insidious ideological dimension with which the war in Iraq was negotiating: from roadways to bandwidth to high-speed downloads, in warfare, and even in theory itself, keeping mobile is what is ultimately at stake. Resource consciousness brings to the fore the irony that wars are fought over speed and perception rather than just by means of them. Resource war in the Middle East, escalating contestation over Arctic sovereignty—the terms of oil security are underwritten by a perceived entitlement to speed itself.

Though it does not share 1991's display of spectacle and grandeur, the current conflict in Iraq is characterized by an equally devastating visual logic that is also based on resources, internal combustion, and mobility. Mike Davis's history of the car bomb points out that the automobile-as-weapon has only recently become a refined method of destruction. It was in 1972 when the IRA gathered together common industrial ingredients and accidentally discovered that ammonium nitrate mixed with fuel oil (AFNO) was as deadly as it was available, and that urban terrorism was elevated from the level of the artisinal to that of the industrial.[43] Inexpensive, effective, simple to organize, and anonymous, car bombs, Davis asserts, are now as "generically global as iPods."[44] This is the do-it-yourself weapon of choice not only of Iraqi insurgents, but of numerous groups and citizens in cities around the globe engaging in forms of undeclared, sporadic, and almost casual warfare. The frequency of car bombs, Davis explains, is increasing at a terrifying, exponential rate, and turned Iraq into a "relentless inferno" which amassed more than 9,000 casualties between 2003 and 2005 alone. Always urban, the car bomb interrupts infrastructures of mobility, delivery, and transport, transforming the ostensibly innocuous automobile into a weapon of "indiscriminate" destruction.

What Davis describes not only suggests 1991's culminating oil inferno, it also clearly corresponds to the other do-it-yourself dissident strategy that defines the conflict in Iraq—digital video. As "globalized as iPods," Davis writes; the rhetoric of cost-efficiency and availability, typically ascribed to digital technology, is similarly applied to the car bomb, equalizing both tools, calling out and making ironic their "democratizing" potential. Like the car, the viral digital image explodes and disperses; harnessing these technologies and turning them into weaponry hyperbolizes what they are—expendable commodities, inherently disposable and intended for destruction. The pervasiveness of DV technology allows for the proliferation of amateur homemade images, enabled by relatively inexpensive domesticated equipment once uploaded onto the Internet or released on DVD; bypassing typical routes of distribution, the digital image of war, like the moment of the car bomb's detonation, cannot be tracked or contained. The numbers of those affected, the collateral damage of viewer and victim, are indiscriminate and unforeseen. The similarities between the "high-tech" digital camera and the "low-tech" car bomb do something to align the former instrument with Vertov's theorization of the camera as an instrument as capable of dismantling life just as surely as it could construct it. Mediated, mechanized vision, in other words, retains a destructive force, particularly when it has been domesticated: the dissident digital video, like the car bomb, capitalizes on the very associations that otherwise cast it as benign or innocuous. The immaterial, erasable digital image, like the moment of the car bomb's destruction, is fleeting, random, so quickly "disappeared" as to become as expendable as it is uncontainable. Meanwhile, the bomber is also the victim of his own violence, just as consumers of digital images are equally their producers and viewers; these identities and roles are not only conflated, but both bomber/victim and filmmaker/viewer are concealed and rendered anonymous, within the car bomb's total destruction and the digital image's potentially untraceable origin.

Speed is a surfeit of mobility, an overconsumption of motion, and so is nothing if not a form of excess. But car bombs embody a symbolic logic that destroys speed itself; operating according to a principle of internal combustion, they simultaneously present this engine system with a metaphorical challenge, exploding as they do the ultimate symbols of consumer culture—the automobile and the fuel that drives it. A feature of occupations rather than anything as short-lived as an attack or as total as an enemy's annihilation, car bombs refuse the temporal designations of this century's resource war. On the one hand, they belong to a war of ambient occupation, while on the other hand, the weapons themselves operate according a logic of the momentary, fleeting, brief, but often irreversibly interfere with infrastructure, puncturing holes in the operations of the urban landscape. But as a collectivity, as Davis's history points out, the concerted strategy of the car bomb renders an "inferno" and a single, uncontainable mass. Both oil wars make spectacle out of consuming, combusting, and destroying the basic ideology and sense of entitlement that is at the heart of these greed- and now need-driven resource wars. *Lessons of Darkness*'s portrait of the profligate waste that characterized Desert Storm's deliberate oil spills and infernos is now transferred to the symbol of the exploding automobile. So expendable as to be decimated and then shoveled up and discarded, the automobile's disposability is used against itself, rendering the very idea of car culture and internal combustion not only inherently dangerous on any number of levels, but defined by the capacity and the destiny not only to destroy others, but to destroy itself. Like the invention of the internal combustion engine, the inherently unsustainable nature of war sees that its beginning is little more than the anticipation of its own end. By means of cheap fuel and cheaper cars, the resource war is a unilateral, endogamous contest that reserves for its prize the maintenance of ideologies of speed and expectations of mobility. Indivisible from this is the technological dimension of obsolescence that sees the digital camera quickly becoming the disposable camera; this symbol, with its disposable images, shares a similar developmental trajectory with the disposable, exploding automobile; as such, they reinforce and inform each other as complementary units within a cultural system of resource waste and abuse. And it is in Iraq, the unfortunate theatre of these messy fusions and interconnections, where the contest over the spoils of internal combustion and its toxic residues were painfully and angrily not just played out, but purely and totally waged.

CHAPTER 3

EXTRACTION

The contemplation of the photographic image—digital or analog, moving or still—is an encounter with industry, the ephemeral nature of the commodity and, by extension, the accumulation of trash or waste, the byproducts of resource-based consumption, and its correlate, technological advance. Industrial culture's present albeit belated preoccupation with minimizing its carbon footprint is, curiously, also a bid to erase what has become the very mark of human culture, namely industrial residue. Because reducing the production of trash, waste, and commodity glut includes shrinking the image economy, the expanding genre of the environmental documentary finds itself in the curious position of being both a direct expositor of and indirect participant in the open-ended flow of consumption and waste that is at the heart of what is broadly described as a global environmental crisis. Because it is as resource-dependent as any other facet of industrial culture, all cinema can be considered "environmental" insofar as filmmaking technology is constituted by the biophysical world, its residues contribute to atmospheric health, and how it is represented on screen has a hand in determining human interaction with that nebulously defined realm called nature. Those films that consciously assume a politics of environmentalism are particularly instructive, and never more so than when they also actively and reflexively include the discursive specifics of the cinematic medium within aesthetic, formal, and narrative frameworks. Jennifer Baichwal's 2006 *Manufactured Landscapes* exemplifies the burgeoning subgenre of the environmental documentary. What distinguishes the film, however, is that it is above all an investigation of a photographer and, therefore, a fixed meditation on both the nature of the image and its relationship to the environment.

Manufactured Landscapes is an investigation of Edward Burtynsky's monumental photographic portraits of large-scale industrial incursions. Depictions of mines, quarries, and landfills define Burtynsky's career, which is devoted to making visible the ways in which hydrocarbon culture is transforming what was once natural terrain into a converging sprawl of artificial or anthropogenic landscapes. Burtynsky's more recent expedition in search of fresh fodder for his ongoing series of resource images occurred in May and June of 2010, when the photographer flew over the Deepwater Horizon disaster zone. The resultant series of aerial portraits depict the drilling platform ablaze as well as the sickened surface water; these images graced the cover of national newspapers in his native Canada and in early fall 2010 were exhibited in a Toronto art gallery—for show, for elucidation, and for sale. As Baichwal is invested in contextualizing Edward Burtynsky's work, consistent reference is made to the photographer's previous projects (one of which gives the documentary its name); yet the principal focus is the photographer's study of China's momentous industrial growth and resultant environmental transitions, if not degenerations. Tracking Burtynsky as he navigates his crew and equipment through China's rural, urban, and industrial zones in search of altered or humanized landscapes, Baichwal does not approach the photographer or his intentions critically but instead clarifies the political dimensions of his project. What emerges is a broad examination of the relationship between the environment and the image, and, ultimately, the processes of industrialization that bind them, inexorably, within a circuitry of mutual invention. By using a movie camera to reshoot the images generated by Burtynsky's large-format, manual apparatus, Baichwal also meditates upon the ontological dimensions of her own medium and, specifically, its ability to represent and absorb the photograph. *Manufactured Landscapes* testifies to how entrenched cinematic technology is in both the physicality of nature as well as in the politics of environmentalism—as a perpetuator of ecological incursion and as a means of making visible what seems an inexhaustible list of environmental causes and causes for concern; indeed, as the increasing number of environmental documentaries confirms, the movie camera and ecological politics are now virtually inextricable. Notably, Baichwal is an adherent of analog technology. *Manufactured Landscapes* was shot by cinematographer Peter Mettler in Super 16, edited in HD, and printed on 35 mm. During this 2005 China excursion Burtynsky was, like his documentarians, also a proponent of analog, chemical-based photography. Since then, however, Burtynsky has embraced digital image making, while Baichwal continues to espouse what she maintains is, as far as image resolution goes, a superior format.[1] Though they are now divided between digital and analog, *Manufactured Landscapes* captured a distinct technological parallel between Baichwal and her immediate subject, wherein Burtynsky's pictures of ecological incursion become less the subject of a documentary than the protagonists of an essayistic narrative on the politics of the landscape image. The difference between her moving images conflate a common discursive enterprise: exposing our culture's perhaps irreversible dependency on the industrial processes of extraction, manufacture, consumption, and, finally, disposal. But what is less obvious and perhaps more problematic is that this self-reflexive film implies how the same circuitry of resource consumption and waste production applies not just to the conventional material good, but to the image maker and his or her images alike.

Baichwal's camera captures the antiquated photographic apparatus that Burtynsky still favored, making *Manufactured Landscapes* function as a trajectory of mechanical image making from the late nineteenth century to the present. When Baichwal's project is juxtaposed against Burtynsky's recent digital work, as well as alongside *Still Life* (2006) by Jia Zhang-ke, a digitally-rendered narrative feature set against China's massive Three Gorges Dam project, the continuities and conflicts between digital and analog, industry and post-industry, and a manual means of production are called out, and on levels aesthetic and as well as ideological. Additionally, and as a direct result of this implied presentation of image history, *Manufactured Landscapes* can be regarded as an interrogation into how "landscape" has developed as a primary photographic genre as well as an aesthetic, cultural, and environmental category. The processes of industrialization have inarguably altered the earth and continue to do so, but they alone do not bear responsibility for the manufacture of landscape. Rather, it is the image, personalized point of view, and culturally inscribed vision that have formulated landscape as a specific way of seeing and thinking about nature and, by extension, managing it. Though Burtynsky and Baichwal acknowledge that landscape is a fluctuating concept, what both take for granted is that it is a naturally occurring term. The representation of nature in cinema mostly escapes critical discourse, making it among the most "naturalized" of categories.[2] According to Timothy Morton, any enterprise of eco-critique must strive toward conceptualizing an ecology that is, paradoxically, not conceptualized. That is, it is not intellectually or culturally constructed by humans—"ecology without nature," as he puts it.[3] Whether such a category (or lack thereof) is even possible, or is merely an example of the orphic conundrum, the inability to preserve purity or authenticity without compromising the same is a factor necessary to how visual artists have long dialoged with and about the biophysical world. Burtynsky's lack of self-reflexivity implicitly suggests that an objective representation circumvents culture-specific ideology and that underneath the industrial slag piles and heaps of junked electronics he depicts is some pre-industrial neutral essence that might be (or once have been) called nature. The images a camera yields cannot be neutral. As an industrial invention the camera is intimately linked to the extractive process, as Burtynsky makes clear; but its lens, that which the practitioner uses to represent land as landscape, is inscribed with his particular set of cultural assumptions and ideologies and so must be factored into the equation of how landscape and image are deeply entangled human ideas—and ideals.

But that the images and technology that turn nature into landscape are also located in the zone of the disposable—the terminus of throwaway commodities—foregrounds and also challenges the idea that the camera functions as a recycling implement itself, for it is capable of rejuvenating the discarded subjects it depicts and, perhaps, the physical world beyond them. What ultimately binds Baichwal, Zhang-Ke, and Burtynsky's various and fluctuating currents of discourse is the conflation between documenting the "site" of manufacture and also, as an unavoidable consequence, engaging in the manufacture of sight. Furthermore, what distinguishes this critical rela- tion and renders it almost insidious is how the cultural perceptions of land and nature are created via images. The ideology of the camera, then, and the behavior it engenders, informs the real, direct practice of how the biophysical world is shaped, altered, and therefore manufactured.

From Yosemite Valley to Silicon Valley: An Image Trajectory

Edward Burtynsky wears his influences openly. The German Romantic land- scape painter Caspar David Friedrich is one such example, as are numerous pioneering landscape photographers. An earlier Burtynsky series, "Railcuts," has been compared to both Carleton Watkins's and William Henry Jackson's photographic documentation of the American railway's incursion into the Western frontier. Importantly, however, whereas these nineteenth-century photographers tended to focus the camera's point of view into the direction the iron tracks were heading—that is, into an implied course of progress— Burtynsky refuses to heed such representational conventions as direction or horizon.[4] The resultant rigidity if not defiance places the photographer's point of view as standing in the way of both spatial orientation and move- ment itself. What Kenneth Baker calls the "monumental inertia" and "stasis" of Burtynsky's positioning effectively rebukes the progress suggested by the railroad and forces the viewer to see the land in a way that the speeding train's passengers do not. Such a bridling gesture speaks to the conservative tendencies within Burtynsky's putatively innovative work and renders the photographer curiously resistant to his own technological future—but also, curiously, to what was the future of the medium's past. In other words, though they inform Burtynsky's work aesthetically, Watkins, Jackson, and Eadweard Muybridge were unabashed technological innovators. Muybridge in particular dedicated his life to the invention and the creation of what would come after him; as Rebecca Solnit points out, his legacy has culminated in nothing less than motion pictures, Silicon Valley, and, by extension, the digital camera that *Manufactured Landscapes* implicitly rebukes. But though Baichwal's politics clearly sympathize with those of her subject, as she chooses to document an austere and static image-making project with a buoyant medium, the filmmaker is less aligned with Burtynsky's gestures toward an analog past than with China's—and the world's—unforeseeable future.

Landscape photography emerged in the late nineteenth century as a response to the pervasive public anxiety that recognized how the same rapid industrialization that was building European and American economies was also taking an irreversible toll on the natural world. The idea of documenting the biophysical world before it was lost to industrial development might be situated within the "recovery narrative" that underlies the relationship between nature and Western culture from the conception of a lost Eden to the present moment.[5] Solnit describes a Victorian culture caught up in just such a conflicting set of desires, the urge to discover and recover nature: to maintain the sweeping momentum of industrialization while at the same time preserving and having access to the natural realms which large-scale innovations in manufacturing and transportation were actively diminishing.[6] Train excursions through as yet untouched countryside, as well as the proliferation of pristine photographic landscapes that became commercially available, are some of the superficial ways in which concern over the hastening decay of the natural world was alleviated. But these same measures of comfort in fact contributed to the further erosion of environment. The train, for example, which conveyed citizens on what seemed environmentally innocuous sight-seeing journeys, also enabled the pernicious activities of the mining industry. Beginning in the 1830s, Lewis Mumford points out, the railway universalized the place of mines, such that "wherever the iron rails went, the mine and its debris went with them," effectively degrading not only the immediate vicinity of the mine but also the terrain that had once separated industry and the city.[7] But train travel not only brought industry to the city, it also conveyed urban citizens and photographers into the country. Each trip, of course, only further entrenched the deleterious effects of the new mode of transportation. Trepidation about what was an unprecedented amount of environmental deterioration was firmly assuaged by the commercial production of pictures of natural vistas and, for photographers, by the picture-taking excursion itself.

And of course, the means of nature's representation—the seductive invention of the photograph—was itself not separate from but a direct result of the industrial revolution and its extractive processes. This nineteenth-century moment is characterized by the startling irony wherein the railway, photography, and the rhetoric of what Leo Marx terms the "technological sublime" developed concurrently, sharing an obsession for those same natural spaces that transportation suddenly made available (and vulnerable, therefore) to the whims of human interests.[8]

More immediate or direct impositions of photography upon the natural world, however, were attributable to the toxic chemicals, including mercury and cyanide, used in the photographic process, as well as to the photographic factories that had come into existence by the end of the nineteenth century. But what this narrative merely suggests about the relationship between the technological image and the environment, Burtynsky's project calls out and considerably deepens. The legacy of late nineteenth-century landscape photography established a critical precedent that saw the image as a means to divert anxieties away from ecological problems and replace them with an ideology of limitless expansion that directly translated into more, not less, environmental abuse. This, photography's indirect impact on the natural world, is also the paradox that underwrites Muybridge's seminal, genre-defining landscape photographs as well as Edward Burtynsky's consciously contradictory ones. In addition to the famous motion studies that eventually resulted in the invention of the moving image, Muybridge's career is defined by his photographic exploration of California's Yosemite Valley. In 1851 the area was opened up to developers and photographers alike, with Muybridge making his debut in 1867. After the Civil War, the practice of photography in the American West, with its intersection of art, technology, and commerce, became a burgeoning industry. Most, however, was the result of commissioned government surveys that were, paradoxically, used to guide further industrial development.[9] The landscape image directly contributed to the depletion of the very spaces it was idealizing, diminishing them physically while propping them up mythologically. Yosemite was eventually sanctified as a National Park, a system that, as Dean MacCannell argues, is only protective by appearance, while in essence is but a token gesture to placate the "guilt" that attends the unrelenting human impulse to obliterate what occurs naturally on earth.[10] By confining "authentic" nature to specific areas like parks, we grant ourselves license to spoil anything left unprotected—but of course, as MacCannell argues, parks are not "nature," but rather, like the landscape photograph, a "museumized" version of the same.[11] The iconic photographs of Muybridge, Watkins, and later Ansel Adams continue into the present moment to shield Yosemite in particular and the idea of "land-scape" in general within a shroud of mystery that proves pernicious to those spaces that have not been sanctified by the camera. Unseen, unconsecrated land is fair game, therefore, only to be rendered visible upon its destruc-tion, at which point Burtynsky and other photographers of the industrial landscape swoop in and expose it, closing the loop of manufacture as they frame it with their cameras. Because of Burtynsky's implied connection to Eadweard Muybridge, *Manufactured Landscapes* offers something of a trajec-tory for the development of image-making technology—from Muybridge's still camera to his motion studies, which eventually resulted in the innova-tion of the movie camera, and culminating in the digital medium in which Baichwal's film now largely circulates. In her astute study of Muybridge's technological contributions to the development of the mythology of the American West, Rebecca Solnit narrates how Muybridge's photographs of Yosemite and his credentials as an inventor won him the challenge of using his high-speed imaging techniques to determine whether or not all four of a horse's feet leave the ground while in full gallop. The horse's owner was Leland Stanford, project sponsor, president of Central Pacific Rail, and California politician. The eponymous university that Stanford founded would later generate the technologies industries concentrated in what became Silicon Valley. Furthermore, it was Muybridge's motion studies that provided what was necessary for the later invention of moving images, the Hollywood film industry, and cinema as we know it. Silicon Valley and Hollywood are intimately linked by the collaboration between these two men; the industries they inaugurated work together to transform concrete realities into dematerialized representations, forged in light and now codi-fied in ones and zeros. An epic network to be sure, and yet this same series of connections—between digital culture, mechanically reproduced images, representations of landscape, and a nation's industrial fever—resurface in Baichwal's detached study of an environmentally dedicated photographer and his medium's (and hers by extension) relationship to culture, tech-nology, and nature.

Like landscape painting, landscape photography's creation and then cultivation of idealized natural spaces was eventually invaded by glimpses of industry; a train, for example, would be visible in the distance of otherwise untouched terrain.[12] With modernity, though, came full-scale enthrallment with industrial form and eventual modification of the landscape's conventional depiction. Burtynsky's work, as critics consistently point out, bears a striking resemblance to not only to that of early landscape photographers but also to industrial photographers of the 1920s and 1930s such as Charles Weston and

Margaret Bourke-White—not surprising given that the industrial landscape appropriated the same conventions as early landscape work, including composition, framing, shot distance, and the absence of human figures. But whereas the landscape painting and then the photograph initially located the inspiration of awe in what is a natural occurrence, the industrial image increasingly found majesty in machines, the city, and its monuments of concrete and steel. The mountain gave way to the bridge, the river made way for the roadway, and the landscape was transposed to the cityscape, streetscape, or urban skyline.[13] And so Edward Burtynsky's industrial landscapes occupy a middle ground; oscillating between and often conflating modernist and romantic zones of interest, dismantling one only to prop up the other.

The images unfolding on screen as well as those that Burtynsky hangs on gallery walls and publishes in magazines are sustained by the same plastics, metals, and chemicals that render post-industrial culture's electronic waste— one of the film's focal points—a serious environmental hazard. Choosing to spotlight the relationship between technology and nature, *Manufactured Landscapes* is inextricably bound by a particularly entrenched sense of self-reflexivity, intentional or otherwise. This principle is not lost on Burtynsky but instead is articulated, with some variation, several times over the course of the film. Within the first quarter, for example, Burtynsky's voice-over describes the moment of epiphany in which he realized how his medium and therefore his environmentally committed projects were complicit with the same systems he was attempting to expose. In was then that the photographer accepted there was no route by which to circumvent industrial infrastructure. Citing everything from film stock's use of mined silver in its nitrate compound to the fuel his vehicles burned as he pursued his desiccated subjects, every aspect of Burtynsky's photographic enterprise could be mapped back to the same deleterious processes he was determined to bring to society's attention. It was thus that Burtynsky turned to documenting the oil and energy industries specifically; now, however, he was equipped with an awareness of their insidiously entrenched presence both within everyday life and also in the photographic image. And so Burtynsky's photographs (and Baichwal's moving images) cannot document the ills of industrial expansion without becoming implicated within the circuitry of those same techno-industrial infrastructures. The suggestion that the human idea that nature must be untouched or un-thought by humans if it is to be unspoiled is as unproductive as it is untenable; image practitioners who engage with the environment as subject or as matter must remain self-reflexive and self-aware, for images, moving or still, analog or digital, are vital to communicating any kind of political or social awareness about environment in the first place.

Creating Geography

Because she is filming a photographer and his images, Baichwal's documentary reframes still pictures within moving ones and can therefore be understood as a literal instance of film-within-film. This is only one dimension that draws Dziga Vertov's superlatively self-reflexive 1929 *Man with a Movie Camera* into *Manufactured Landscapes*' discursive proximity. Given that China's industrialization and its immense social, political, and physical energy is her subject matter, the spirit of Baichwal's project can be located alongside Vertov's vision of a similar moment in Soviet history. While Vertov's film is in part an explosive celebration of industry, and Baichwal's a restrained lamentation of the same phenomenon, what unites these two films is that they capture two countries' negotiations with or anticipations of massive industrial, economic, and cultural transformation. With this in mind, points of comparison proliferate: urbanization; the transition from a local, often manual, mode of production to one that is centralized and industrial; replacing nonmotorized transportation with vehicles powered by internal combustion engines, to name but a few. But in addition to content, the formal and aesthetic strategies that inform *Manufactured Landscapes* are explicitly suggestive of Dziga Vertov's, and include montage techniques, consistent self-reflexivity, and the fixation on certain thematic tropes and editing tricks. These formal commonalities give way to a larger, specifically theoretical, comparison from which emerges how the technology of the moving image and its manipulation can transform inert ideas of space into "geographies," approximations of that which is real or "natural."

Man with a Movie Camera documents a day in the life of a cameraman as he negotiates the new dimensions and experiences the fresh contours of an industrializing Soviet Russia. All the while, the film is self-reflexively intent on revealing the creative processes that convert the raw stuff of the image into an artificially derived cinematic city. Baichwal's film is, similarly, an exposition of the processes that transform life in contemporary China into an Edward Burtynsky photographic essay. Burtynsky's medium is of course distinct from that of Vertov and his film's eponymous cameraman; and yet, equipped with their respective image apparatuses, tripod mounts, and political vision, these heroic image-hunters share a symbolic logic that turns them into nothing less than metaphors for industrial and now post-industrial civilization. That Burtynsky is a photographer and not a filmmaker lends an important dimension of friction to Baichwal's project. She is often at odds with her subject, specifically the anxiety of industry that belies the mechanical and almost misanthropic gaze Burtynsky has cultivated in his brand of landscape portraiture.

From the creation of composite "cinematic" environs to the more indirect relationship between image technology and the transformation of the natural environment, what ultimately aligns Baichwal's film with Vertov's, and also keeps them separate, is the idea that making images, still or moving, both directly and indirectly alters the physical environment as well as its conceptual counterparts: what is "landscape" for Burtynsky and "geography" for Vertov. One of the montage experiments Lev Kuleshov conducted in the 1920s at his famous Moscow State Film School Workshop juxtaposes the image of a man in his own city with an iconic shot of Washington, D.C, then with another shot of the same man walking up a set of stairs. Though the stairs were really located in a Moscow church, Kuleshov's audience took for granted that this series of images was continuous, inferring that the man's ascent must have occurred in the capital of the United States. Kuleshov's conclusion was that such basic editing principles make it possible to create a spatial and temporal unity that does not exist in reality. The construction of cinematic screen space seemed infinitely more flexible and significant than espousing the contours of "real" or referential space. As Vertov understood it, the filmmaker was quite literally the engineer of space rather than just its representative or mediator. The kino-eye "built" unique spatial realities out of shots taken in different geographical locations or at different times. What came to be known as "creative geography" is one of the fundamental principles of Soviet montage that continues to play a significant role in how films are edited. The term's powerfully evocative intersection of art and environment insists that film theory revisit these basic principles of Soviet montage, where it will find an analytic that incontrovertibly roots the industrial essence of cinema within an external, physical environment. Theorization of cinematic space must exceed the immaterial or the conceptual and also consider how the tangible external environment is shaped and determined by the world of manufactured images.

It is with enthusiasm that Vertov locates himself within Russia's juggernaut of political, social, and industrial upheaval. Often termed a cinematic essay, Vertov's film is an argument about the essential role that industrialized vision could play within the futurism of the Soviet project. *Man with a Movie Camera* shrank spaces both visually and conceptually and also minimized divisions among, for example, ethnic groups, ages, occupations, and genders. Derived from footage of Kiev, Odessa, and Moscow, and thus transformed into a composite city, Vertov oriented the viewer within a single urban space and a shared vision for the future. Within this framework, Vertov's documentary traces the circuitry of relations that bind the image to industry on the level of aesthetics, economics, and basic technological mechanics. For Vertov, the cinematic image was nothing less than the connective tissue that glued the cells of industry together. Relating all people and all parts across space and time, the cinema could, according to *Man with a Movie Camera*, negotiate the complexes of industrial culture, orient the citizen within its broad topographies, and ultimately render Soviet society conceivable, functional, and possible. As the film gracefully demonstrates, montage associations such as creative geography relate the automobile to the factory, the factory to the street, and the street to the camera, all of which are traced back to the editing table and the film factory. Vertov's film theorizes that the cinema's facility to create and thus manage geography would compose the new industrial society's sense of space and place, if not of the new society itself. Just as Edward Burtynsky insists all aspects of the photographic process are derived from the lamentable practices of resource mining, Vertov's kino-eye theorizes nonfiction filmmaking as a process of extraction. The camera operator "gropes" through "the chaos of visual events," mining and harvesting the raw material of images which are then subjected to the processes of editing, refining, and organizing into cohesive bodies of discourse.[14] As Vertov describes it, "if one films everything the eye has seen, the result, of course, will be a jumble," but if one "skillfully edits what has been photographed," and "scraps bothersome waste," what remains is not only a refined approximation of reality, but an improved version.[15] The result of this production system is an impossibly artificial cinematic universe. The manufactured landscape that *Man with a Movie Camera* effectively and self-reflexively constructs is as spatially continuous and temporally cohesive as it is politically idealized and even utopian. Kuleshov's basic experiment in creative geography and the resultant editing techniques thus create a spatial continuum on behalf of forging political and ideological counterparts.

Baichwal's film makes it a priority to call out this vital reflexivity between the camera apparatus and its subject matter. From early portraits of Alberta homesteads to his aerial snaps of the 2010 BP disaster, Burtynsky's consistent spatial abstraction inspires an overriding sense of detached objectivity that effectively subtracts Burtynsky and his medium from direct interaction with his landscapes. The signature lack of horizon, as well as vast shot distance, a flattening of dimensions, and the absence of contextualizing features are consistently employed formal manipulations that contribute to and likewise participate in Burtynsky's subtle critique of hydrocarbon culture. Baichwal's portrait of the artist's work upsets the balance, though, stepping in as just such a horizon line or reference point—but still withholding substantial contextualization. The heavily abstracted portraits of environmental devastation that have made Burtynsky's vision something of a brand do not moralize, nor do they assign blame. Though it is this lack of didacticism that Baichwal claims attracted her to her subject's photographs, her documentary reverses many of Burtynsky's neutralizing techniques, including a rigid and limited perspective that separates the industrial from the social, and from the individual human therefore. Baichwal, however, collapses this divide, insisting that industrialization and the technology it produces is layered with human life and spirit. Baichwal brings human figures into the Burtynsky realm, and a frequent use of close-ups radically reverses, if not compromises, the photographer's efforts to attain high vantage points. Meanwhile, and most obviously, the animating factor of motion undermines Burtynsky's static images. Though she is sensitive to the post-ideological space of Burtynsky's work, Baichwal's film cannot do other than denaturalize and de-neutralize Burtynsky's photographs. Baichwal therefore positions the photographer within the landscapes he is rendering and makes incontrovertible the fact that without technological interface and human perspective, the idea (and ideology) of "landscape" would not exist. Like Vertov, Baichwal ventures into the framework of the cameraman and so documents the physical labor that manufacturing involves, that of the factory employees, street workers, and other toiling citizens, including the cameramen and their assistants. These behind-the-scenes exposures pinpoint the origin of the image and so denaturalize it, forcing the viewer to consider how industrial spaces are borne within the image's representation.

The theoretical and aesthetic legacy of Vertov's film resides in how it simultaneously constructs and deconstructs the cinema as a material system and does so by rendering a film that in many ways is not a film: a film that puts itself together only on behalf of taking itself apart. Like his contemporaries within the Soviet montage school and the Constructivist movement, Vertov was motivated by the need to demystify the cultural icon and reveal it as an object, seams and all. The film-factory logic behind *Man with a Movie Camera* is ideologically committed to revealing process and production. Baichwal and Vertov are equally invested in overt and implicit exposition of industry and in revealing that which is invisibly embedded within the images that are finally projected on screens and consumed by viewers. But the demystification process at the heart of *Man with a Movie Camera* should not terminate when the viewer is brought into the site of manufacture. Establishing the provenance of the image is the foundation of Vertov's film, and yet this reverse-trajectory can be pushed back even further. The point of origin is not the image-extraction process, but the rawness that is extracted—that which is literally derived from the material, physical environment. Baichwal's film is thus, like Vertov's, about the derivation of the image, but it goes the distance, forcing the viewer to look beyond labor and urban and industrial infrastructure when attempting to locate the image's primary resource field. What anchors Baichwal's assessment of Burtynsky's work comes early on, when the photographer describes the moment of epiphany that allowed him to connect his photographic medium to the extraction sites that compose his subject matter. This revelation also draws Baichwal's camera into the same self-reflexive bind, but her film reconfigures the parameters of sourcing so that it asks not about the origin of the images that make up Vertov's composite city, but about the origin of the city itself. From where and what is industrial culture derived? How do we obtain and then maintain the roads, traffic, trolleys, goods, services, and factories that Vertov captured on film and edited into an artificial urbanism? At the beginning of a century that is becoming defined by environmental decline on the one hand and digital incline on the other, Baichwal picks up Vertov's documentary impulse and takes the camera beyond the street and beyond the factory, and, as an addendum to Vertov's 1929 film, all the way back to the extraction pit where the image is forced to confront industry at the site where hydrocarbon culture is derived.

Nikolaus Geyrhalter's *Our Daily Bread* (2006) is a notable example of the eco-conscious society's urge to render transparent the industrial processes embedded in our common consumer goods—in this case what we eat. Globalization has made it impossible to locate or cognitively map, as Fredric Jameson might call it, the origins of that which fuels our bodies, our vehicles, clothes our bodies, takes our pictures, and so documents our history. The dialectic gap between our own knowable reality and our place within that of a totalizing, unmappable globe manifests as alienation, disorientation, and ultimately disempowers the subject, leaving him or her beholden to the nebulous unknowability of social, political, and economic structures. But we can think these structures through, and render them visible, Jameson argues; through the imagination, consciously or otherwise, within the sphere of cultural production.[16] The idea is not just to represent a problem but to offer a solution, smuggling it into the form and aesthetic of the representation itself. Of course making visible has always been the mandate of the documentary or nonfiction mode, since Vertov in particular, whose legacy is palpable in Geyrhalter's studied mediation upon industrialized food production. Clearly reminiscent of those sequences in Vertov's *Kino-Eye* (1924) which use reverse motion to trace raw beef from the butcher's, back to the bull in the slaughterhouse, and then to the stockyard. Bread is given a similar treatment, traveling backward from the bakery to the wheatfield. Geyrhalter's film is notable for its silence, restraint, and an aesthetic as sterilized as the meat-rendering plants upon which he casts his camera eye. Unlike *Kino-Eye*, this is not a celebration of collectivization and socialized labor but rather an exposure of the guts of what might be considered quite the opposite—industrialized agri-business, whose cheap and anonymous migrant workers put cheap food in the mouths of anonymous citizens located offsite, off camera, elsewhere—perhaps here, where we sit and watch, as Geyrhalter thinks through or maps out the social and political divides that drive global economics. What is remarkable about *Our Daily Bread* is that as it isolates and then follows laborers through their working day, each episode closes with those laboring people, alone or in groups, consuming a meal—some form of the daily bread that is the subject of the film. And so Geyrhalter refrains from easy moralization, for although the work itself is often as horrifyingly unappetizing as it is dehumanizing, these farm hands and slaughterhouse employees must, like us all, eat. And so they do, crouched in the field or in the factory cafeteria; and as they face Geyrhalter's intimate camera and quietly consume whatever they have brought or bought for lunch, the viewer effectively joins them. *Our Daily Bread* and *Manufactured Landscapes* include the camera, the practitioner, and the viewer within the imagination of the cognitive map; all are complicit and equally dependent upon the very systems these films are making visible and, more obliquely, critiquing. But though the guts of industry are exposed, if not mapped, we cannot live without technology, and we cannot live without bread. How does the global citizen protest BP's egregious oversights when the company's fuels disappear into a global supply chain, where they become undetectable drops within an already abundant flow? Geyrhalter's film so carefully argues (as does Baichwal's and Zhang-ke's) that the solution to closing those dialectic gaps that numb the brain and disable the human subject is to make films, and thus expose the gaps, and make a map. Second, as these three filmmakers do, is to insist on humanizing industry rather than, like Burtynsky, adhere to a predictably detached, disorienting logic. Where, Geyrhalter and Baichwal and Zhang-ke ask, is my spot within this totalizing economic structure? Just seeking out one's place, if not finding it, as Jameson argues, is itself a political act.

Zhang-ke's *Still Life* (2006), made the same year as Baichwal's film, is a map in and of itself and bears no shortage of stunning moments, but one of the most resonate, for the purposes here especially, features a group of workers from the far stretches of China who gather together and show each other their home provinces, as depicted on the paper Yuan they have earned laboring along the Yangtze River in anticipation of the infamous dam which has dislocated their families (and which Burtynsky was perhaps at that moment photographing). These displaced men literally locate themselves using currency, a gesture that masterfully reflects back upon the viewer, insisting not only upon economic stratification but, more deeply, that there is humanity in industry, economy, and in history, a dimension which Burtynsky's pictures of the Three Gorges Dam and its environmental consequences minimize. Zhang-ke's digital camera is fluid and intimate, its long takes allowing the filmmaker to locate his subjects amidst the vast landscapes and complex cityscapes—and then via its buoyancy, he sticks closely by as these same subjects orient themselves within what is called a juggernaut of industrialization, a program and process so totalizing and enormous it seems to lack reference points and sightlines and places called home. But how do we cognitively map cultural production itself, from whence the digital camera comes? Burtynsky and Baichwal, as they expose our industrial culture's ecological footprints, inevitably leave behind a set of their own. We can keep moving, as Gilles Deleuze might suggest. Not as exiles, but as nomads, whose capacity for "absolute movement" buffers against the sedentary confines of the state apparatus that seeks to absorb and ultimately immobilize—dam up—such sources of fluidity as the waters in the Yangtze River and the movie cameras that expose the "striation" process as the state harnesses the river's energy to power its seemingly unstoppable—and umappable—industrial growth.[17]

Old Is New: The Encroaching Camera and the Incursive Image

Burtynsky favors the same large-format viewfinder cameras as the nineteenth-century landscape photographers whom he claims as his influences. His prints are unusually large as a result, typically 30 by 40 or 50 by 60 inches, and are defined by a hyperrealism achieved by his camera's particular capacity to gain clear focus and a profusion of detail. Because large-format images are excessively sensitive to movement, shooting requires the use of a tripod mount, which imposes stasis upon the photographer and his or her perspective. Standing still at a tripod, and viewing a given scene as it appears on the glass screen shrouded under a black cloth, not only enables a more "contemplative approach," as Lori Pauli claims, but also imbues Burtynsky with the iconographic associations of the nineteenth century's photographic heroism.[18] The sensitivity of the antiquated device is perhaps complemented by its operative complexity, substantial physical weight, and cumbersome nature. Burtynsky typically carries 150 pounds of gear to his sites, which have been carefully selected after months of scouting and negotiations with corporate or government bodies. The need of a crew surely resonates with associations of a much earlier mode of landscape photography, but his process is an improvement on the wet-plate method of the 1860s and 1870s that demanded that all necessary chemicals and developing equipment accompany the camera. Carelton Watkins, Solnit points out, traveled through Yosemite's rugged mountains with 2,000 pounds of equipment; Muybridge, meanwhile, might have been accompanied by four assistants as well as a pack train.[19] And yet not only does Burtynsky align himself with photography's earlier practitioners, but because his large-scale photographs reference paintings rather than mechanically produced images, he often exceeds them. The symbolic logic of Burtynsky's antiquated apparatus thus situates his process as well as his images squarely within the traditions of past centuries and, by extension, their ways of seeing.

In 2006 Burtynsky embarked on *Australian Minescapes,* a project documenting mining operations in that county's remote west. In order to gain an even greater vantage over his subjects, he hired a helicopter and took to the sky. Not only did the rigidly analog photographer go aerial, he also converted to digital, if only temporarily. Burtynsky describes his large-format manual process as unforgiving, and yet he will not tolerate a less than perfect image. But the great expense of helicopter rental forced spontaneity upon the calculating Burtynsky; shooting on the fly required a more responsive, predictable format than that which has been his signature. So Burtynsky invested in a digital camera and shot his pictures from a height of four hundred feet. While the photographer still clings to the rigor and commitment that film demands—he had made a mass purchase of the discontinued Polaroid and Kodak stocks—as opposed to the expendable digital image, digital accords with the air in achieving even more enhanced distances. That the same digital-helicopter combination was used during the Deepwater Horizon flyover speaks to digital as a necessity rather than a choice. As industry grows increasingly vast and instances of environmental incursion take on a real-time urgency—exemplified by the BP disaster—the tools of representation seem to shift, and come to speak the same language of that which they record. While Timothy Corrigan argued that videotape's mobile logistics both responded to and likewise shaped the "emergency geography" of the U.S. public sphere in the late 1990s, Manovich similarly (but less politically) describes the way in which the portability and massive storage capacity of electronic media transforms all culture (and the cultural production that responds to it) into an "open source."[20] Likewise, the vastness of digital memory, its lightweight flexibility and instant processing, is part of what accounts for the success of Zhang-ke's portrait of the Three Gorges Dam: the format can handle the physical scope and spatial depth, and thus map out the complexities of the monumental initiative in a way that defies Burtynsky's analog efforts.

A discourse of encroachment is the glue that binds *Manufactured Land-scapes'* layers of narrative and authorial perspective; innovation upon tradition, industry upon nature, urban upon rural, Chinese economic might upon the faltering West, and the West's moral judgments of China's environmental and social policies are some of the binaries pitted against each other as the new encroaches upon the old. Burtynsky's aesthetic, formal, and mechanical choices situate him as a proponent of stasis rather than motion, and thus position his vintage conceits in opposition to what is current if not futuristic: velocity, movement, and the *cine* that is at the heart of Baichwal's camera, China's idealized present, and perhaps untenable future. What emerges, however implicitly, and perhaps unintentionally, is that part of what is being encroached upon is Burtynsky himself. Baichwal's gaze invites the viewer to essentially invade Burtynsky's privileged side of the camera, and this overriding theme is put into practical, literal terms. The rather unyielding dimensions of Burtynsky's venerable manual medium are concisely articulated by an image strategically situated within the concluding moments of Baichwal's film. A lone, dilapidated tenement building stands in sharp contrast against the hard, freshly chiseled edges of the Shanghai cityscape built up in the distance. As Baichwal's camera cuts inside for a closer look, a defiant tenant remains: a woman, elderly and crippled, sitting in a cold concrete stairway, unwilling or unable to rise and meet either the camera's gaze or China's future, both of which hover imposingly around her. She is impassive but not immobile, for her hands are occupied, sewing fabric with a needle and thread, a representation of a manual, perhaps artisanal mode of production that exists simultaneously but not harmoniously with the high-speed rates of innovation benefiting—and befitting—certain of China's (and the globe's) social strata more than others. Like the stubbornly implanted elderly tenant, a particularly illustrative anecdote describes how, in order to accommodate Burtynsky's request for a photograph, an entire chicken processing plant was shut down, the conveyer belt stilled, and the workers instructed by floor managers to freeze their motion or risk blurring the inscription of their image. Such instances of the photographer's imposition of stillness are repeated several times in Baichwal's film—a particularly resonant example features Burtynsky assembling milling crowds of factory for a group shot. When the factory is thus tranquilized by a technology as refined as it is outmoded, the implication positions the photographer as an interventionist within the transformative march of China's industrial project.

The large-format camera is, like the old woman's manual task, a symbol of defiance, embodying a reverence and a nostalgia for a medium that came before global warming but is now considered more threatening to natural and human health than the digital imaging technology that is—for now—the summit of hydrocarbon cinematic culture. The sustainability differences between digital and analog is at the heart of environmental politics, as choosing the former over the later is generally perceived as more "green."[21] But while engineering innovations might introduce more energy efficient and thus less harmful technologies such as digital devices and various other electronic objects, their very production, as critics point out, not only requires the use of energy petrochemicals and other toxins; replacing extant analog forms perpetuates the capitalist circuitry of consumption and obsolescence that are the heart of environmental degradation.[22] But there is a rich complication here, for as green film initiatives—in both dominant and independent sectors of the industry—search for modes of sustainable film practice, reverting back to earlier (analog) forms might be progressive. If curbing the consumption of hardware is at all a consideration, not innovating camera technology and using extant forms seems the innovative choice. For example, as Leo Enticknap has argued, because the essential technology of the analog camera, printer, and projector are basically unchanged since the 1890s, nineteenth-century films, if properly preserved, could be shown today with only minor modification. But can we go back? Though Baichwal strictly adheres to the film camera, her documentary's post-production was digitally rendered and it readily circulates in DVD form. Indeed, outside of institutions committed to upholding celluloid cinema traditions, there are fewer and fewer moving images untouched, at some level, by the ones and zeros of binary code. As Nicholas Rombes argues, there are none.[23]

Improving the quality of the celluloid-based image involves changes to the stock itself and not, like achieving better digital resolution, the retooling of the entire computer-based system. The digital camera is just a front-line worker; computer hardware and software—and therefore industry in and of itself—lurk behind the scene, giving shape to our pictures. But as Burtynsky discovered hovering above the Australian minefields or the oil-slicked Gulf waters in a helicopter, the time and space occupied by resource extraction projects exceeds a format born in the nineteenth century. There is no time for contemplation, the suggestion goes, when the pipeline ruptures or when time and space, the push and pull of globalization, further "compress," as David Harvey imagines it. Increasingly rapid rates of commercial and technological innovation, rapid shifts in the patterning of uneven development, and the forward thrust of global economic development all manifest, Harvey argues, in a shrinking of the scope of time both in private and public life—as well as in a fundamental melding of these once separate realms. Meanwhile, electronic communications have coupled with ever-expansive travel networks, aviation in particular and now cyber-based, rendering the distribution of information both instantaneous and ever more far-reaching.[24] A manually rendered large-format photograph presents itself as an obstacle to the rapidity of global shrinkage. Ephemerality, volatility, the collapse of barriers—such are the terms that Harvey bandies about and that Burtynsky's images, equally resistant to whatever we imagine postmodernity might be, firmly resist.

Jia Zhang-ke is, as Dudley Andrew argues, a modernist. Though he favors a digital camera and exploits the special effects available to that technology, what cinema *is*, Andrew insists, does not depend on the format of the camera. Andrew counters the divisive tendency of new media theorists to foist binary opposition upon analog and digital by citing differences rather than continuities; the fallback suggestion seems to be that one is more or less cinematic. Indeed, there is nothing "new" about digital forms of media, and so Andrew indentifies the persistence of cinema amidst emergent media technology. Citing Jia's *Still Life* as an example of cinema's robust spirit, the film is exemplary, informed as it is by layers rather than a totalizing dialectic that ruptures past and present. A key moment when the film brings together digital, televisual, and black-and-white newsreel, Andrew argues, highlights the film's larger discourse about history as overlapping layers and patterns rather than a series of fissures. This vision of history is articulated through Zhang-ke's consistent use of various modes of representation and the aggregate references to layers and gradation. This composition works counter to "compositing"—Lev Manovich's description for the new media's telltale integration of various mediums into a single, discrete media "object" (typically involving original footage seamlessly integrated with CGI or special effects).[25] But at the same time, there is an accord between the emphatically modernist composition, the expansive capacities of digital memory, and the industrial thrust that Zhang-ke's film negotiates. He is in control of the camera, obviously; his masterful compositions insist that they are first of all cinematic rather than "digital," as is not always the case (or goal) with this mode of filmmaking, what with its CGI, on-the-fly associations. But that industrialization and the levels of "compression" it introduces come with set of representational questions must be acknowledged, particularly as these same questions haunt representations of environmental catastrophe and resource disaster (deep sea drilling, mine collapse). How and by which form is such content as the Three Gorges Dam or other monolithic projects of environmental engineering suitably represented? It is a practical, material question more than an aesthetic one, as Burtynsky tellingly realized in the helicopter above the Australian mine sites and the Louisiana Gulf Coast wherein the subject itself, the moment of ecological crisis, exceeded the "warmth" of the celluloid format.

Manufactured Landscapes' opening shot defines the central ideological ambiguity that frames the relations between Baichwal and Burtynsky and also between both documentarians and the environmental politics they together engage. The film commences with a mobile long take that is exceedingly, frustratingly extensive, maintaining as it does an unbroken frame for over eight minutes. As her cinematographer Peter Mettler plods along a factory's production floor—the Factory of the World, as the viewer learns later—he covers a surface space so vast and sprawling it becomes clear that combining a moving camera and an open aperture is perhaps the only method capable of documenting this expansive terrain while also embellishing its sense of limitless growth. While Burtynsky chooses to capture this factory's immense frontier by assembling employees out of doors, Baichwal's medium is equipped to explore the factory's sprawl as it exists—indoors and in the moment, caught up in the throes of production. But the fact that Baichwal's long take does not manage to establish the full scale of the factory's interior only heightens the magnitude of the industrial project of which this specific site is but one example. To do otherwise—to contain Chinese industry in a framework, even one that is mobile—would minimize the daunting immensity that *Manufactured Landscapes* intends to foster; so too would a sense of orientation undermine the implicit anxiety that escapes from Burtynsky the photographer and *Manufactured Landscapes* the film. The point is not to understand the Chinese industrial juggernaut, but to leave it mystifying and defiant, and so Baichwal's camera cuts away before the panorama of the factory is fully determined. It is an aesthetic choice and an ideological one. Baichwal's enormous opening frame thus competes with the excess of China's current moment of industrialization. Not unlike Burtynsky's unusually large prints and the images that defy horizons and bleed beyond their frames, Baichwal's film manages to situate rampant, large-scale development in the realm of decadence, surfeit, and overabundance simply by means of the ideological associations that exude from her equally excessive shot choice.

Digital media's voluminous capacity for storage—and thus the ability to shoot continuously without stopping to change film reels—has made the long take a defining shot choice for digital filmmaking, as I discuss at length in chapter 4. Manovich has argued that the turn toward digital compositing involves a similar turn away from the cut, which has long been the dominant aesthetic choice or default organizational principle of the cinematic imagination. Sequential montage techniques passed down from D. W. Griffith's narrative ingenuity and then the early Soviets' economical and ideological imperatives give way to what is for Manovich a "new language" of seamlessly layered fragments and nonlinear narrative flow.[26] But to what ends? Manovich pointed out at the turn of the twenty-first century that just when digital was beginning to take hold, (dominant) cinema embraced digital forms almost exclusively as productivity tools alone—but the desire to adhere to proscribed convention and produce reality-driven narratives remains essentially unchanged.[27] While Daniel Rombes insists that digital memory's capacity for deep storage can absorb hundreds of hours of footage without interruption (power permitting), it is inaugurating a new "organic" grammar of film, and with it a viewer more receptive to imperfections and signs of randomness. But these examples fall under the category of style, and so it seems that Manovich is correct: significant changes that digital technology instills affect where and how users (not viewers) make and access (rather than view) moving images.[28] Or, as Timothy Murray's examples of what constitutes the "digital baroque" point out, digital's transformation of narrative is happening outside of cinema itself, in the realm of interactive media arts.[29] Jia Zhang-ke's digitally-rendered representation of the Three Gorges Dam makes frequent use of the long take, but does so with such grace that we look at what is in the shot rather give attention to the length of the shot itself. The image that closes *Still Life*, of a tightrope walker suspended between a pair of abandoned apartment complexes, is about nothing if not a balance between polarities, as well as faith and wonder in what the lone human being can accomplish—on his or her own, with body and mind alone, well outside of the industrial thrust. The image defies that which is concrete, including the buildings themselves as well as the idea the categories such as nature or cinema are diminished by change. The tightrope walker is thus a symbol of the persistence of cinema itself, as Dudley Andrew might see it, and therefore of the necessary and inevitable coexistence of old and new. But as *Still Life* and *Manufactured Landscapes* both insist, such massive and totalizing projects as Three Gorges Dam—the largest electricity-generating plant on the planet—leave no room for such things as balance, flow, or pursuit of intuition rather than the political imperative. Innovation comes from above, and Zhange-ke embraces the medium now most closely associated with what is new; but he masters it, creates a modern portrait of what might be called a set of postmodern problems. Zhang-ke's camera does not represent China's forward drives with any degree of finitude, but it steps up to match them, thus proving the digital mode well suited for negotiating the magnitude and velocity of industrial and post-industrial culture, the very set of conditions from which it springs.

Outside In: The Interiorization of Cinematic Spaces

Space, Henri Lefebvre has written, is not neutral, but rather is produced through social action. Like history, geography is constructed out of lived conditions and underwritten by economic and political circumstances, including the creative geography that continues to inform cinema in all its formats and modes.[30] *Still Life* is replete with moments that occur neither indoors nor out. As cities and villages along the Yangtze are dismantled brick by brick, the characters, their lives displaced, wander through a shell-shocked landscape in the state of suspended dilapidation that, like the tightrope walker, hovers between inside and out. Cityscapes, though, have never been about exterior space; they are all about interiors—the indoors and environments that architecture creates. Conventional long-shot representations of urban skylines do not just foreground architecture's visibility, but also the opposite: what is invisible—hidden inside the structures that compose the horizon line. Jia Zhang-ke reveals throughout his film that human lives are what constitute abstract categories—history, industry, civilization, environment.

The narratives that frame *Still Life* feature a coal miner and a forsaken wife who solicits the help of an archeologist with the Cultural Bureau as she searches for her husband, lost to the pursuit of dam construction. The contrast between lives and professions is part of the film's neat binary logic between those who extract (memories, resources) and those who construct (shards, bones, buildings). From Deepwater Horizon to the San Jose mine, the availability of live feeds featuring resource disaster and subsequent heroic rescue introduces a new awareness about the extent to which our culture—and our images, by extension—literally come from the ground. While Burtynsky has referred to marble quarries as "inverted architecture," Lewis Mumford's theory of mining and extraction-based society is premised on the concept of unbuilding. A form of creative destruction, the term describes how extraction-based civilization is sustained by nonrenewable forms, and thus characterized by discontinuous, counterproductive processes that unravel what it weaves and condition what Mumford calls downward evolution.[31] As *The City in History* imagined it, unbuilding would see its final manifestation in the form of underground cities, a shift that Mumford determined to be the logical contribution to urban planning from a civilization whose significant inventions come from down the mine shaft. Mumford observed that subterranean infrastructure begins with water pipes, gas mains, sewers, automobile tunnels, subways, and air raid shelters, and eventually attracts shops and restaurants, which then give way to entire commercial zones, and, finally, communities—perhaps something akin to Chris Marker's postwar underground in *La Jetée*. An "extension and normalization" of the conditions familiar to the miner, the underground interior city was, according to Mumford, extraction society's inevitable environment. But what is effectively our civilization's "premature burial" underground is sustained by the artificial lighting and ventilation systems that are, of course, generated by nothing less than continued resource mining and extraction.[32] But, Mumford argues, life submerged in the earth sees its more refined and insidious equivalent above ground, in the skyscrapers and towers that are equipped with such artificial environmental features as air conditioning, heating, and lighting; indeed, the inverted mines Mumford describes differ little from their underground counterparts. Similarly, Baichwal's narrative consistently posits China as a country in the process of physically sealing up. The dominant conceit that structures the Shanghai sequences that end the film, for example, is a dichotomizing shift back and forth between the interior of a freshly constructed and comparatively lavish home, and what are the eroded backstreet dwellings of Shanghai's laboring class. Without windows, doors, and often walls, the traditional residences are in such profound disrepair that their interiors are visible from the outside, so there is little distinction between the indoors of private living and the outdoors of the public street. Mumford's prediction of a shift from above ground to below ground and outside to in finds a visual match in Baichwal's representation of interiorized landscapes and Zhang-Ke's portrait of the Three Gorges Dam relocation project as a process of unbuilding—of architecture, social relationships, and natural landscape.

The cultural and technological genealogy that connects Muybridge's landscape photographs to Burtynsky's, and from there links Muybridge's motion studies to the movie camera, the Hollywood film industry, and, via Silicon Valley, the proliferation of the digital image, is both intricate and abstract. And yet is it is neatly, richly, contained within the narrative framework of *Manufactured Landscapes* in general and its discursive consideration of interior/exterior conflation in particular. Though the film industry that would become Hollywood relocated to California partly to take advantage of abundant lighting resources and variation in landscapes, the studio era that remains the pinnacle of Hollywood's achievements is not characterized by outdoor, on-location shooting. Rather, the industry standard was localized and on-site, and rather than contend with the temperament of the sun, production was contained within manageable, controllable interiors. The "studio," then, was premised around the production of specifically nuanced artificial environments. John Alton's *Painting with Light* gives rare insight into how the ecology of the studio set functioned. Soundstages and the reliance on arc lamps are detailed, as are the ways in which artificial weather was produced by wind, rain, and snow machines; what appeared on-screen as a sea could in fact be an indoor pool. Back lots, meanwhile, took advantage of both sun and lamps, and the extensive use of sets and props to create offsite, often exotic, locations. Further aspects of this environmental apparatus included background projection and animation cameras that granted miniatures, puppets, and other replicas with the illusion of a full-scale reality. Servicing the needs of any number of film projects, sets were exchanged, revised, and ultimately recycled from one picture to the next, and the studio's back lot became a virtual schizophrenia of artificial geographies, shifting between the backdrops of various locales, landscapes, and terrains. Exemplary of this factory system was MGM, which was, in 1947, Hollywood's most prolific studio—a status achieved by the employment of numerous soundstages to manufacture as many as six different films at the same time.[33] From the carefully managed darkness of Edison's Black Maria to the luminous back lots and studios of Hollywood, contemplating the final film product necessarily involves understanding how cinema is defined by those simulated or manufactured habitats where the raw stuff that will become an ideal image is initially extracted, processed, and then finally refined. The self-contained space of the studio speaks to cinema as an "environment industry" and an "industry of environments"; such an analogy makes it possible to reformulate filmmaking's basic theoretical and practical terms. The extraction-based society's eventual convergence of interior and exterior space described by Mumford combines with environmentalism's current dominance and trickles down to penetrate and finally alter entrenched assumptions that cultural expression might somehow be environmentally neutral. With the real-time images of thirty-three men emerging from their months in a collapsed copper mine barely digested, the latest news from the San Jose mine disaster involves, at the time of writing, book contracts and movie deals. The world was watching—the globe, they say, was galvanized, riveted to monitors and screens of all sizes and shapes as the excavators were themselves excavated. Without the innovation of digital image making and its dissemination capabilities there would be no San Jose mine—not as we know it. It is only now, using the summit of available technology, that we are privy to the origin of our culture and the source of that summit itself. The question now is whether that technology provides a solution to the ecological, social, and political problems of extraction-based culture by making them visible.

In chapter 1, I discussed cinema as an art and industry of light, the resource (natural and artificial) upon which image generation most essentially depends.

The purpose-built greenhouses in which films were typically shot during the 1910s and into the 1920s were more common on the east coast, where sunlight was at a premium. In California, open-air stages were conventional—at least until the introduction of sound cinema and its heightened sensitivities shifted production to enclosed studio spaces.[34] Greenhouse is indeed a useful term, with its environmental associations, as way to describe the process by which radiative energy leaving earth's surface are absorbed by atmospheric or greenhouse gasses and re-radiated in multiple directions, including back down to the earth where it is reabsorbed. Solar radiation, or the greenhouse effect, is an elemental biophysical process. The anthropogenic greenhouse effect is of course not natural; human activities—burning fossil fuels, razing forests—produce abnormally high levels of carbon dioxide or CO_2 and contribute to global warming, entrenching further the eco-political associations which trump the intended meaning. But even without this specific terminological fortuity, greenhouse remains an instructive way to conceptualize studio filmmaking, for it also describes an artificially derived environment that fosters the cultivation of an organism or product onsite, and so precludes having to import its equivalent from elsewhere. The term includes both economic and climactic conditions and is properly understood, like the Hollywood studio era's mode of vertical integration, in specifically Fordist terms: highly efficient and decidedly localized production and working methods perfected by Henry Ford's factory system. But the protective space of glass walls and roofs has long been reconfigured by post-Fordist economic conditions that transfer production from that single site of production offsite, where it is dispersed across any number of economically competitive intercontinental or overseas venues.[35] Transnational cinema is organized around transience; it lays few roots, enabling movement to the next locale where resources are available, cheap, and labor markets flexible. What Harvey terms flexible accumulation is not random, however; rather, it tightly organizes its geographic mobility. The bottom line of transnational commerce is remaining flexible to changes in consumers markets and labor processes, whether political or technological.[36] While such aesthetic factors as authenticity—settings and climate—remain motivation for shooting movies offsite, it is commerce and network culture's global trade routes that perpetuate the standardization of film's cross-border activity. Because transnational cinema, like flexible capital, dissolves borders not only in terms of the circulation of products to new consumer markets but the production of them, the compositing Manovich theorizes is underwritten by the flux and flow of capital circulation. The images that layer new media objects, a CGI-dense composite such as *Avatar*, are drawn from those sites offering the most attractive tax incentives or from the more affordable animation house. So while Manovich's argument that Vertov's "database" imagination and the "universalizing equality" of his montage effects provides the foundation for a new media language, the Fordism that informed the Soviet production model—from cigarette factory to film factory to theater—has diffused.[37] Vertov's vision of the singular film factory where time shrinks, space is produced, and cultural differences erased still resonates theoretically, but the language of the new media, as Manovich calls it, needs to account for the economic factors that have disrupted local economies and spread the manufacture of cinematic environments across borders, languages, cultures, and terrain.

At its most foundational level Vertov's practice of spatial rather than temporal montage creates composite environments via processes of extraction and refinement. For Vertov what constitutes "cinema" is not determined by the referential space where the image is extracted, but is instead derived from its various stages of production, none of which is so valuable as the interior space that glues *Man with a Movie Camera* together—the film factory that is the editing table in Svilova's workshop. A studied exposition of the cinema's power to create artificial and composite spaces, which overcome their indexical nature, Vertov's film makes an important contribution to the overlapping discourses of interior/exterior collapse and industrialization's violation of spaces otherwise considered natural. As anxiety heightens over the disappearance of geography—coastlines swallowed by rising sea levels, forests consumed by fires, fertile farmland receding into desert—cinema's artificial spaces, so often taken for granted, come to assume a distinctly utopian role: a barrier between the post-industrial and industrial citizen and the consequences of unprecedented environmental erosion. Like the landscape photographs of the nineteenth century, the prevalence of CGI in dominant cinema, from the passing glimpses of idealized landscapes of the past to extravaganzas like James Cameron's eco-epic *Avatar*, turns the composite into the compensatory. Derek Bousé points out that the maligned genre of so-called nature films has escalated in popularity since the 1960s and 1970s, paralleling public awareness of ecological decline and species extinction. Though typically dismissed by media scholars and scientists both, these films, he posits, could become archival evidence of a disappeared world, and thus acquire new scientific and cultural value. CGI technology already manipulates nature films to the extent that animal are reanimated, their movements and actions enhanced and altered for dramatic effect; if necessary, Bousé posits, species could be brought back from extinction and made to live virtually, in a world purely cinematic.[38] In light of heightening eco-consciousness, Vertov's film factory can be situated within the dimensions of the meteorological, privileging it as a vision of industrial culture's potential to house or hide itself within the architecture of cinematic space—the zone of the shot and the territory of the image.

Digital technology similarly localizes image making, condensing the production, dissemination, reception, and consumption into the single space of the privately owned desktop computer—all phases of filmmaking can be accomplished without leaving one's workstation. Barbara Klinger argues that digital recording has increasingly shifted cinema into the insular sphere of the private home, producing what she terms a "fortress of solitude." But this sense of confinement is founded on paradox, disguising as it does how private image consumption is inextricably embroiled within a complex system of social, industrial, and economic relations.[39] Because communications technologies exist in conjunction with industrialization processes, the private home is opened to the outside, collapsing its distinction from the public sphere. Thus domestic film cultures do not exist in isolation from other external cultural forces, but as technology extends into the home, the democratic possibilities of inclusion and open access can become oppressive, particularly as communications technology transforms the private dwelling into a job site and a marketplace. Michael Hardt and Antonio Negri might argue that the domestication of cinema is symptomatic of the capitalist economy's insatiable search for new consumer markets. "Capital," they write, "constantly operates through a reconfiguration of the boundaries of the inside and the outside."[40] Capitalism, then, does not operate within the boundaries of "a fixed territory and population, but always overflows its borders and internalizes new spaces."[41] As they understand it, economic expansion is always in need of an outside—a frontier to tap and subsume. "Limited" imperialist expansion drives capitalism forward by means of maintaining an imbalance between the internalized capitalist environment and the external, noncapitalist outside. In these specific economic terms, then, what the physical interiorization of cinema—the confinement of the viewer and the practitioner to the home via increasingly convenient and inexpensive mediation devices and platforms such as Netflix—represents is a fresh outside, a vast frontier just now in the midst of being developed. The interconnected realms of economics and environment—both biophysical space and the composed environment within the moving image—open up a complex system of relations that digital technologies bring to the production, reception, and theorization of images. And when these dimensions are allowed to interact, what emerges is that the outside space that capital needs in order to grow finds a cinematic equivalent in environmental politics and the greening of the film industry. What Rupert Murdoch's monolithic News

Corporation's self-imposed mandate to become carbon-neutral by 2010 attests to is that ecology is the latest zone of intrigue and opportunity to which both the independent filmmaker and the nebulae of Hollywood turn their exploratory desires, banking, cynically or otherwise, on the fact that environmental consciousness is acted upon in the marketplace, in patterns of consumer spending.

The Disposable Landscape: The Image Value of Garbage

Both Burtynsky's China portraits and Baichwal's documentary demonstrate that large-scale recycling further entrenches rather than ameliorates the harm done by industry's environmental negligence. The focus is the residues and leftovers that have been cast aside, relegated to zones of obscurity, including the abandoned site of extraction: landscapes that are used up, broken down, and then discarded are, according to Burtynsky's portraits, also a form of garbage. Like any other good that is manufactured according to the ideologies and processes of throwaway culture, the landscape is also commodifed, and thus, when its use-value is depleted, becomes subjected to the conditions of disposal. The quarry or the mine site loses worth once it has exhausted the limits of extraction and is rendered barren, no longer able to yield either a natural resource or the image resource of a conventional landscape composition. What Burtynsky's project manages to do so well is to reinvigorate waste by inscribing it with a new value. Taking a picture of garbage is a transformative act, insofar as subject matter becomes concretized as a picture—a new object in possession of a distinct function, meaning, and value. Sontag argued that cameras "fix" moments in time, transforming what is transient into that which can be devoured.[42] Reframed, recast, and ultimately re-commodified, waste is rendered a photographic print only to be (once again) reproduced within catalogues, magazines, book plates, and promotional advertisements, or digitally recorded by the documentary filmmaker, and then projected on any number of theater, television, or computer screens. Burtynsky's exposure of China's industrial behaviors has heightened his artistic status and created more demand for his work as a result. Not only does Burtynsky implicitly theorize how an image's transformative dimension can recycle waste into a new commodity, he also participates in the same circuitry, rendering the referential site of extraction a photographic print and therefore a tangible commodity item. Burtynsky's medium aligns him with the extraction process, as well as with his few human subjects, the recyclers of electronic waste or the breakers of oil-tankers. Because taking a picture of waste transforms it into an object to be displayed, exchanged, or purchased, it is recycled and is therefore waste no longer. But by aestheticizing waste, reframing an expanse of used tires as a desert or a heap of rusted sprockets as a mountain range, Burtynsky performs a critical intervention wherein his photographs do not allow either trash or dispensable landscape to be finally discarded. What his project ultimately recycles is the image itself, infusing it with what is an inherently ecological and economic dimension: the potential to recycle used commodities and expired terrain simply by containing them in a framework and objectifying them as a tangible, transferable, saleable good.

Baichwal's images of Burtynsky's fussy mechanical instrument equate the photographer with the mountains of obsolete rotary dial telephones and vistas of electronic wastes that are his subjects. But the manual process of photography parallels not only the obsolete goods Burtynsky and Baichwal put on display, but also the crude recycling practices that have grown into one of China's most durable and important subeconomies. Because of its human health risks and environmental dangers, much of China's recycling industry is sustained by an underclass and is at least nominally illegal. Capitalism, according to Hardt and Negri, requires instability and imbalance, the outside of noncapitalist environments that are its "new frontiers."[43] Global economics depends on this principle of uneven development, as profitability lies in the ability to trade with societies and underclasses that continue to operate outside a capitalist model.[44] Baichwal highlights this essential economic imbalance as she continually employs visual juxtaposition to capture the interdependent relationship between the outmoded and the ultra-modern, the so-called un- or underdeveloped and the developed. Images of bare hands and simple tools dismantling the toxic electronic parts that were, until recently, considered high-tech make visible global capital's necessary economic overlaps between divergent worlds and modes of production.

Because the photographer's camera, the movie camera, and the digitally formatted film can reproduce a potentially vast number of landscapes from a single negative, an inherent dimension of renewability is built into the ontology of mechanized and digitized image reproduction. Indeed, Baichwal's intervention guarantees that the dissemination of Burtynsky's images will rejuvenate his spent sites, for they are now and forever renewable, commodifiable, and limitlessly reproducible as digital images. But they do not just represent garbage; they are also objects, also embroiled in a circuitry of commodity consumption and waste production. Lisa Parks's discussion of media artist Ivo Dekovic's installation *Monitors*, in which the artist submerged a series of television sets molded in cement in the Adriatic Sea, points out how by molding the cement televisions from discarded monitors the artist not only mimicked the manufacturing process but instantly turned the end product into a ruin. The artist's gesture signals how useless the television set is once it has fulfilled its function; but it can be reborn, through the artist's imagination and, of course, through the photograph, one of which appears as a still in Parks's essay.[45] While Dekovic's installation forces us to consider television as a material object, the connection Burtynsky makes between his mechanically reproduced image and the mounds of commodity items—"residuals" as Parks terms the electronic discards of networks culture—is implied rather than overtly broadcast.[46] Because Burtynsky desists from making the connection between image culture and garbage concrete—as Dekovic does, and literally so—his science-fictional glimpses of the earth's changing landscape offers his spectator no solutions. Gay Hawkins insists that images that communicate with us indirectly about our relationship with waste have more potential to introduce a new ethical approach to so-called garbage than in those top-down calls to self-regulate and discipline the ways in which we consume and expend. How, she asks, would we react to waste if it was not regarded as such?[47] Does the image of waste reinscribe how we interact with commodities? While he might be compared to photographers Andreas Gursky and Thomas Stuth, Burtynsky's work is not about the social alienation that comes with bulk and magnitude; the "mass" the Canadian photographer represents is that of the energy buried in and burned up by the objects consumed by an implied humanity. And we consume image objects with increasing ease and fervor. Burtynsky, like Gursky especially—whose massive portrait of a big box interior, *99 Cent II Diptychon*, sold for over three million dollars at auction, the highest price paid at auction for a photograph—carries in his work two competing lines of discourse: the photographic image as an agent of social and political critique and an object caught up within the larger cultural and economic forces of industry and the consumer marketplace. And this is especially so when the subject is garbage, waste, or detritus, the effluvia of waste-making civilization of which the mechanically and digitally reproduced image is its dominant mode of artistic and cultural expression.

The photograph, like celluloid film stock, is, of course, an impermanent means of representation. Photographs not only "antique reality" by turning it into an instant past, but they themselves are also "instant antiques," especially now that manual processes have been radically outmoded by digital innova-tions.[48] This ephemeral dimension further imbues the analog photograph with value, rendering early filmstrips and vintage photographs as artifacts and thus worthy of preservation. In other words, certain images accumulate value with deterioration, but only when cultural sensibilities intervene and transform into relics what might otherwise fit the description of the exhausted or the expired. That photographic paper or film stock is in disrepair, and perhaps ready for disposal, is also what could measure its perfection as an aesthetic object and thus inscribe it with social and monetary value. The film industry has exploited cinema's lost classics and thus created a mystique of limitation, a climate of scarcity, and therefore, consumer demand.[49] Haidee Wasson describes how the turn toward film archiving in the 1930s transformed our culture's relationship with moving images. By collecting and screening films within the space of the art museum, the Museum of Modern Art (MoMA) film library, for example, lent cinema a cultural pedigree and curbed its disposability factor. MoMA's initiative turned movies into *films,* a harmless entertainment into an elevated form of artistic production, forgotten features into invaluable cultural records.[50]

Film stocks (moving and still) and their printed manifestations have always been fated with the inevitable destiny of expiration and eventual disposal. Until the 1950s nearly every film was made on nitrocellulose film stock. Though not immediately detectable, as soon as it is produced nitrate begins to disintegrate, limiting its average shelf life outside of a climate-controlled environment to no more than one hundred years.[51] The technology of industrial image making and reproduction is, it appears, made to break, its (re)productions intended to disintegrate. This dimension of scarcity and the nonrenewable reformulates Benjamin's theory of the mass-produced image in that the disintegrating photograph or film stock achieves the distance necessary to infuse it with a sense of the auratic. Burtynsky's photographs are as ephemeral as the dead goods that are his subject matter; photos of waste are only temporarily salvaged, reenergized, and concretized as valuable art objects. On the level of aesthetics, then, images of garbage, waste, and recycling must be appreciated for their power to critique and transform but also to re-commodify in accordance with the same systems of obsolescence and disposability that will inevitably use them up and toss them away. Discussing Bill Keaggy's photo-essay "50 Sad Chairs," Gay Hawkins contends there is inherent possibility in trash; but reversing the easy resentment of our garbage means learning to recognize its potential use-value, an acknowledgment which would ultimately disturb, and disrupt, the "shit end of capitalism" which trash, and we, its progenitors, ultimately represent.[52] We must learn to live with our reflection if we are to continue to live at all. But Hawkins's critique is based upon looking at the chairs in the photograph, not at the photograph itself. She argues that the photograph of trash is important because, reframed by a lens and an aesthetic, the trash-object asserts itself, upends our conventional expectations, and forces the way we experience the "anterior physicality of the world" to fundamentally shift.[53] But the photograph itself, the image's support surface and all the physicality it represents, is taken for granted, rendering it less valuable, perhaps, than the trash it depicts.

Part of what distinguishes the cinematic and photographic image from pre-mechanical methods of reproduction is its potential to proliferate and therefore to create an overabundance of visual material. But as Jonathan Sterne argues, anything that is called a medium must have a physical infrastructure attached to it.[54] "New" media's material dimension is growing exponentially, in part because of constant replacement of devices required to achieve the sense of the immaterial or the disembodied, and in part because these same devices are made of material that will not biodegrade. The inherent contradiction of throwaway industrial culture resides in the fact that the disposable is also the durable. The nature of trash has transformed, wherein industrial and techno-scientific goods are so well made they will not break down.[55] The image, however, is about preservation, but is, conversely, also destined to decay and disintegrate into little more than illegible surfaces or empty bits of storage space. But it (the image) is also about reproduction, and the digital image especially so. Built into this technology is the capacity to continually rejuvenate itself, incrementally extending an image's life span each time it is reproduced and reissued. The "original" image might then be saved from the fate of disintegration and disposal, but as consumers are beginning to discover, digital photographs are vastly more time-sensitive and fragile than manual photography's paper counterparts. Even when stored on disk, digital images will only endure for five to six years. A possible recourse is to print digital images as hardcopies, though these too are fated to fade. What is more, this diminishes an essential marketing feature of digital technology—the provision of durable and enduring storage capacity. But as discarding objects is, as Susan Strasser argues, a demonstration of power, the question becomes whether or not techno-citizens really want to preserve their myriad of images.[56] What is truly valuable about digital imaging is not its capacity for storage or preservation, but for erasure. Manipulation and exploitation of its most distinctive feature means that images can be reaped, gleaned, consumed, and then deleted, gotten rid of, and discarded without much consequence. This, then, is the current gauge of an image's perfection. Freedom and ease, even democracy, are equated with the potential for vast consumption and excessive disposability, an ideology that is compressed within the form of the digital camera—the latest measure of the image's total perfection and total destruction.

Using disposability as an analytic, the final shots of *Man with a Movie Camera* depict the film's cameraman-cum-camera as a perfected innovation that is measured by a self-annihilating capacity for autonomy and ubiquity. But though the camera has reached a state of refinement, it is not rendered disposable. Rather, it is the human filmmaker who becomes redundant and is essentially discarded, absorbed into the very form of the technology he has helped develop. What is more ambiguously insidious is that as the human becomes disposable, filmmaking as a distinct process is also discarded, usurped by the ontology of the autonomous camera that is the kino-eye. Framed thus, cinema as a category is rendered depleted and defunct, replaced only by what might or might not be the disposable perfection of technologically derived vision. The gaming industry, for example, has at the time of writing super-seded cinema in terms of its total economic worth and is growing even more immense as a form of social, cultural, and economic interactivity.[57] But does the growth of gaming signal the end of the indexical image? Perhaps not, for Baichwal maintains the heroic, and human, dimension of the image maker. The final shot of her subject finds him astride a high peak, alone but for an assistant, the wind sweeping his hair and clothes as Baichwal's camera encircles him from above. It is a monumental image, reinstating the photographer's power to remain distinct from his images and his apparatus and to maintain dominion over his subjects.

CHAPTER 4

EXCESS

The long take is a single uninterrupted shot that occupies more cinematic time and space than any other single unit of exposure. According to Barry Salt, the measurement of a long take is a relative exercise, for it depends on whether or not that given shot is considerably longer than those occurring alongside it or in other films made contemporaneously.[1] For a take to be long, in other words, it must stretch beyond the status quo as far as exposure times go. The implication of all this is that a long take's execution depends upon—and is ultimately indicative of—the capabilities of available cinematic technology and its accessibility to the practitioner. Concordant with this is how the history of the long take's growth, from several minutes to several hours, is determined by technological innovation, namely the amount of raw celluloid a camera's magazine can actually hold before it runs out and the shot terminates. In terms of digital cameras, the amount of available or writable support surface (memory) will not typically limit a take's length; limitations come in the form of how much power a battery is packing. So, apart from what are obviously diverse sets of intentions and circumstances, the difference between Alfred Hitchcock's prototypical single long take in *Rope* (1948) and Alexander Sokurov's record-setting 96-minute digital run that comprises *Russian Ark* (2002) is first of all technological: the cameras and stocks in existence and available for each filmmaker.

Taking measure of the long take is a viable and productive way to map out the trajectory of cinema's material history, which is itself a narrative of industrial culture's access to natural resources, their subsequent conversion into technologies, and expendability as material wealth. Because cinema is technology and therefore materially determined—that is, it comes from the minerals, metals, and compounds mined from the earth—the filmic text and each of its shots not only measure a duration, they also present an inventory of

121

the amount of raw stock or support surface consumed by the camera and the practitioner. Shot length, then, gauges the relationship between a filmmaker and his or her access to materials, and can work as a subtle, even eloquent, signal of excess or lack thereof, visualizing as it so often does the economic power of the culture that ultimately produced it. There is an ideology of limit-lessness, expansionism, and unfettered expenditure built into this specific formal decision wherein the camera aperture is opened indefinitely and seem-ingly indefatigably. Theorizing it as such establishes a direct correspondence between cinema and its position within hydrocarbon culture and so speaks not only to an audience's expectations, but to resource consumption and, concordantly, casts filmmaking as an intractably environmental practice.

Though digital technology sees the trend reversing radically, the long take in the analog cinema is still a relatively rare occurrence, attributable to its organizational challenges, logistic intricacies, and budgetary feasi-bility.[2] Particularly when mobilized by tracks, cranes, or vehicles, the long take requires tremendous technical coordination among camera operators, lighting technicians, and actors. Such demands translate into high material and labor costs, especially as the long take is does not forgive mistakes easily and therefore requires a retake to begin from scratch, at the shot's inception, even if a flaw occurred at its end.[3] As, arguably, feature film audiences are so accustomed to narratives guided by the editing cut, the lens of the long take is typically framed by aesthetic decisions rather than continuity ones. The long take—as it occurs in the context of American and Western European traditions especially—can be read as a gratuity, an opulence of choice and an indulgence in materials, as well as in space, time, and energy—and on the part of the producing filmmaker and the consuming viewer.

Analog cinema's use of the long take might pronounce its excess more readily than digital, as the former mode typically expends more physical, economic, and material resources on achieving the proper take than does the latter, whose ability to record until the camera's batteries expire to some extent reconfigure the long take, and in its practical, aesthetic, and also theo-retical dimensions. Indeed, the open-aperture aesthetic has come to dominate mainstream cinema's peripheral realms—home movies, YouTube shorts, news footage, and innumerable independent documentaries—but so has rapid-fire cutting. André Bazin extolled the use of deep focus, recognizing in it a democratization of viewing. The theorist's commitment to cinematic realism and in particular the pronouncement that cinema would not become just that—cinema—until freed of the burden of its own infrastructure in many ways anticipates digital cinema's buoyancy, unobtrusive physicality, as well as its capability for lengthy shot duration—the true continuity that minimizes the difference between image and the indexical world.[4] Of course, realism always depends on artifice, as Bazin recognized; but while montage guides the viewer into accepting a predetermined meaning, what Bazin called deep focus allowed the eye to linger over an image as the viewer made his or her own sense of it. Deep focus brings the spectator closer to reality because it requires a "more active mental attitude" and a "more positive contribution on [the viewer's] part to the action in progress."[5] As the ease and ubiquity of digital filmmaking diminishes cinematic infrastructure and the size of the camera itself, the format might very well finally remove the "hand of man" from the image. However, because such small cameras do not as yet deliver high-resolution images, their presence is paradoxically enhanced. An additional obstacle that stands between digital and Bazin's mythical ideal of a total cinema is that the ease and liberation by which digital captures a presumably pure, unadulterated reality is supported by a highly complex production infrastructure. So what must accompany an investigation of the long take—beginning with analog, concluding with digital, and all along founded on Bazin's evocation of a cinema's democratization of vision—is the desire to consume and expend images and imaging technology. The so-called "access culture" that comes with digital's expansionism is equally a culture of excess.

The Measure of Excess

In "The Concept of Cinematic Excess," Kristin Thompson maps out the development of an ambiguous and esoteric term—cinematic superfluity or "excess." Thompson's imperative is to counter certain militant tendencies within structuralist film theory, specifically its mandate to resolve the irresolvable and finalize "meaning" through application of external (Marxist, psychoanalytic) systems. The term's theoretical origins, Thompson argues, are located in Russian Formalism, specifically the conviction that poetry's incomprehensible layers are both inherent and necessary to the structure of a given work's very form, if not to the genre itself. The first proper use of excess as both an aesthetic and cinematic term is found in Stephen Heath's "Film Systems: Terms of Analysis," which, Thompson contends, is itself likely informed by Roland Barthes's analysis of Sergei Eisenstein's *Ivan the Terrible* in "The Third Meaning." Loosely understood as those unmotivated, perhaps baffling, and seemingly gratuitous bits of stylistic flourish that "puncture" or "exceed" a film's otherwise homogeneous and comprehensible structure, Thompson's loose definition fuses aspects of Barthes and Heath from which "excess" emerges as a specifically cinematic category. The value of excess for Thompson is that the term itself is, like the cinematic texts it describes, stubbornly ambiguous and necessarily irresolvable. Beyond its immediate intentions, Thompson's essay is instructive not only in its evocation of this potent and discursively rich term, but because in doing so she places emphasis on "materiality" as the inherent determination of excess. Though used vaguely, materiality seems to be understood as the cinematic apparatus and the technological dimensions of image production, from equipment to editing—all those properties which classical Hollywood cinema, for example, intended to conceal from the viewing audience.

"At that point where motivation fails, excess begins": such is Thompson's most comprehensive summation of the elusive term that is never fully resolved within the space of her article.[6] Resistance to definition is at the heart of excess; and so it is defined negatively, by what it is not rather than what it is. Excess, for example, does not simply mean an accumulation of gratuitous formal indulgences. Rather, it is that which makes the viewer aware of the very materiality of the film itself, drawing attention to itself as a consciously conceived system. In Heath's terms, excess describes those incongruous parts which do not fit the otherwise homogeneous filmic system, and it is this nuance that Thompson traces to Roland Barthes's evocation of "obtuse meaning," whose self-reflexivity and self-effacement signals a form of excess in that it actively subverts and thus challenges the very system from which it arises—not unlike the long take in extremis.[7]

Thompson's arguments focus on Eisenstein's *Ivan the Terrible Part I* (1944), a film defined by self-conscious stylization, the materiality of which calls it out the film as an exemplar of cinematic excess. *Ivan* is also a striking departure from Eisenstein's pre-Stalin cinematic practice and a lucid instance of how excess is hyperbolized and thus used against itself, in extremis. But in contrast to *Ivan*, Eisenstein's earlier career and the practice of Soviet montage that he helped define was laconic and marked by brevity. Though the material strictures imposed by the post-revolution civil war could have proved otherwise, Soviet practitioners such as Eisenstein managed to produce an impressive body of agitation films and from them a cinematic language that was as passionate as it was didactic. Without the civil war and its scarcity of resources, film among them, the Soviet cinema would not have produced the striking and distinctive style that remained its aesthetic foundation.[8] So it was that the science and the political intention behind Eisenstein's particularly rigid editing system were committed to ensuring that the images and the political associations were not ambiguous but instead incontrovertible. Subtlety and suggestion were luxurious; in a climate of political transformation and material impoverishment nothing could be left to randomness or chance. If the audience did not respond as predicted, the entire enterprise would be lost to its anathema: the gratuitousness and decadence of narrative cinema.

For Thompson, excess is specifically and homogeneously cinematic, but resonates all the same with suggestions of Georges Bataille's essay in what he calls general economy. It is in *The Accursed Share* that Bataille describes how excess is a surplus of energy (also understood as wealth) that humans and their societies strive to produce and then accumulate in various material forms. But because there is a limitation to how much wealth can be amassed without devaluing it, excess energy must be expended, lest it becomes destructive, such as in acts of war.[9] Purging such surplus is therefore desirable, processes of which have mutated into socially and culturally inscribed behavior, often in the form of visual displays. Important to note is that Bataille distinguishes between different registers of purging. One manifestation qualifies as "extension," wherein surplus or excess energy is transferred away, relocated off-site, and thus potentially engenders growth elsewhere. Removed rather than destroyed, extension is understood as giving excess back to the system from which was it born; what Bataille describes is not negative but rather a positive expenditure of surplus, a productive form of waste. Bataille's taxonomy is not unlike what industrial ecology describes as the "closed system" or symbiotic loop of consumption and waste. An opposite model, however, wherein all the flows are unidirectional, is what underwrites industrial society: this linear or open system, though quick and efficient, is only sustainable until the waste that accumulates at the other end finally spills over.[10] Bataille's understanding of extension might be compared to the open loop ideal, wherein resources and waste are mutually inclusive; what is waste in one component of the system serves as resources in another.[11] Industrialization, as Susan Strasser argues, has made uni-directionality dominant, but because extracted resources are industrially converted waste cannot be reabsorbed by the system and thus destroys rather than facilitates the potential for regeneration or, in Bataille's terms, extension.[12] But Bataille is not concerned with describing models of sustainable ecology, but rather with theorizing how societies maintain values by limiting their growth. "Luxury" or "squandering" function not only to dispose of excess, but its spectacles also affirm a given society's power: military aggression, and colonial and industrial expansion are conventional examples.[13] In order for excess to accumulate, growth's boundaries must be recognized: excess, in other words, can only be as such when there is a set of limitations to breach. Cinematic excess performs particularly well as a model of this same dialectical tension, articulating as it does in visual and aesthetic terms how limitations are erected only in order to be dismantled or destroyed.

Jonathan Sterne writes that the electronic waste haunting the technology industry might be called, in Bataille's terms, the "accursed share" of the digital economy—those stubborn leftovers that threaten to rise to the surface and so must be disposed of, either in a feat of "glory" or "catastrophe." Indeed, cinema itself might be viewed as a glorious expenditure of energy, and the long take an aesthetic marker of the same—one way in which to burn off surplus wealth and resources (both the material and emotional or intellectual, placing it on display but only on behalf of destroying it.[14] Bataille's theory is not unlike Thorstein Veblen's influential notion of conspicuous consumption, wherein surplus that is excised or wasted through ritualized cultural performances become naturalized within patterns and conventions of habitual (and therefore inconspicuous) behavior. What immediately differentiates the personal and political freedom of one individual from another person's restrictions is the ability to conspicuously consume and, therefore, to conspicuously waste.[15] Eisenstein's *Ivan* exemplifies how the material and technological possibilities of cinema can be harnessed in order to simultaneously exploit and display excess before it becomes what is waste for Veblen and the accursed share for Bataille. The film's coronation scene, for example, and specifically those shots in which Ivan is ritualistically showered with coins, use editing not to elide the temporal duration of the narrative, but rather to extend it. Because the same shots are repeated, and gratuitously so, the decadence of the diegetic event is given accent, as is the power that is inherent in wealth itself and, more profoundly, in its symbolical wasting. The use of cinematic resources to lengthen time rather than to accurately espouse it signals a flourish and an indulgence that exceeds considerations of style. This moment is particularly potent, signaling how Eisenstein's own aesthetic was forged during a time of material shortage and limited resources. The repetition of the image here is not done out of material necessity but rather as a covert demonstration of the political decadence that Ivan the Terrible's (and Stalin's) Russia would attain. Eisenstein's repetition thus forges a political allegory on a purely formal level.

Cinematic excess acquires further relevance when situated alongside Bataille's insistence that wealth and power are located in the waste of the ostensibly benign cultural display. Cinema has always functioned as an exhibit of technological progress, a demonstration of wealth and power, a squandering of resources on something that is still so often considered a transitory, momentary, and disposable entertainment. Kristin Whissel points to the Pan-American Exposition held in Buffalo, New York in 1901 as an articulation of modernity, newfound power, and the wealth of a nation caught in the throes of industrializing itself. As Whissel reads it, the event gave shape to the mechanistic and imperial imagination of America at the turn of the twentieth century. From incandescent light to moving pictures, Thomas Edison's array of converging inventions were front and center of the Expo, and their various overlaps bring into view the intricate relationship between cinema, systems of mobility, and hydroelectric power—the latter sourced from the nearby power station on the mighty Niagara River. The City of Buffalo, the exposition it hosted, and the Edison moving pictures shot from on board electrically powered rides that toured the exhibit grounds served as outlets for hydroelectric power, ultimately providing citizens and spectators with a "dematerialized and disembodied" sense of power which seemed "omnipotent, omnipresent, and potentially limitless" in its breadth and universal applicability."[16] The seemingly invisible force that powered cinema, streetcars, or factory assembly lines inspired the spectator's imagination with the awe that might have been reserved for nature—the source of that invisible power—an instance of what Leo Marx terms the "technological sublime."[17] Viewed through the lens of environmental politics and accompanying resource consciousness, such displays assume, if not a whole new meaning, then a new sensitivity, one that signals a pernicious and unsustainable consumptive decadence. The American imagination, then, is a hydrocarbon imagination and a hydroelectric one. The resource image is similarly powered by a faith in energy, but only if energy's circuits, sources, and dirty politics are kept invisible; the subordination of nature by industry, its excess power unleashed in such displays as the moving picture, come to a confused head in the image of resource, for it displays rather than disguises the energy economy's less than sublime origins. Oil politics and attendant environmental contingencies completely renovate excess as both a cinematic and a cultural category, positioning it as a strategic way to make visible, in varying degree, the resource energy that powers the means and ends of industrial culture's cinematic representation of itself.

The long take is typically analyzed in terms of its aesthetic and ontological dimensions rather than its material value.[18] It does far more, however, than measure real time; it is also a gauge for the length of the reel, and therefore the celluloid, upon which the shot itself has been recorded. Films of cinema's early period (1895–1905) are characterized by a point-and-shoot formal practice and usually consisted of a single shot of considerable duration. After the emergence of continuity editing during cinema's transitional period (between 1905 and 1916), technological advances, and the studied commitment to standardizing a cinematic means of storytelling, the shot was significantly shortened; narratives, as a result, become more refined, and the development of plot and story reflected the increasing sophistication of the cinematic medium. During the late 1910s and early 1920s, for example, the average shot length (ASL) was five seconds. After the introduction of sound, however, this figure was lengthened to ten. In the United States as well as abroad, the mid-1930s witnessed a tendency to increased shot length. But though long takes became a "major resource" for filmmakers, the factors that account for this shift cannot be fully understood, as David Bordwell and Thompson concede; it is assumed that the reasons were simply practical, as a means to achieving narrative ends.[19] But increased shot length could very well indicate cinema's technological advancement—sound cinema's introduction of conversations, for example, necessitated longer shot lengths—which in turn signals that cinematic resources, from stock to lights to labor, were increasingly available and that filmmaking had become consolidated as an industry. Eisenstein's *Ivan* exemplifies that access to more than just the most basic materials effectively extended and therefore liberated the duration of his shots. Likewise, the direct cinema movement of the 1960s was in part made possible by the affordability of cinema's raw materials, film stock in particular; not only were long takes indulged, but certain filmmakers were able to be incredibly prolific in their documentary output.[20] Somewhat divergently, *Russian Ark*'s long take is a particularly potent example of how the liberal indulgence in technological innovation can showcase, and unequivocally so, the political, aesthetic, and economic freedoms that come with it. The decision to completely eschew editing makes *Russian Ark* exemplary: a one-day shoot required four years of planning, the organizational logistics of which escalated the cost of production to the point of lavishness. Obviously the correspondence between an extreme long take like Sokurov's and economic or resource abundance is not a universal rule; extended takes are notable in both amateur and low-budget filmmaking as a way to offset the costs of crews and equipment rather than, like Sokurov, to indulge in them. Early cinema, meanwhile, consisted mostly of long takes, which does not imply that film stock or equipment was inexpensive, but rather that cinema at that developmental juncture could not do much more than point and shoot. And so it is a decrease in shot length (but increase in total shots) that corresponds with cinema's industrialization and growing material abundance. And yet the long take of the B film or the independent digital documentary still indicates inclusion within a larger economic structure that allows for cinema in the first place, wherein the open-aperture affect acts as a deviation even, thus signaling the essential availability of movie-making resources. Those long takes that are defined by something other than logistic or aesthetic need but rather by self-conscious reflexivity and hence a discursive ambiguity are most notable. These subversive instances will be taken up here, for when used against itself, the extensively bloated shot can be harnessed as a means to undermine and critique the cultural behaviors that are manifested in the long take's conventional employment. This self-effacement foregrounds a long take in order to undo it, hyperbolizing and thus upending a culturally dominant aesthetic of excess by means of what might be called the long take in extremis. Choosing to open the aperture and leave the camera running (walking away from it, as Andy Warhol claimed to do) suggests a waste of both raw material and operational energy. Such extreme cinematic behavior implies a deliberate indulgence intended to foreground the ideology of consumption by means of it putting it on show. This is what is at stake, and at odds, within extreme use of the long take: excess is employed in order to denaturalize it, thus rendering its terms problematic if not grotesque.

Barry Salt's exhaustive study of the history of film style is founded on the premise that above all else, style is dictated by the advancement of technological capabilities. The development of sound technology, for instance, exemplifies how the introduction of a new technology can totally transform the way films are manufactured, which in turn alters their aesthetic manifestation and, with this, audience expectations. The introduction of synchronized sound in the Hollywood cinema of the late 1920s and internationally into the 1930s is a notable example of cinema's industrialization process and represents a significant contribution to what has become feature filmmaking's aggregate impact on the biophysical world. As the conventional history goes, after the debut of Warner Bros. *The Jazz Singer* in 1927 studios clamored to meet the demand for talking pictures and were forced to retool—top to bottom—with sound compatible infrastructure, including new film stocks, cameras, studio sets, actors, and theaters. The economic and technological implications of sound technology's standardization were complex; the process occurred over time, varying from one country to another. On an aggregate level, sound fundamentally rewired cinema and is readily comparable to contemporary analog to digital switchover.[21]

Salt's history, meanwhile, uses empirical evidence to chart how various technological factors contributed to the fluctuation of the average shot length (ASL) of American and European films from 1895 to the 1980s. Obviously, the study is premised on technological determinism and disregards social and cultural dimensions, as well as economic questions such as the cost value of cinematic technology and materials. And because focus is trained on American and Western European cinema, the study makes the assumption that cinema is privileged and inherently affixed to systems which yield abundance. Indeed, because cinema is so plugged into an energy economy, it is assumed that it could not exist without direct or indirect access to a technologically determined, resource-based infrastructure. If, as scientists, economists, and environmentalists continue to argue, oil commodities continue to radically diminish, perhaps drying up in as few as fifteen years, every dimension of cinematic culture will be forced to modify. But looking beyond the dominant mode of large-scale production ameliorates the otherwise fragile future of the cinematic medium, and industrial culture more broadly. As I argue in this book, particularly in the concluding chapter, the so-called Fourth Cinema of Indigenous populations is a particularly relevant model of sustainability, as it is so often positioned at the crossroads between ecology and video technology. As Indigenous filmmakers like Zacharias Kunuk and the Isuma TV initiative use the latter (digital communications platforms) to produce solutions to the former (environmental depletion), they prove that ecological crisis does not threaten cinema, but it does challenge the feasibility of dominant modes of filmmaking—and living, by extension—to continue in their current dispro-portionate forms.

The Open Aperture Aesthetic

Faced with the ascendancy of television and the fallout of an apostate audi-ence, the feature film industry of the 1950s and 1960s struggled for redefinition. Following an imperative to outmuscle the comparatively limited capabilities of the black-and-white medium's technological support systems, the Hollywood film industry conventionalized highly saturated color values, consolidated widescreen pictures, produced lengthier features, and in general embraced any post-production process that could maximize the silver screen by exploiting every last dimension of space and time. The expansion of screen space that began in the 1950s peaked in the 1960s, as, ironically, it "thinned" back down to accommodate a new subsidiary market, broadcast television sales. Movie attendance fell dramatically after World War II. America's postwar middle class both worked less and spent more money on higher priced recreational activi-ties. Hollywood cinema, as John Belton argues, stepped up to meet the demand for outdoor entertainment experiences, redefining itself as an amusement park or recreation center rather than a place of passive activity—television now had that market under control. Expensive renovations enabled movie theaters to accommodate innovations such as the wider screens and multitrack stereo systems needed to deliver Technicolor, Stereoscope, and stereophonic sound to the audience. All of this came with higher admissions, for, after all, Cinerama prints, shot on three cameras, were projected onto twenty-five-foot-high curved screens using three separate projectors, while a separate strip of sound played on multiple speakers behind and surrounding the screen. But while the wide-screen revolution of the 1950s saw cinema literally grow in size, content remained constant.[22] In addition to cinema's presentation,

Hollywood also fought for its share of the entertainment market by funneling budgets into a handful of monstrously ostentatious and costly productions intended to appear distinctively cinematic rather than banally televisual; but beefy, expensive fare proved a spectacularly failed strategy and precipitated the industry's near collapse.[23] This expansionism is analogous with the new spatial demands of North Americans and North America in general. While widescreen technologies extended the girth of the image, suburban sprawl was likewise beginning to increase the amount of space occupied by individuals, municipalities, and transportation infrastructure and locating it within the larger narrative of postwar economic, spatial frontierism—and, thus, material prosperity. The North American home was caught up with Hollywood movies in a parallel pattern of expansion, exemplified by the inherently disproportionate nature of suburban growth. The extension of floor space in the average North American home is one way to expose such patterned decadence. For example, while a bungalow lot might have measured sixty by one hundred feet in the 1940s, by 1950 the floor space in the average home in the United States was one thousand square feet, rising to two thousand by the year 2000. This growth takes on added dimension in consideration of the fact that the family units occupying such generous structures were likewise dwindling in size.[24] While unbridled amounts of consumption can be measured in such terms, the space of the shot likewise takes on a similar set of implications. The point is that the amount of time and space that the units of film occupy directly correspond with a consumption of energy and resources that go into the production of what Barbara Klinger calls the "film good"—including the physical, tangible constituent parts (DVDs, promotional tie-ins, and public and private screening infrastructure) that accompany the cinematic image.

The emergent democratization of the filmmaking medium is at the heart of Andy Warhol's 1964 long-take extravaganza, *Empire*, a film which uses its own banal excess to foreground and ultimately upstage the decadence of the culture from which it springs. *Empire*, bearing an appropriately expansionistic title, does not make overtures toward the gloss, editing speed, or technical endurance that were to come to characterize the 1960s film industry as it raced to fill up what was left of the cinematic frontier. Rather, the film is unequivocally restrained and even austere in every aspect except its length and its intentions, thus allowing the filmmaker to make ostentation plain, and excess restrained. In an interview featured in Chuck Workman's documentary *Superstar*, Warhol laconically explains how his approach to filmmaking involves little more than turning the camera on and walking away from it; leaving the static camera to run, the operator entrusts his labor to the machine. That the movie camera captured time mattered far less than that it saved time, and in the most practical, banal sense, allowed the practitioner or the viewer to "multitask," engage cinema while performing some other kind of leisure or labor. Consider how cinematic technology was harnessed by turn of the twentieth-century industrialists as a way to analyze human motility and then improve worker productivity.[25] Warhol's early "entropic" films returned cinema to the ostensible purity of a primitive cinema, and thus inaugurated a phase of liberated filmmaking that countered and then radically altered dominant cinematic culture.[26] *Empire*, therefore, functions as a trajectory of cinematic history; it is everything the Hollywood feature film industry once was and, despite itself, would always be. Warhol's open aperture opened the 1960s and made the consumptive foundations of cinema conspicuous, signaling the reversal of the Hollywood studio system's principles of Fordist conservation which restricted innovation in style, rendered formal practice parsimonious, and subsequently prospered by its trademarks of quality and consistency. As in any similarly inspired Fordist system, there was no room for experiment within the classical Hollywood cinema and it is because of this mode's predictability that Salt is able to establish trends within average shot length (and numerous other formal devices). *Empire* would of course corrupt Salt's search for reasonable, technical explanations as to why film style has developed as it has. Yet it also represents the industry's totality, conveniently compressing roughly sixty years into eight hours of near stasis. After all, what has been called the longest establishing shot in cinema's history is a spectacular display of a basic Hollywood principle of continuity editing. *Empire* is all continuity: eight hours' worth—it is all Hollywood, too much Hollywood; enough Hollywood to burn.

The cinema of 1960s America is not characterized by the long take. In fact, the converse is true, for shot length slowly decreased throughout the decade, when American feature films reached a historical low. The underlying reasons for this shift are attributable to a combination of increasingly accurate editing devices as well as the ascendancy of the role of the editor in the post-production process. The so-called New York School of editing is the American feature film industry's realization of Vertov's insistence on the vital contribution of the editor to the creation of the on-screen environment. With Dede Allen's virtuoso editing of Arthur Penn's *Bonnie and Clyde* (1967) and resultant radicalization of feature filmmaking's conventions and expectations, emphasis shifted to the post-production stages and rendered the editor less a hack and more, in the spirit of Vertov, a hero. Paul Monaco argues that creativity in editing became acceptable, and the pacing and spacing of a film was transformed into an aesthetic and an expressive device. So while feature films in the 1960s veered away from the open aperture, displays of excess shifted to the editing commitments that would have trimmed the establishing shot that is *Empire* from eight hours to less than eight seconds. Warhol's superfluity would seem like anathema to the New York School, yet the extremities of editing's subtraction and the long take's extension function as complementary manifestations of excess. The rapid edit epitomized by Sam Peckinpah, for example, is largely informed by a Warhol-esque dedication to extravagance both in terms of resource indulgence and 1960s on-screen expansionism. Rather than being measured strictly by what appears on-screen, Peckinpah's intemperance is defined negatively, by how much he cut away. Composed of 3,624 separate shots, the director's 1969 *The Wild Bunch* set the record for number of shots in a feature film and thus serves as a fitting contrast to Warhol's single long take. Peckinpah's trademark editing style required an expansive amassment of necessary infrastructure in order to achieve the weightlessness of his rapid cutting speed. Not only did his system require the use of multiple cameras, but his editors paradoxically extended shot length through slow motion, then sprawled these same images across a widened screen and over the course of his films' unusually long running times.[27] The sheer abundance of montage virtuosity thus complements rather than contrasts Warhol's open aperture as excessive display. Exploiting his available cinematic resources by ridding his aesthetic of the waste that separates one shot from the next, *The Wild Bunch* is an orgy of exudation, a monumental suggestion of paring down and then discarding the surplus footage that does not contribute to a film's hurried pace. The polarities represented by Warhol's opening of the 1960s and Peckinpah's closing of the same decade are both exemplary of an overuse of available techniques and, correspondingly, of resources.

The shortening of the shot in American feature films during the 1960s suggests that this basic unit of film was being absorbed by film technology as its capabilities expanded and were increasingly refined. Technological innovation, as Paul Virilio argues, corresponds with a decrease in the physical size of a given apparatus, a diminution process that culminates in disappearance or fusion with a given set of extensive realms.[28] A dimension of this is how the sophistication of a technology is gauged not by its longevity or endurance but rather by how quickly it succumbs to obsolescence. The fetish of innovation and disposability that is really at the heart of Virilio's disappearance theory is neatly summarized by the ad slogan for the Apple iPhone 4 (released in 2010): "This changes everything. Again." As everything that came before is cancelled out, the ad's call to action is to throw the previous model away, disappearing it in favor of the new specs of the latest platform. Warhol's attempt to remove editing from the filmmaking process signals the obsolescence not only of editing but of cinema, making room for a democratic culture of image making and image makers that collapses its mythological statue. When a total amateur can make a film so easily—and without any mistakes—as Warhol contended, the medium is naturalized, easily integrating into the fabric of everyday life. Thus the casual point-and-shoot aesthetic forges a link between the fate of cinema and the relative cheapness that comes with its ubiquity, a logic that applies as much to an image as to any other consumer good. As Leo Enticknap points out, beginning in the 1950s film camera technology was motivated by the desire to reduce costs and improve efficiency for film studios, the result of which spilled over into the broader realm of amateur and independent filmmaking practices.[29] So, while 35mm technology remained stagnant, the portable and affordable 16mm camera flourished, particularly within television production and eventually within documentary filmmaking—direct cinema in particular. Both the new documentary style and live television approached editing, like Warhol, in the moment rather than in post-production. The 16mm camera was then replaced in the 1970s and 1980s by video—an even more accessible, user-friendly medium. Initially used by television producers and surveillance systems as a means of copying and storing content, video was rather expensive until the early 1970s and thus limited in use. But as video innovated and became more user-friendly, it gained a greater market, and the price of equipment fell. In terms of documentary practice, lighter and more affordable equipment has consistently had a democratizing effect. With the advent of compact cameras such as portapaks, as well as basic editing equipment, suddenly almost anyone could make quality moving images—and more and more people did. There was no laboratory processing involved, no need for special lighting either, and low-cost tapes could be reused, such that video tape "could be expended almost as freely as a novelist uses paper."[30] As one person could be his or her own production unit, and with video distribution networks opened up, the result was a decade of tremendous documentary and independent filmmaking activity. The parallel to digitally captured documentary is obvious. The difference is that analog video was often regarded as marginal, the grainy low-resolution medium of radicals and artists, while the digital video that has replaced it occupies both the peripheral and the mainstream. Digital editing is likewise polarized as it is either over indulged or completely dismissed. As cinema is downsized or democratized by technology itself or by circumstantial necessity, viewer expectations also experience a shift, if not a complete renovation. Warhol's excess clearly celebrates the democratizing possibilities inherent in his movie camera, and he duly makes a spectacle of the material wealth that allows the sacred mythology and technology of cinema to be manipulated by such amateur, unqualified hands (or, in his case, total lack thereof).

The Cinematic Pyramid

The "useless" pyramid, Bataille writes, consumes the resources it uses without turning a profit and is therefore "a monumental mistake."[31] Skyscrapers, like the pyramid, weigh heavy with overt symbolic logic—as well as large financial costs, in part because they are so inefficient at generating revenue. For example, no floor space can be rented until after the entire building is complete, meaning that large sections stand empty in the meantime, often for years, earning no returns; height also demands more operating infrastructure such as elevators and safety features, which more grounded structures do not require.[32] Likewise, the empty vessel that is the grand architectural wonder does nothing apart from tax energy reserves (materials, laborers) on behalf of satisfying the observer. Moving from the mammoth tomb markers of Ancient Egypt to the cult of church-building that characterized the Middle Ages, Bataille continues his architectural history of excess with the industrial era's equivalent, the factory, into which the dominant middle class concentrated the spillage of its manufactured excess, thus symbolizing the wealth and power being generated within.[33] Of course there is a precedent of analogizing the movie theatre and the church, the former supplanting the latter, and of conceptualizing the Hollywood studio system as an analog of the Fordist manufacturing plant. *Empire* is a pyramid, but a cinematic one. Most obviously, the film locates the skyscraper as American society's particular interpretation of the pyramid. But because the "useless" film is so intentionally analogous to its subject, the artist the situates cinema itself as the so-called immaterial version of the Ancient Egyptian pyramid.

Though an unedited film, *Empire* takes for its structuring conceit the generation of waste itself—all the stuff that Dede Allen or Vertov's wife and editor Elizaveta Svilova would snip off, casting into the archives of stock footage, or simply sweep away. *Empire*, then, is a film to be disposed of, a fact that seems to directly contrast with its subject's solidity, longevity, and sense of permanence. The Empire State Building, for such is the film's protagonist, embodies the visual logic that a society in access to a plentitude of material resources, labor, and technology is burdened by a wealth so great its surfeit must be released, uselessly and in grandeur. The building's construction was part of New York City's intense competition for the title of tallest building, unofficially launched in the late 1920s. Two other projects vied for the distinction: 40 Wall Street and the Chrysler Building were still being erected when work on the Empire State began. Completed just over a year after ground was broken, the Empire State Building outstripped its competitors in terms of height and the speed of its construction. Officially opened on May 1, 1931, U.S. President Herbert Hoover marked the event by turning on the building's lights from a control switch located remotely, in Washington, D.C. There could be no more perfect a display of the technological sublime—although it was short-lived, for as the building's opening coincided with the beginning of the Great Depression, the impracticality of its dimensions expanded as the majority of its available office space was left vacant. It was not until 1950 that the Empire finally turned a profit.[34] But because economic downturn precluded other rivals from joining the competition, the depression in fact guaranteed the Empire State Building's retention of its superlative distinction as New York's most iconic monument of conspicuous consumption. Only in 1972 with the construction of the World Trade Center was the height of the Empire State Building surpassed, though it would regain its former title in 2001.[35]

In its ideal pre-Depression moment, the Empire State Building's monumentality and the sheer speed of its construction functioned as a narcissistic assertion of power and prestige, plainly and obviously symbolized by the ostentatious squandering of the energy, labor, and resources required to finish the project and secure the title of the biggest and, therefore, the best. But that the building was destined to stand for so long as an empty shell of drained wealth and entropic energy transformed its symbolic power into a fiction that radiates with unintended irony. That is, even if the building was not burdened for so long with associations of lost prosperity, its moment remains an exultant enactment of Bataille's theory of the ritualized exudation of excess. The monument that is Warhol's film performs the same rite not only because wealth and power radiate from the building itself (as the film's subject) but because the actual form of the film matches the Empire State Building in all its symbolic value. Both the architectural showpiece and the cinematic icon use the form of their material existence to make symbolic their culture's access to and conversion of natural resources into energy, wealth, and then excess that is necessarily and "uselessly" lost.[36] Likewise, the island of Manhattan is itself characterized by the limitations of its geographical surface space; the result, of course, is the Empire State Building and the architectural genre of the skyscraper—buildings whose occupancy of the only available space—the air—symbolizes the precarious terms of growth. Meanwhile, the stock market crash that turned the Empire State Building into a ghost of its former prosperity is nothing if not an example of the restricted nature of economic expansion: without the release of enough surplus, the system bursts its seams and collapses. But while the architectural blockbuster that Warhol took for a subject exemplifies the basic terms of Bataille's economic study, the film that results points specifically to cinema's lack of growth rather than its progression, for its structure is defined by a limited amount of change or transition.

Bataille writes that the energy that emanates from the sun is "the origin and the essence of our wealth." But what distinguishes solar power is that it "dispenses energy—wealth—without any return"; the sun, as Bataille describes it, "gives without ever receiving."[37] *Empire*'s only source of illumination is the building's gratuitously illuminated exterior, which directly corresponds to the open aperture of Warhol's idling camera, matching the filmmaker's own display of conspicuously consuming (squandering) available excesses of energy. The Empire State Building has made a career out of its light shows; President Hoover's christening set something of a precedent that continues on in the building's various seasonal and celebratory costume changes. From light to images to operative energy, *Empire* is not only about the ability to artificially derive resources; it also exalts in the spectacle of their squandering. The extreme self-consciousness of *Empire* denaturalizes cinema and the skyscraper, deflating these monuments and replacing them over the course of eight hours with ones that are exultantly artificial. Of course, what for our contemporary moment is increasingly a glaring signal of wasted energy and environmental negligence did not have the same resonance in 1964 when *Empire* was made. And yet the building, like the film, is not innocent of the associations of waste and excess that our heightened ecological awareness makes more apparent. The point of reformulating excess as a term is that it bridges cinema's emergent environmental politics with the behaviors of the past; the current moment has finally caught up to the environmental implications that both the term excess and *Empire* possess.

The Empire State Building itself does not exude physical energy, though like any manufactured good, its value resides not in its particular use or function but in the labor power that is concentrated in the very fact of its existence. And so the building remains inanimate and therefore as seemingly lazy and lifeless as the fixed camera. But *Empire* is premised on displaying a lack of energy in order to reveal energy's totalizing presence in culture at large. The film is dominated by a resource-conscious subtext to the point that the availability of natural light dictates what might in another film be called a script. Shot from dusk until dawn, the departure and arrival of light are the film's only "events." More importantly, the absence of natural light makes the film not about night or darkness but about how technology precludes ever shutting down, allowing an energy source to rest or restore itself. On a strictly formal level (for the film is nothing if not pure form), as *Empire* narrates the passage of an artificial night it also showcases how cinema is, like the Empire State Building, wholly dependent upon technologically produced resources. It is excessive, this nocturnal long take that is fuelled by generated power and artificial light, and we call it such, now and here, in our eco-conscious moment, precisely because these feats of overconsumption within cinema and in all spheres of life are becoming totally unfeasible. *Empire* is thus understood as ritualized performance of cinema as a gratuitous self-indulgence, a self-conscious demonstration of the capabilities of the camera, as well as a manifestation of the autonomous vision machine that produces images without the assistance of a filmmaker's mental or physical energy. The cinematic pyramid, of which Warhol's is only one, behaves not unlike the resource image. The difference, though, is that the display of excess is arguably intended to be self-reflexive in its hyperbolization of cinema's material, temporal, and visual excess and thus subversive in its homage to the very culture and society that has produced it as such.

Ruhr: *Empire*'s Twin Tower

Because American experimental filmmaker James Benning has spent his forty-year career meticulously mapping out cinematic duration in conjunction with natural and constructed landscapes, his work can be contextualized within the larger history of the cinematic long take.[38] The Ruhr Valley is the largest urban agglomeration in Germany, known principally for its industrial developments and manufacturing, and *Ruhr* (2009) is Benning's portrait of its variegated social, industrial, and natural landscapes. The film is a first for Benning in two ways: it is his first complete work in high definition digital video, and the first he has shot outside of the United States, whose open landscapes have served as consistent discursive and aesthetic inspiration throughout his entire artistic output. The changes are critical, both for the filmmaker and the history of his art form, for they conflate two interrelated currents that are transforming cinema, its economics, culture, and aesthetics, namely digital technology and globalization. The film is divided into seven shots and two sixty-minute parts. The first hour is comprised of six static long takes (each about fifteen minutes), featuring a traffic tunnel, a factory interior, a worker sandblasting graffiti from a Richard Serra sculpture, a mosque during afternoon prayer, a wooded area near the Düsseldorf airport, and a residential street. In the single one-hour take (also still) that makes up the second part, a brutal industrial tower spews what could be either smoke or steam, all set against the sound of a wailing siren and a setting sun. Points of contact between *Ruhr* and *Empire* are numerous; the final long take is particularly suggestive of Warhol, as well as of the catastrophic—even iconic—events known now as 9/11. More than just the subject matter, though, the comparative terms of the films' production and use of technology are worth outlining. *Ruhr*, of course, bears its own rich and detailed set of discourses and should be addressed in its own right, but as it also functions as a powerful addendum to *Empire*, inscribing the 1964 film with new resource-conscious currency.

Benning has long remained a proponent of a 16mm camera and analog filmmaking as the most purely cinematic. The filmmaker converted to digital only recently (in and around 2008) less by his own volition than because of recurring problems with the diminishing quality and availability of both film processing labs and projection systems. Because shots for his earlier 16mm films maxed out at eleven minutes before a change of reel, a large part of his structure was determined by his technological limitations. For example, Benning's rigorously structured works *13 Lakes* and *Ten Skies* (both 2004) consist of takes ten minutes in length—each of which corresponds to a four-hundred-foot roll of 16mm film, shot at twenty-four frames per second. The digital medium of course changes Benning's shooting and editing style, as generous memory cards allow for shots of up to several hours.[39] And while each of *Ruhr*'s long takes appear unedited, they have in fact been cut together, thus speeding up the passage of time—though digital editing tools seamlessly disguise the differences between amassed shots. But time does not move quickly here. The shot's time seems to be the event's time, as Bazin might say it ought to be; but, then, there is no "event." While Warhol used the eight hours of night to impose some kind of narrative order on an otherwise ceaseless flow, Benning's mathematically divided time restraints limit the film. Though, like *Empire*, the sun sets and dusk descends, limiting his visibility, it seems that Benning must find additional reasons to shut off the camera, cut the shot, or else his subject matter could—it seems—continue on indefatigably; for, like the industry it is filming, the camera Benning employs will not or cannot shut down. While the "technological sublime" in this case depends upon obscuring the source of technology's and industry's power, thus consolidating its potency in a sense of the divine, Benning's cinema strategically overexposes and undercuts the same. Each of *Ruhr*'s ground-level long takes force the viewer to confront the complexity within the taken-for-granted simplicity of the environment—natural inseparable from the industrial—that surrounds. While each shot seems random, we are given time to forge relationships between such things as a mosque, airplanes sweeping across the sky above a gently rustling forest, and the production floor of a pipe making factory. As Benning has commented when presenting the film, the suggestion he forges is how migrants working in the Ruhr Valley, many from Turkey and the Middle East, are transforming Germany's cultural fabric. Presumably, as we piece the shots together, those in the mosque and on the airplanes are those invisible humans laboring in the coke processing plant, whose smoke stack is seemingly "destroyed" at regular intervals throughout the final sixty-minute take. After belching its cloud of smoke, obscuring the structure, the stack rematerializes only to disappear into its own belched effluvia once again. It is the narrative of industrial capital, and of Bataille's theory of general economy: wealth destroys itself so as to create itself anew.

Coke is what remains after coal is burned down to a pure tarry essence. After superheating it in blast furnaces for periods of twenty-five hours, the dense residue is used in the manufacturing of steel (such as the pipes in the factory in *Ruhr*'s second shot). While such coal-fire processes are now associated with the industrializing world and the so-called BRIC nations, it endures in Ruhr.[40] Benning's film dismantles the myth of post-industrialization, forcing the viewer to confront and ponder at length how historical periods and attendant modes of production overlap rather than come to an abrupt end. The world in this film, which includes people, transportation systems, and the experience of nature, revolves around that coking tower. The tower featured in *Ruhr* is located in Duisberg, and is considered one of the world's top such production facilities. As Benning has explained, seventy-two furnaces cook the coal for twenty-five hours, after which a machine pushes the coal out of the coking oven into a train car. The noise of the siren signals that the train is beneath the tower; ten thousand gallons of water is poured on top of that coal, which creates enormous plumes of vapor. This happens every ten minutes; the sixty-minute take captures the process five times. All the while, Benning's camera stands firm, pitting itself against the coke plant; for sixty minutes they face each other down in a contest of stasis and of power, the viewer oscillating between the two summits of industry and energy, the coke tower and the HD video camera. Michael Ned Holdte notes that the film's subtle action occurs literally and figuratively on thresholds between nature and industry.[41] While the structure is dialectical, positioning industry against nature, and dominant German culture versus the Muslim Other, the nexus or point of axis is the movie camera itself, and in particular digital imaging technology. Because the DV camera has the capacity to record at length without stopping could seem the ideal mode by which to narrate industrial capital's accelerated social and procedural dimensions—what David Harvey might recognize as a compression or "collapsing" of space and time.[42] But the choice to shoot in high definition is being made *for* and not necessarily *by* analog filmmakers like Benning. Yet digital image-capture has the capacity to tell this very story of technological hegemony: how culture and artistic means of representation are determined by the tools that technology industries make available to us in response to market demand and what are constructed social needs. As Edward Burtynsky likewise discovered when the BP oil spill rendered his analog apparatus inadequate, even antique, Benning's film asks whether digital is necessary to tell *this* story, draw *this* map, probe *this* topography, which industrialization will only deepen as it further penetrates the layers of nature and society in search of new frontiers to tap for human and natural resources.

In practical terms, Benning discovered that HD bears much more precise resolution and steadier registration than 16mm. And so he exploited that capacity for stability by looking at things "in a much closer, deeper way than before" and "at much more subtle things that were happening."[43] The technology accords with telling of the story of *Ruhr*, exploring and conflating its layers of globalization, industry, and nature, and the complexity introduced by digital technology, all of which come together in a film hinged around coke processing—which is or ought to be an outmoded even antiquated industrial process, one of which is at the heart of seemingly sleek technologies like cars and postmodern architecture. Situated alongside Warhol's bold long take of a monolithic office tower disappearing into darkness, Benning's digitally captured film pits the camera against industrially derived energy embedded in the long take image and speaks to continuity between analog and digital rather than absolute difference. Warhol's exploration of what was at the moment a newly "liberating" movie-making technology suggests that not much has changed in the four or five decades since he opened up the terrain of experimental filmmaking.

Final Cuts: The End of Editing

Warhol's film is a portrait of a monument of wasted energy but is itself constructed according to a principle of total "entropy"—energy saved, kept latent, held in reserve.[44] Empire's energy is spent not in the process of filmmaking but, conversely, in avoidance of the same. As part of the amateur trappings of the film, editing is abandoned altogether, creating a void matched only by the camera's lack of movement. The energy of the cinema is thus negatively defined, wherein the removal of the energy that editing and cinematography typically require are highlighted by their absence. Contemporaneous with Warhol, and also enabled by 16mm film cameras, direct cinema was likewise a dedication to achieving pure and unadulterated depictions of live events, but for political ends rather than ostensibly apolitical ones. Filmmakers such as Robert Drew, Albert and David Maysles, and Frederick Wiseman aspired to invisibility, sacrificed seamless aesthetics to allow events to unfold naturally, without interference, and thus delivering them to audiences. Beginning in the 1950s, cheaper, lighter 16mm equipment began to displace both the standard 35mm and the tripod. While mobility improved, documentary filmmakers in particular still found sound recording a burden, for in order to be synchronized, camera and tape recorder had to be connected with a cable. Thus tethering sound operator and camera handler, maneuverability was hampered. By 1960, however, Robert Drew and his associates had, through assiduous experimentation finally worked out an assemblage in which camera, recorder, and microphone moved independently of each other. This, in addition to the lightweight 16mm camera, enabled Drew's unit to—ideally at least—shoot on-location, in the moment, and, in the spirit of Dziga Vertov, disappear the cinematic apparatus into the living environment. Direct cinema, like observational documentarians since, strove to lay bare political and social reality in all its grittiness; a philosophical imperative echoed in a roughshod style, which still has the rhetorical power to convince viewers of the practitioner's objectivity. As the commentator's voice gradually disappeared along with other paternalistic conventions that interfered with truth-telling, such as montage or supplying contextualizing information, the subject was allowed to speak freely, in real time, without interlocutor. Developments in synchronized sound recording contributed to the political imperative of observational filmmaking, in that allowing the subject to speak directly and at length resulted in longer shot duration.[45] But what is not obvious in the ostensibly uncut aesthetic of direct cinema is that editing choices remain integral, except that they were made in the moment of shooting and so are hidden in the instructive spontaneity of the camera operator's way of seeing—such as the decision to zoom in on a subject or even to physically turn a corner, thus cutting from one space into another. Accessing truth or reality, such as it is, by opening the aperture and recording freely results in the accumulation of large amounts of unusable footage. Before digital video made "delete" a viable choice for movie making, practitioners of direct cinema whittled hundreds of hours of material into the length of a feature. Editing imposed cohesion and patterning on amassed spontaneity, all the while radically cutting away unseen objectivity. Likewise, as Paul Monaco points out, for all the apparent flexibility and randomness of direct cinema, accessing that same casualness was anything but, as it put huge physical demands on the filmmaker. On the one hand, such innovations that enabled nonfiction filmmaking to flourish—faster films stocks and zoom lenses were also key technological ingredients—were far less taxing to the operator's energy supply; but on the other, as the body of the camera operator could now replace the tripod, crane, dolly, and track, unhindered filmmaking came at the expense of increased physical exertion. The camera operator, who was also usually the director, needed to be physically agile, respond quickly to actions, and possess the stamina to record long takes.[46]

Vertov's *Man with a Movie Camera* is a remarkable exhibition of the energy that is poured into and absorbed by all stages of the cinematic process, from the energy of the subjects to that of the camera operator, the editor, the projectionist, the audience and the film itself, playing out on screen. Then there is the energy of the camera, which assumes physical liberty and independence, superseding its former dependence on the anthropod who birthed it. Vertov's unfettered camera liberates human energy rather than burdens it with further demands. This ideal, while not attained by the observational filmmaker of the 1960s, reflects the founding ambitions of cinema's early innovators—the study of the energy exerted by human bodies, what Jules Étienne Marey called the "animal machine."[47] Though his films are replete with bodies in motion, Vertov does not celebrate human movement, or even document it; rather, he is documenting how the camera itself records movement. The early Soviet's experiments in film truth were premised on a transcendent camera. The vision machine, as Vertov's montage principles imagined, did not just use energy, it supplied energy; the movie camera brought the industrial world to life. The question that Vertov posed is still incredibly relevant, for it is as yet unrealized. How, indeed, can we unplug technology from a power supply? Wind energy or solar power? As Google Energy's massive investments in wind power suggest, perhaps such renewable energy sources will institute a more balanced, even seamless, relation between nature and industrial culture. While the ambiguity of the autonomous camera at the end of *Man with a Movie Camera* typically provokes readings about the ubiquity of the camera and a surveillance society, there is another option for interpreting Vertov's richly layered text: technology does not control us, the image seems to say, but its need for power, energy, and natural resources, such as "rare earth elements," certainly does.

A cinematic *Sputnik*, Alexander Sokurov's *Russian Ark* was at the time of its release in 2002 the longest single take in cinema's history. Enabled by digital's vast memory stores, a customized Steadicam was anchored to the cinematographer and, thus energized and stabilized, the camera takes the viewer on a 96-minute transhistorical tour of the Hermitage gallery in St. Petersburg. By overlapping the real-time of the long take, the first person perspective of the protagonist (represented by the camera's eye and Sokurov's own voice-over narration), as well as the gallery's witnessed history, the film's multiple historical fragments accumulate organically into a narrative whole. But *Russian Ark*'s subject matter is eclipsed by the director's famous exploitation of digital's facility to both record for an almost infinite length of time and also to indulge in relatively unrestrained mobility. Digital enables an ambulatory camera, rendering literal the suggested omniscience of Vertov's aesthetic, wherein the kino-eye's invisible presence saturates all places and at

all times. The film has been called an "anti-*October*," and indeed the mobility
of Sokurov's liberated digital apparatus clearly challenges the Marxist politics
that informed the Soviet avant-garde in general and Vertov's and Eisenstein's
systems of montage and conceptions of the camera in particular. The DVD's
accompanying "making-of" documentary *Film in One Breath* points out that
the lead-up to the ball scene which concludes *Russian Ark* is partly shot on the
same staircase that Eisenstein featured in his 1927 film. Returning to the scene
of the crime, as it were, the staircase pits the two filmmakers against each other
in terms that are historical and ideological but enacted on the level of technologically determined aesthetics. Sokurov's digital portrait somewhat restores
the relationship between Russian cinema, with its iconoclastic legacy, and the
venerable tsarist institution know as the Hermitage. Perhaps paradoxically, it
also does something to align Sokurov with Eisenstein, for what *Russian Ark*
ultimately highlights is the way in which the very technology of the camera
and the formal dimensions of editing (rather than what is being represented)
can be directly engaged as a means of political discourse. While Bazin understands montage as an attempt to "rule out the ambiguity of expression," he
extols depth of focus for its democratization of vision, wherein the image's
extended space and time allowed the spectator to construct a distinct and
even personalized meaning.[48] Conversely, however, amidst the political fervor
and social turmoil of post-1917 Russia, the imperative of the filmmaker was
to inform, educate, and ultimately agitate a vast and mostly illiterate population. Soviet montage did not allow for such liberties as ambiguity, nor the
luxury of an image's measured contemplation. But Sokurov can luxuriate, it
seems, for *Russian Ark* does just that: maintaining the momentum of the open
aperture and likewise avoiding editing (or intending to) effectively negates the
early Soviet cinema's theoretical intention to produce in the viewer not only
a specific, unswerving ideological direction but, like Vertov, a new spectator, a
new human being, and a new society. The purpose behind Vertov's theory of
the kino-eye, for example, was to "create a man more perfect than Adam" and
from that prototype "thousands" more.[49] Vertov's cinema, like Eisenstein's,
and *October*'s staircase sequences in particular, similarly ushers out Russia's
reigning political, social, and cultural structures and uses the camera to replace
them with a politics and a people entirely new. Sokurov, however, returns to
the past that the Soviets dismantled, revitalizing it with the cutting edge of
the digital camera.

The Steadicam's ability to freely roam thus signals the end of the aesthetic
tyranny of montage and the ideological and political repression that its Marxist
ideology came to represent. The film maximizes the digital video camera's
capacity for girth, multiplicity, and protracted duration, resulting in "semi-

otic excess," as Thomas Levin terms it.[50] In material, practical, and aesthetic terms, Levin's assessment is really about an excess of vision itself. While the film depends upon the abilities of digital video technology (from shooting on DV cameras to the editing technology that inspired the project), it is also unrestrained in its self-conscious display of the improvisational capabilities of this medium's fortitude and flourish. Digital or analog, the long take is defined by a disinclination to interrupt: it will not break apart or disguise the simultaneity of concurrent (or disparate) actions, while it is the actual exposure that the virtuosic long take will not interfere with. The refusal to cut, edit, or otherwise interrupt results in the production, occupation, and then maximal exploitation of cinematic time and space. Manovich's seminal concept "composting" describes a transition from the linear sequencing of "modernist" Soviet montage to the layering of "postmodern" new media narrative, wherein the principle of assemblage by cutting is superseded by the digital "morph" or "composite." The result: a layered cinema of fluidity instead of one premised on rupture (however invisible or well concealed).[51] Digital cinema is also about what the camera itself can do in the moment of capture—open up and roam, cover more than 4,265 feet of floor space and three hundred years of history in less than ninety minutes. The effect of the ostensibly unedited long take experience is that we are confronting waste—excess—that which should or would have been eliminated if conventional editing, narrative patterns, and shooting strategies had been observed. What might it mean, Sokurov's mobile framing asks us, to abandon or be dispossessed of our typical means of production and to make cinema without cutting, pasting, and perhaps without wasting a cell or digit of support surface? The question is whether or not film becomes waste when it is or is not edited. Does the long take hoard waste and thus overindulge in visualizing excess, or is editing a process that relentlessly trims excess away, and is responsible for producing waste? In other words, perhaps the avoidance of editing is more wasteful than editing itself. This difference is subtle, and somehow counterintuitive, but it belies what is a fundamental paradox in Sokurov's film: namely, what seems a liberal indulgence in technology and style in fact depends upon premeditation and authorial control. Factor in as well that the digital images are then transferred to 35mm for theatrical distribution. Of course this extra step is a common practice in feature filmmaking; even films shot on film stock are edited in post-production in high definition and then converted back to analog form, a fact that illustrates how digital technology adds both complexity as well as simplicity to moving image production. The digital long take narrates the prowess, power, and saturation level of that mode's capacity to consume time and space to the point that indulgence itself results in its own specific aesthetic.

With digital, however, the conception that it is purely immaterial encourages a surfeit of images, such as those accumulated when making a film that requires multiple takes before achieving one that is ideal. The principle sees an equivalent in flawed recycling programs, wherein the knowledge that something can be discarded responsibly contributes to the creation of more waste, not less.[52] Guilt assuaged by the blue box, consumers are granted permission to consume more, and so they do. The same psychology contributes to a glut of digital images, their so-called immateriality permitting increased production and consumption, precisely because they are apparently immaterial and superficially inconspicuous. The fallaciousness of digital's immateriality resides in the fact that the technology that enables its support surface might prove more materially dependent than that of the analog cinema it is eclipsing—if for no other reason than the troublingly rapid pace with which the DV camera and all its attendant parts are rendered disposable by the economy of planned technological obsolescence—an essential dimension of capitalism's operative principle of creative destruction.

Is *Russian Ark's* claim to be a single take viable when the film itself consists of 30,000 "digital events"? David Rodowick points out that getting at the nature of the digital event—consisting of digital capture, synthesis, and compositing—is essential to understanding how digital technology is shaping cinema. He exposes the true complexity and labor intensity behind the crisp simplicity of form that digital images impart, and thus shows how the energy "saved" by the ostensible absence of editing and reduced production infrastructure is simply displaced, exiled off the set to the post-production phase. Rodowick's discussion of digital's "algorithmic transformations" concludes that *Russian Ark*, and all digital cinema, bears an "aesthetic of post-production" that is as dependant on the structures of montage (understood as editing or a combination of events) as the analog form.[53] Rodowick rightly reminds us that *Russian Ark's* mythical status as a one-take digital feat was the result of marketing ingenuity rather than critical assessment. Jay David Bolter and Richard Grusin ought also to be evoked as, once again, the paradox or double logical of remediation presents itself, wherein digital culture strives to both increase media and likewise erase the evidence of mediation.[54] Behind the phantom image composed of touchless binary code is a pulsing, energy-hungry data processing center, or slag pile of obsolete CDs. The caveat should be applied to other received wisdom about digital technology—particularly that it is less wasteful and "greener" than analog or that access to vast amounts of digital content implies political freedom and that content is not regulated. So the full dimensions of Sokurov's indulgence are not always readily conspicuous; just as the unscripted films of Warhol or direct cinema result in an overabundance

of footage, so the apparent spontaneity of *Russian Ark* required four years
of energetic planning and choreography, not to mention three partial takes,
before the ideal of a spacious, cinematically liberated film finally material-
ized. Sokurov's ostentation requires both the energy derived from the camera
post-production, and the energy involved in preproduction phases. Added to
this is the energy that is surrendered by the camera operator, a dimension
that is perceptibly minimized by *Russian Ark*'s laudable use of the Steadicam.
The ambulatory camera that structures the film formally, characterizes it
aesthetically, and also sustains its real-time pretensions speaks to a greater
amount of resource consumption, not less. Digital's seeming effortlessness in
fact introduces a new set of burdens, or at least replaces old ones—batteries
running low, the cameraman taxed to near collapse, unforeseen production
costs—which seems to defeat the intended aesthetic of open-endedness and
unfettered liberation. The unrestricted autonomy promised by the digital
camera proves to be anything but. On a procedural and material level,
technologies necessarily leave behind a tangible impact or physical residue.
The ecological dimensions of cinema now substitute the Bazinian "hand of
man" with our own contemporary God term, the "ecological footprint." The
"cinematic footprint" is a juxtaposition of these terms—it closes the circle,
and thus makes it possible to engage a set of heretofore divergent lines of
inquiry: moving-image technology, environmental erosion, and the hydrocarbon culture they all, together and separately, define.

For Sokurov the grandeur of his shooting location is matched by the
democratic promises of what has become industrial and post-industrial
culture's dominant mode of expression and communication, the result of
which might be called a digital baroque. It is baroque in terms of its unrestrained technicality, flamboyant range of motion, and stylistic flourish that
Sokurov unabashedly delights in; and, second, in Timothy Murray's sense of
the digital "conditions" that shift towards a "labyrinthine continuousness"
(the Hermitage as the maze of the digital fold) rather than in the "deceptive cohesion" of analog projection.[55] But the opulence Sokurov indulges is
accompanied by a distinct air of insecurity. Murray finds in the interactive
media arts an unbounded subject position that thwarts the tight regime of
analog linearity wherein time can only move forward, even when montage
makes it appears otherwise. Sokurov, likewise, sees possibility in the state
(or statelessness) of Deleuzian becoming that digital image-capture seems
to embody. When *Russian Ark* was released the former Soviet Union in
2002, the ascendency of the digital camera, the new Russia, and the new
media, such as they were, seemed to be charting new terrains of political
and artistic expression. Technology was equated with redemption and the

coming of democracy; post-Soviet governments and emergent middle and upper classes displayed status and likewise unfettered political freedom in the acquisition of computers and cameras and other digital devices that enabled open-access communication systems and handed control of content production and dissemination over to the user (consumer). From the telegraph to the VCR, the equation between technology and social and political freedom is one of modernity's recurrent themes, and one that continues unabated.[56] But the political opulence Sokurov was celebrating is accompanied by a distinct air of insecurity and, in light of Russia's regressive, repressive, and anti-democratic political climate, even trepidation. While the protagonist's interlocutor (Astolphe de Custine, a discriminating French marquis) constantly derides Russia's attempts at cultural and intellectual sophistication, the digital showcase that is *Russian Ark* counters the insinuation that this country is backward. The film itself, like its protagonist, seems intent on responding to both Western Europe's perceived superiority over its easterly neighbor (a longstanding theme in Russian society and culture) as well as the apparent end of Soviet montage in favor of the "democratic" digital long take. Ronald Deibert diligently reminds his fellow network citizens that with new media communications technology comes insidious forms of political and social repression. Cyberspace, for example, is an increasingly militarized zone; its open terrains—the utopian labyrinth of interactivity, video streaming, and file sharing—are in fact heavily patrolled by state powers and nonstate insurgents (never mind commercial players) whose interest is to control and limit access to information and, where interstate security is concerned, sabotage it. The moving image is now rarely untouched by digital technology or the Internet, the platform by which it is accessed and traded. And, like other vestiges of electronic communications systems and accoutrements (cell phones, cameras, Global Positioning Systems), the Internet has undoubtedly empowered de-centered groups around the world and given tremendous voice to the politically and socially marginal. Indeed, the space of instantaneous communication seems at times uncontrollable, shaped only by its legions of private users and their collective imaginative powers, but the amorphous Internet has taken shape, in the form of an "architecture of control." And what it controls are images and information, in both the private and public sphere. "Newtonian physics is as relevant in politics and cyberspace as it is in the physical realm," as Deibert argues; regulation and control exercised by a form of "political calculus" has inaugurated a new geopolitical information environment that inhibits rather than fosters social and political freedoms.[57] Cyber filtering systems—the "Great Firewall of China" is a prime example—have become the new paradigm of security and privacy invasion that clever Apple advertising campaigns and media scholars fixated on image ontology and subject subjectivity consistently obscure. Deibert's interventions make stunningly clear that scholars of media also need to address the political realities of the network culture that is changing not just how and where we interact with images and information, but global politics and all our security interests in turn. While artists and filmmakers harness digital technology and dissemination forms such as the Internet, the scholars who track them need to at least acknowledge how the manufacture and disposal of electronics is exploitative in terms of labor and environmental abuse but also how, as Deibert consistently demonstrates, the freedom principle of open communications and expression is in fact politically restrictive. So while *Russian Ark* celebrates the possibilities of its technological and historical moment, it also, like Vertov, suggests the trepidation of what is an ambiguously defined political and social future.

Surveillance Screens: Vision as Excess

Vertov's *Man with a Movie Camera* ends, famously, with the undying image of the autonomously powered movie camera which uncannily anticipates many things, both literally and metaphorically, one of which is the long take. Because energy is generated by the cinematic apparatus itself, the autonomous camera's omni-voyance suggests a perpetually open aperture as well as the ability to make films without a separate editing process. Whatever the camera sees is cinema, and the camera—towering above the city with its bobbing searchlight head—sees everything, always. Without the discernment of the editor and cinematographer, an unencumbered camera apparatus such as those used by closed-circuit television systems relies on chance, seeming objectivity, and its unfailing energy to dictate the dimensions of the images it produces. Not unlike the "vision machine" that functions, as Virilio describes it, according to "kinematic" or "observed" energy, the camera is fuelled by nothing less than sight itself, the ability of the machine to see rather than merely record.[58] The end of the cameraman inaugurates the beginning of something else; however ambiguously positioned, Vertov's prescient image sets the stage for what became Soviet Russia's police state. But as digital technology renders the camera and communications forums ubiquitous and post-industrial society increasingly surveyed, vision's proliferation has material manifestations: the sheer amount of images available to us and the infrastructures they are tethered to is as significant as what they depict.

The apparent effortlessness of Vertov's "kinematic" kino-eye transfers the energy saved on the part of the human operator to the machine, the result of which is an unprecedented amount of unedited and unscrutinized visual and physical material. Theorizing the long-take image must involve discourses of surveillance and, specifically, questions of storage space and the archiving of unwatched reels of real-time footage—the physical residue of omniscient, unmediated vision.[59] Paolo Cherchi Usai points out that only a fraction of extant moving images (of which these are only a fraction of moving images actually made) could possibly be seen in a viewer's lifetime. Importantly, "the unseen" is for Cherchi Usai films and images made with the intention of having an audience.[60] What of the images made for nothing and no one? Or for limited audiences? What of pornography, for example, or home movies? Within that unseen is another unseen or invisibility, all those so-called amateur images ever made that escape the cinematic canon that is the historian's conventional reference point. Patricia Zimmerman argues that home movies and other forms of amateur filmmaking (industrial films, travelogues) are visual evidence of social and political realities of de-centered groups and cultures left out of dominant historiographies. Home movies are always fractured and incomplete, but taken together comprise an "imaginary archive" that is vast, even infinite.[61] If we mine even deeper, venture further outside dominant realms of what is and is not cinema so as to include surveillance footage and its oceans of long-take images, both extant and wiped, we would render the archive of the unseen both unmanageable and unimaginable. The long take is inseparable from the visual dynamics of security systems and what might be called the genre of closed-circuit television (CCTV). The resultant aesthetic (reality television among the most obvious example) showcases how normalized is post-industrial culture's great submission to being monitored and monitoring in turn, as well as the tremendous excess and indeed glut of images that continues to be so zealously produced and reproduced by digital activity. As film storage was and remains costly, a principle reason why analog video technology prevailed in both the television and security industries before being modified for home use was that cassette tapes could be re-recorded multiple times.[62] This practical fact speaks to the reuse value inherent in video as well as to the amount of footage accumulated before it was erased; however, what was once embraced as video's advantage, the ability to erase images and reuse tapes, archivists now blame for the loss of what might have been culturally relevant material—professionally referred to as "missing, believed wiped." Because Warhol's *Empire* assumes the trappings of a surveillance tape, its cold eye tirelessly and without relent safeguarding the integrity of the iconic building in the distance, it likewise introduces the dimension that this film, like the security tapes that were becoming standardized in the 1950s and 1960s, would eventually be erased. Suggestive of the solitude of the security camera and the recordings it produces which are only temporarily retained, Warhol's surveillance aesthetic impairs the chances that *Empire* will even be viewed. What the "closed circuit" of security television refers to is how its signal, unlike broadcast television which is openly transmitted, is received only by a specific set of monitors. The implication is that the closed circuit is a self-consuming display, deprived of an audience apart from its own operator (the camera itself or the absent human). In the contemporary urban environment, a surfeit of surveillance cameras have come to control activity, time, and space, and with relentless intensity, 24 hours a day.[63] Because the amount of information these cameras gather is so great, most of it is useless, and even with digital's capacity for organization and storage, "the sheer mass of data [is] impossible to handle."[64] Because of the prevalence of webcams and live-streaming available on the Internet, the closed circuit is more easily accessed and distributed, transforming what was once an endogamous self-consuming display deprived of a viewership apart from its own cameras or hired surveyors into the "open circuit" of multiple perspectives and an exponential field of screens.[65] Images—especially digital ones, as the CCTV aesthetic tells us—are cheap, ubiquitous, and, because of their unmanageable volume, necessarily expendable. So, when the long take is multiplied, made available round the clock and in innumerable iterations—televised, streamed live on the Internet, featured as still images in print media—*its extremity* undermines the liberation imparted by the open aperture and the invitation for the viewer's eye to linger. The relationship between excess and vision is no longer Bataille's a "vision of excess" (of transgression, subversion, perversion) but, more literally and immediately, an excess of vision itself. It is not the image itself that shocks, but the amount of images we have to choose from. An abundance of choice and accessibility, such as it is, can be transformed into a tyranny of the same. Excess, paradoxically, can also impoverish.

In May 2010, one month after the fiery collapse of the Deepwater Horizon drilling rig in the Gulf of Mexico, British Petroleum (BP) finally capitulated to demands from scientists and members of the U.S. Congress and posted a live video feed from the ocean floor where oil gushed without cessation. The demands were formalized in a congressional hearing in which BP was accused of withholding information, thus impeding independent scientists from assessing the real amount of crude that was churning out into the ocean waters each day. The magnitude of the spill was highly contested, and BP, the

U.S. Coast Guard, and the Obama Administration were all accused of gross minimization; but as the slick spread its reach on the ocean surface, it was clear that the accident was in fact a disaster. A thirty-second clip taken from a camera-equipped remotely operated vehicle (ROV) or submersible robot that had been released to the public in April, again under pressure, sounded the alarm. Marine scientists gleaned from the low-resolution images that the flow was far greater than the estimated 5,000 barrel per day figure provided by BP, the Coast Guard, or the Obama administration. Using a technique called "particle image velocimetry," which tracks the speed of objects traveling in the flow stream, mechanical engineer Steve Worely analyzed the clip and expanded the range of the spill to about 70,000 barrels a day. A computer code assessed the swirls and vortices of substances (methane and oil) pumping out of the end of the ruptured pipe and then calculated the volume of flow. But that initial thirty-second clip was not enough to accurately gauge what was happening thousands of feet below water level.

As BP was forced to turn its camera on itself, the resource image conflated with the surveillance image, opening up for public scrutiny the murkiness that is the oil industry. In addition to the now iconic photographs of oil-slicked waterfowl and the burning drilling rig itself, the public's angry response to events in the Gulf Coast in the spring and summer of 2010 was fuelled by images sourced by those same submersible ROV cameras which BP used during its standard drilling operation. A remotely operated vehicle is about the size of car; it is unoccupied, its movements controlled by a technician on the water above. The ROV is tethered to a mother ship by an umbilical cable, by which electrical power, video, and other data is carried between vehicle and operator. An ROV will typically have at least one camera; among BP's gaggle of ROVs, there were a dozen cameras capturing images from different perspectives of the ocean floor—images which U.S. Representative Ed Markey, the chief player behind the Congress's hearings, angrily demanded be made available for scrutiny. Markey stressed that "this may be BP's footage, but it's America's ocean. Now anyone will be able to see the real-time effects the BP spill is having on our ocean."[66] When the oil giant finally bowed to pressure, and the live feed became standard public fare, images of the murky plume went live on BP's site as well as the site operated by Markey's Select Committee on Energy Independence and Global Warming, which he chaired. News agencies around the world hosted the Spillcam's feed, which became something like an interrogation light that we viewers at home could train relentlessly on the BP nebulae. But unlike the image of the oily seabird, the plumes of oil deep in the ocean were abstractions. The long-take images—for that is what they amount to as far as formal elements—made little emotional impact.

But because these images were available, or eventually were made so, the BP oil spill did something to shift power relations wherein the consumer/citizen seemed to be granted the power to monitor the behavior of the heretofore invisible corporate/government bodies that, unbeknownst to us, have taken control our environment.

At the time of writing, BP's official website is replete with friendly efforts at damage control in the form of highly selective videos and photo galleries depicting images of the spill, cleanup effort, and, now, the drilling rig's business as usual. While there are still live feeds available from the ocean floor where the accident occurred, most are inactive. The Spillcam is also still live on Representative Markey's website, though images are limited. Not surprisingly, YouTube is the go-to archive to trawl through for fragments of live feed video, some of it accompanied by ironic musical scores, as well as of broadcast news reportage on the spill and testimony from all and sundry witnesses. Undoubtedly, the BP spill was a defining event for the citizens of hydrocarbon civilization; our imaginations were forced to grapple with the inherent danger in our need for and abuse of nonrenewable fuels. While it was difficult to reconcile with the abstract nature of the silent plume pulsating on the Gulf seabed, the live-feed long take put on display not only the volume of liquid fuel spilling into the water, it also exposed the monstrosity of the infrastructure—the brain power and people power—invested in getting that oil out of the ocean. But the BP disaster leaked into our consciousness slowly. When the magnitude began to register, the Spillcam was instrumental in galvanizing media, scientists, and citizens against the criminal oil giant caught on its own surveillance video red-handed, in real time, taking from "our" ocean and leaving its effluvia in return. The long-take resource image united the globe, making us all industrial citizens in general and members of hydrocarbon civilization more specifically. The Spillcam "caught" more than just BP in transgression; it caught the hydrocarbon world.

Mary Douglas forcefully pointed out in her seminal study of how culture constructs and categorizes things as waste that "where there is dirt there is a system."[67] Douglas denaturalizes waste and argues that effluvia are produced through cultural codes and social rituals. Dirt is necessary, she shows, because it makes visible that which is pure and ordered. A given society can recognize what is pure and what is, in her terms, a danger because of dirt; it makes the binary logic of Judeo-Christian culture possible. While the discourse of waste and image making will be taken up in the next chapter, it is necessary to anticipate certain questions and ask how it was that something that is in fact naturally occurring and so embedded in every conceivable dimension of our culture—from fertilizer to plastics to motor fuel—can come to disgust us when it gushes full throttle into the ocean. The Spillcam made a spectacle of watching waste, our waste, the terms of our own excessive needs; global citizens watched in disgust, and were quick to create a distance between ourselves and the debacle. When oil performs for us as it should—powering our vehicles, growing our crops—it is not a pollutant. It is the excess of the fuel that the Spillcam relentlessly monitored that struck fear and revulsion in our hearts and turned oil into a waste product, but one that would not flush away—the accursed share of hydrocarbon civilization.

And even with the days and weeks and hours of accumulated images fed to us from five thousand feet below, this disaster, like environmental erosion in general, is impossible to map—both in terms of time or space. There is no method to represent the spill accurately, for to do so would contain it, as BP claims to have done, thus limiting the legacy of pollution and erosion, environmental and economic, that the Gulf Coast faces. Perhaps the most productive way to capture or represent the terms of the Deepwater Horizon disaster is simply to open up the aperture of an ROV camera and let it run and run and run, monitoring its own operations twenty-four/seven and spoiling us with all its—and our—excess.

CHAPTER 5

WASTE

The free market economy of industrial and now post-industrial culture is enabled by the ability, if not the right, to dispose of our personal and collective undesirables and have them disappear—forever. As Gay Hawkins shows throughout *The Ethics of Waste*, the industrial human's relationship with refuse is steeped in social and political complexity. Environmental concern is only muddying relations further, inscribing waste disposal with an evolving set of self-regulating considerations that moralize such mundane habits as placing household garbage in the proper receptacle. Ridding our lives of dirt orients us as subjects, defines our social position, and—if we do it properly, at the proscribed time and via the proper channels—ties us to the state, which ultimately determines what is and is not dirt. Hawkins, like Michel Foucault and Dominique Laporte, describes a biopolitics between state power and the self-regulation of the human body. The garbage we generate and then manage draws decisive lines between our private and public lives and mediates the relationship we have to our physical bodies and through them, to others. Such social determinants become visible only when we step back and gaze upon the way we behave towards our refuse. Having our garbage exposed in public, for example, is a personal humiliation that often registers in feelings of violation and exposure.[1] Thus because our own waste must be secreted away, so must that of others; anything less disrupts the rules of social order. Hawkins is careful to differentiate between types of rubbish—human waste inspires a different set of psychosocial responses than a junked automobile. Yet material culture is inseparable from the fact that it generates waste of any kind—the excess that is transformed into useless garbage the moment it is thrown out. But while we fear confrontation with our refuse, and in any form, as Mary Douglas argues, managing our waste is not without satisfaction. There is pleasure in consuming, of course, but also in banishing its residual evidence.

"Eliminating [dirt] is not a negative movement," Douglas writes, "but a positive effort to organize the environment."[2] Indeed, one of the most enduring tenets of Veblen's economic theories similarly describes the pleasure of waste, for conspicuous waste is, like its companion conspicuous consumption, a way in which the so-called leisure class demonstrates its status, power, and attendant sense of democratic freedom. Susan Strasser similarly argues for the importance of waste disposal as spectacle of power; as Georges Bataille would recognize the ability to purge what is unwanted or give it away consolidates the rank of the consumer rather than diminishes it.[3]

While the theorization of waste has tended to focus on domestic and personal waste—human organics or the contents of a home's refuse bins—industrialized network culture is producing a new kind of waste—electronic rather than garden variety, the effluvia of what is termed new media technology. Any and every dumpsite exposes the fleeting nature of objects, the speed with which they are consumed, and also the "enduring materiality" of that which has been disposed of and, we assume, left to decay.[4] The challenge is to locate ourselves within the flow of the garbage side of industrial culture. As we saw in chapter 3, Edward Burtynsky's photographs make visible evidence of the volume and seriality of hydrocarbon civilization's excessive waste production. Such glimpses are vital reminders for negotiating what should be an evolving relationship with industrial trash, especially as it is shipped overseas to be recycled and takes on the dimensions of geopolitical economics, moving as it does in accordance with the flexibility of labor markets and lax environmental policy. While recycling is enforced by municipalities around the globe, recyclers passively assume that their compliance is benevolent. Trusting the business of garbage to state and private industry perpetuates the exploitation of laborers and biosphere alike. *Ghana: Digital Dumping Ground* (2009) is just one example of how deleterious—and vital—the recycling component of the electronics industry can be. Because obsolete electronics—cell phones, computer hardware, obsolete digital imaging devices—are sold off to developing and underdeveloped nations whose poor salvage the precious metals and sell it back to the technologies industry, the so-called First World consumer is prevented from reversing this regimented flow of waste. And how much flow is there? The average life expectancy is less than two years for a personal computer in North America, which resulted in Americans disposing of 315 million operable personal computers in 2004, an increase of 500 percent from the previous year. These machines were not recycled domestically, if at all, but shipped offshore where mercury leaches into groundwater and, if burned, becomes toxin that poisons the air. Apart from the ethical issues involved downloading technological waste, the practice itself cannot be sustained. Giles

Slade points out that if e-waste continues to proliferate, the world soon won't even be able to build enough containers to get it to the "have not" economies contracted to deal with cell phones, DVD players, and plasma televisions.[5]

Visual confrontation with trash has the tendency to give pause to our own consumption habits. As Jonathan Sterne reminds us, computer technology is not ethereal, but a junk pile waiting to happen. Jennifer Gabrys makes a similar conceptual move, launching a critique of post-industrial culture's mythology of immateriality by tethering the electronic transference of information to what she terms digital culture's "residual ecology," her way of describing the destructive physicality of ostensibly intangible and therefore innocuous digital realities.[6] The term proves particularly valuable when cinema, in its digital form, is brought into the fold, for the moving image's garbage evolves along with technology and so is immediately located in the solid composition of the film industry's surplus and detritus, those unwanted, unused, or unusable bits—from decayed celluloid to trashed DVDs. These solid wastes foreground moving images as consumable material goods and therefore denaturalizes the perception that cinema, especially in its digital form, is somehow immaterial and therefore does not manifest a tangible biophysical impact. But while theorists like Gabrys, Sterne, and Slade address the need to deal both practically and conceptually with the mountains of trash that accumulate as a byproduct of technological innovation, little is said of how the moving image is and has been thinking through its material life and residues since its inception. Not only is filmmaking an ephemeral art form, it is an art of repurposing—one which, outside of mainstream channels, quite often makes do with limited resources. The practical workings of a "composted" (as opposed to composited) cinema are redemptive and inherently instructive, for it forces hydrocarbon citizens to rethink habitual relationships with the biosphere, industrial culture, and its moving images.

The electronic waste that is shipped overseas to recycling communities has a counterpart in the dumping ground that is the Internet, in that its spaces testify to the paradoxes and contradictions between an urge to preserve and the desire to negate. Computer technology is marketed as much for its expansive storage capacities as for its processing speed, and it is memory which hastens a system's obsolescence as its ability to retain information seems diminished each time technology advances. The technology industry's obeisance to ramped up cycles of innovation and replacement has turned into a law named for Intel founder Gordon Moore's 1965 observation that computer processing power shall double every year (Moore's Law).[7] So it is that the very functions "erase" or "delete" seem fated to be rendered obsolete from the computer's range of features. As a result, both material and immaterial vestiges of digital culture—from last year's Apple to the scratched DVD to the information it contains—never really need to be thrown away, just relocated to zones of seeming dissipation.

Susan Sontag was consistently alarmed by how constant exposure to and consumption of photographic images inured viewers to their content and deadened ethical response to suffering and the human lives contained therein. She concluded her famous collection of essays on the subject of photography with the call for what she termed "an ecology of the image." Published in 1973, *On Photography* is strewn with a resonant environmental rhetoric. Though she challenges the feasibility of her own proposition some thirty years later in *Regarding the Pain of Others*, even though the situation has obviously magnified, what Sontag called for was the application of conservationist measures as a way to minimize the overconsumption and therefore abuse of image resources.[8] Intersecting Sontag's image ecology and Gabrys's residual ecology, the "residual ecology of the image" describes the materiality of images, the direct and indirect environmental impact of moving-image culture, as well as the practice of managing cinematic detritus through such means as archiving, recycling, and reproduction. A principal problem that residual image ecology identifies and challenges is the counterintuitive premise that objects are made according to the enduring principle of planned obsolescence but are at the same time composed of materials (plastics, glass, compressed metals) engineered to endure. This, the structuring contradiction at the heart of the globe's waste management crisis, provides an analytic for understanding and describing the aesthetic and ideological foundations that form and inform the images our waste-making culture produces. Part of correcting the perpetuation of disposability—from human lives to commodity objects—is exposing not only the social and ecological consequences of throwaway ideology but also challenging the fallaciousness of the rhetoric itself. What lies beneath such terms as post-consumer, single-use, throwaway, and recyclable is a set of cultural behaviors normalized by the deceptive idea that the post-industrial is also the immaterial.

Necessary Wrappings: Waste, Cultural Production, and Packaging

Using Michelangelo's description of transforming stone into sculpture, Zygmunt Bauman describes the intractable intersection between cultural production and the creation of waste. According to Michelangelo, it is the sculptor's job to cut superfluous matter away from the "blank" surface that is the slab of stone and thus, through a process of elimination and paring away, reveal the perfect form hidden within. This description is readily applicable

to most creative processes and, as an aesthetic theory, is particularly appo-
site in consideration of Lewis Mumford's contention that modern cultural
production is predominantly modeled after processes of extraction. Bauman's
instructive analogy is equally applicable to cinematic editing, and thus closely
aligns the practicalities of filmmaking with sculpting; both practices are
premised on elimination, paring away, cutting down, and then discarding the
unnecessary waste that envelops the piece of perfection hidden within. With
minor exceptions the very act of cinematic creation inherently implies the
sourcing of resources, and like the mining and extraction society, is wholly
dependent on the creation of detritus. As Bauman writes, "For something to
be created, something else must be consigned to waste."[9] But, "creative" waste
is characterized by an ambiguity in that depending on the context, it can be
both attractive and repulsive. Referencing Mary Douglas's theories of purity
taboos, Bauman explains that waste becomes such only through processes of
separation. Arbitrary social categorizations have the power to cast one object
as repulsive or useless, while another is prized for its aesthetic quality or use-
value. And once waste is separated out, it must be rendered invisible, often
re-enveloped by some other form.

Architecture critic Lisa Rochon points out that how we package our garbage
is one of the design industry's most pressing challenges.[10] The wrapper, then,
requires a new wrapper. Aesthetic practice that is based on making use of
waste similarly and necessarily creates waste, thus perpetuating the circuitry
of production, use, and eventual disposal. We consume more than just the
commodities contained within the foam shell, glass jar, or plastic sheath, but
also the very package itself. Heather Rogers notes that the systematic eradication of refillable drinking containers after World War II inaugurated the
standardization of what is now ubiquitous disposable packaging and radically
transformed the composition of American trash demographics. In the mid-
1970s, packaging accounted for more municipal solid waste than any other
in the United States and by 2006, single-use packages (especially cans and
bottles) composed one-third of American landfill space and have directly
contributed to the doubling of the country's amount of garbage in the past
thirty years.[11] But because it is not typically equated with being a commodity
item, packaging is denied its very essence, even though it is, like its contents,
also made of natural resources and labor. While Rogers argues that we all need
to radically rethink what constitutes a consumable commodity, the initiative
can go further so as to position cultural objects as resource-driven goods that
always come wrapped in some kind of container.

The nebulous entity known as Hollywood thrives on its packaging. Significant portions of a film's budget is reserved for marketing purposes; in 2003,

for example, the cost of producing a movie averaged at $63.8 million, while the standard release cost was $39 million. Notable too is that the release budget had risen 28 percent since the previous year, while production costs had increased by only 8.6 percent.[12] Those figures seem almost reasonable compared to *Avatar*'s global marketing budget of an estimated 500 million dollars, which exceeded its production costs of almost 250 million, the *New York Times* reported in November 2009. By funneling this amount of economic and creative energy into promotional phases (perfecting the wrapper for, perhaps, a less than perfect film), the film industry reverses the logic of Michelangelo's sculpting metaphor: the wrapping that is the ideal form, as the contents they conceal pale when compared to their anticipatory advertisements. Discourse around transnational cinema focuses in part on the changing patterns of theatrical releases as a contributing factor to the homogenization of global culture. As Hollywood studios discover new consumer markets around the globe, the intervals between North American and international release periods have shrunk, even disappeared. A chief motivation is offsetting piracy, but because international revenues continue to grow, there is little reason to stagger global distribution.[13] Additionally, the window between theatrical and DVD release has also radically minimized to the point they often overlap. Robert Davis notes that advertisement for theatrical showings often includes promotion for the DVD, and Charles Acland points out that the theatrical appearance of a big-budget film is only the beginning of a chain of mutations. As the film good moves through formatting stages, from the box to the CD, DVD, book, video game, television broadcast, or Netflix download, each platform represents the chance to wring even more revenue and recoup costs of both production and advertising.[14]

Home theater technology, digitization, and the marketing of released "classics" has reconstructed the cinephile as archivist, consumer, and technophile.[15] Such preoccupation with collecting cinema (tangible or otherwise) is inextricably connected with technological innovation, and directly correlates the purchase of in-home theater equipment with the construction of private film libraries. Unlike other collectables—books or plastic arts—the film collection involves two steps of consumption: the purchase of personal copies of the film itself (including electronic files) as well as investment in the viewing platform. And of course with technological innovation, the film library is subject to consistent modification and updating in terms of keeping formats and interfaces in check. Writing in 1991, Timothy Corrigan describes the effect of the VCR's penetration of the domestic sphere as a cataclysmic redefinition of the relationship between movie and audiences. Not only was the viewer empowered with extra purchasing power, but once the movie good was brought into the home, it became malleable; what was inalienable could be stopped and started, erased, and overdubbed. The VCR likewise made film goods more widely distributed, thus eradicating cultural differences, and rendering cinema heterogeneous, fluid. Corrigan's study adapted Malraux's concept of a "museum without walls," positing that when anyone can own a film, or other cultural object, no one can; authorial rights disappear, and the image-object belongs to everyone, always.[16] But whereas Corrigan saw the VCR as a technology of openness and an agent of dissolution between viewers and practitioners as well as between nations, Klinger reads home-viewing technology as a force that erects walls and reinforces separation between public and private. And though her focus is specifically on a social politics of repetitive viewing in the home, her insights can and should be taken a step further, thus broadening the scope of what is a recycled, "secondhand" cinema to include the environmental politics that are inextricably linked to home-viewing practices. While Klinger points out that unprecedented accessibility and ownership of cinema has been facilitated by digital technology, the relationship between the viewer and his or her repetitive viewing habits must also take into account viewing technologies, including the economics of obsolescence and its attendant production of waste. The empire of home cinema—from VCR to DVD player and, more lately, laptop or other playing device—are supported by a practice of "secondary wrapping," wherein the reissued, rereleased, remastered, recut film is concealed in a fresh container and transformed from used good to a primary commodity. By intersecting the movie good's packaging or wrapper, the guaranteed obsolescence of the machinery that plays and replays it, and the limited shelf-life of expendable film "entertainment," the production of cinematic waste becomes increasingly discernable.

In the same way that digitization atomizes the image, making it possible to create numerous reproductions without compromising the quality of the original, so too does the accompanying technology become commodified and similarly diffused throughout those populations who can afford to purchase it. Walter Benjamin's contention was that technologies of reproduction erode a cultural object's uniqueness, and thus its essential ontological value; it also situates widespread ownership as the force that shifted the religious to the secular and, by extension, public culture to private consumption. Benjamin anticipated a culture of waste, precisely because the cultural object is inseparable from its support surface. On a practical, economic level, the real consequence of reproduction is over-reproduction, the work of art in the age of the digital dumping ground. Consider then how the standardization of single-use packaging refined systems of commodity distribution and, ultimately, enabled commodity markets to reach into the home, shaping the daily habits of the individual consumer. The introduction of the refillable bottle and then the take-home six-pack, for example, replaced the conventional (communal) keg and the local tavern with the more convenient option of imbibing privately.[17] Also, because of the linear flow of the beer bottle that mass distribution made possible, the final leg of the journey was transferred to the consumer who absorbed the responsibility of bringing beer into the household. The idea is that the shift from public to private that is at the heart of democratization and consumerism depends on multiplicity and reproduction; private ownership produces accumulation, therefore, and not only of material objects but also their seemingly immaterial equivalents, the images and information that digital devices generate, display, and ultimately render consumable objects. Like the premise of the six-pack, the task of accessing moving images is literally being downloaded onto the consumer. On-demand video streaming provided by companies like Netflix further privatizes cinema, while also creating a sense that movie goods purchased are somehow seamless, weightless, perhaps inconsequential. But the incredible choice that Netflix offers (17,000 "watch instantly" features at the time of writing) is only half the equation, for users must of course invest in necessary hardware and software support as well as energy power and broadband costs. The introduction of high definition television enables the consumer to stream content directly into their digital units, provided it is a Netflix-approved brand (certain sets still require desktop or gaming console to interface). But downloading content into the home will not completely displace theatrical distribution; rather, it represents only a further layer of potential revenue for studios to exploit. When it comes to blockbusters in particular, the limitations of theaters with finite seating and the fixed number of DVD copies available in stores is sorely felt, for both can and do sell out and thus potential consumers turn away, perhaps opting for other fare. But digital distribution ensures that there is no physical object to get to market; digital exhibition in theaters and video on demand eradicates these limitations and represents huge cost savings for studios.[18] As long as theaters and consumers possess the right tools, big movies can be released simultaneously—reaching everywhere and everyone and through all exploitable channels.

But, again, the consumer at home is downloading more than the movie; he or she is also absorbing the overhead costs associated with domesticated theater. Every home thus equipped parallels the vehicle(s) parked out front in each homeowner's driveway. The private consumption of the image, like individualized modes of transportation, signals unsustainable patterns of single-use and single-user consumer society, a condition specifically targeted by the UN Intergovernmental Panel on Climate Change (IPCC) in its 2007 Assessment Report. The private/public duplicity captures the dialectical tension, and even contradiction, at the heart of a post-industrial culture of access: at once so relentlessly private and so unequivocally public, digitization moves cinema in two simultaneous directions; movies are undoubtedly becoming more open and available, largely for the private consumer. And what is being offered up is not new. While movies are beginning to premier on Netflix, the typical fare is not dissimilar from storefront video chains. Granted, Netflix is being championed as a distributor of independent films—when all other possibility for exhibition and distribution have failed, filmmakers are invited to submit their productions to Netflix—but many features have already been screened or broadcast. Will Straw notes that remediation frames the Internet as being less about what is new than reinvigorating the past with fresh consumer appeal and, thus, commercial value.[19] So, while Netflix was hailed as a force destined to reconfigure how films and television are watched, the content remains the same, as is the logistics of how those films and TV shows are actually made. Recycled, resold, watched again; but the packaging is new, and this time it is called Netflix.

Secondhand Cinema

As Sontag's famous essays on photography emphasize, once selected and aestheticized by the privileging attention of the camera's transformative eye, squalor, deformity, or bits of trash are given value and recast as objects of art or cultural artifacts. Subjects within images (cinematic and photographic) are themselves converted, but so too is the material, physical reality of the image's support surface; it all depends on whether or not the celluloid is original or secondhand—that is, found elsewhere, rescued through reuse and thus rehabilitated. But as Bauman's sculpting metaphor makes relentlessly clear, extraction-based cultural production is always about the materiality of its resource—whether marble or celluloid—and through that resource's refinement, the generation of waste. All cinema, all photo-mechanical image making, is therefore inextricably connected to the process of making waste; the difference is that not all cinema makes active use of detritus.

Agnès Varda's DV documentary *The Gleaners and I* (2000) is an oft-cited essayistic investigation into the politics of consumerism, resource availability, poverty, and scarcity. Varda conflates the investigation of the film's subject with the life of the filmmaker, producing a decidedly subjective discourse that merges the specificity of digital video with her sense of self. Varda's digital medium is defined in part by practical and conceptual dimensions of recycling, and renders hers a specifically "secondhand" enterprise. Structured around the practice of *la glanage* or "gleaning," Varda's film outlines the term's trajectory from pre-industrial rural economies to contemporary post-industrial urban ones. Originating simply as the way farm workers trawled the fields and gathered for themselves what was left after harvest (and thus managing agricultural surplus), gleaning's current manifestation assumes the castigated form of scavenging or, in specifically urban environs, garbage picking. Foraging meals out of the trash, harvesting fallen fruit and vegetables from farmers' fields, or making art out of garbage-picked objects, Varda's subjects—whom the filmmaker effectively separates out and thus scavenges from the wider population—are committed recyclers, marginalized by the social expectations of consumer culture. Transformed by Varda's camera and the insight of her narration, the gleaners of the film function as analogs for Varda herself; indeed, the process of employing images "gleaned" or harvested from the universe at large, scavenged and infused with new meaning once taken home, cleaned up, and edited, together confirms this equation. As the term is unpacked etymologically and socially, gleaning is extended as a metaphor for the mechanics and dynamics of filmmaking and a way to understand how contemporary consumer culture is organized around the accumulation of randomly acquired tokens, souvenirs, and possessions. Outfitted with what is for her brand-new DV technology, Varda reinstates gleaning as a necessary social, economic, and cultural intervention. Theorizing the relationship between cinema and recycling, for Varda "gleaning" describes a specifically digital aesthetic. Varda fits into the subgenre of independent, subjective, autobiographical, and decidedly first-person DV documentary, of which there is an ever-increasing abundance. The specificity of such practice, Varda argues, positions the self-sufficient cinematic document as a composite of ideas and images gathered from the practitioner's immediate universe (real-world, cyberspace, media landscapes) which are then reorganized, restructured, and reformulated into discrete, subjective visions such as Varda's. The digital first-person mode is a limited cinema, extracted from what is within reach, accessible, necessarily close at hand.

Varda's film implicitly theorizes the essentially "impure" or secondhand nature of image-based art. Mikhail Bakhtin's theory of "heteroglossia" and "the dialogic" is a useful approximation of Varda's aesthetic articulation of post-industrial cultural production. In "The Problems of Speech Genres," Bakhtin articulated how language—spoken, written, imagined in our minds—is "already-used," "second hand," and essentially "hybrid."[20] What is, in specifically Bakhtinian terms, "double-voicedness" results from speech diversity, a principle of sociolinguistics in which other words and speech patterns are "gleaned" from the voices and genres circulating in the world at large and appropriated by the speaker. The voice, according to Bakhtin's conception of heteroglossia, carries with it other voices, rendering language dialogic, alive with a multiplicity of speakers. Language is never original; by extension, expressive communication, linguistic (or visual) is always layered with residues and resonances, the leftovers of all its previous users and uses. "Our speech," Bakhtin wrote, "is filled with others' words . . . which carry with them their own expressions, their own evaluative tone, which we assimilate, rework, and re-accentuate."[21] Bakhtin argues that dialogism undermines the authority of an individual's speech, subordinating it to the din of other voices, the fabric from which it is composed, making it impossible to speak purely, "monologically," in one's own voice. The metaphorical value that infuses Varda's discourse on gleaning achieves a similarly subversive vision of how the individual and the filmic product are manufactured in direct relation to the culture from which they spring. Varda effectively upends the privileged naiveté of consumerism, exposing the junk heaps, garbage dumps, and disenfranchised citizens that maintain the conditions necessary for a society and economy to be structured around the ability to throw away and continually renew itself without apparent or visible consequences. Just as it is impossible to imagine a pure articulation, so, Varda argues, the post-consumer is seeping into our sensibilities, aesthetics, and selves. The garbage bin is not the end of the discarded item; the dump, rather, is an accumulation of resources and potential for reuse. What, after all, is cyberspace if not a dumping ground? Just as Bakhtin was invested in analogizing the impossibility of speaking with a single voice and the contradictions of totalitarian monotheism, so Varda uses gleaning-as-metaphor to approximate a similar discourse on the fallacy of the pure image, the pure subjectivity, and on the impossibility to conceptualize the object without also accounting for the provenance of its origins and the trajectory of its demise. In other words, Varda's is a cinema of leftovers and remains; the concept of disposability thus banished, what is placed in its stead is a residual ecology of the image.

As Varda explains to her camera/viewer, the guiding formal principle of her determinedly digital project is "to use one hand to film the other." Thus describing what is here conceptualized as a "secondhand cinema," the term compresses multiple possibilities by which to understand and critically assess digital cinema's technological and ideological core. To begin, separate from but also attached to "gleaning," Varda's intended meaning of "filming one hand with the other" articulates one of the structuring conceits that informs much of her essayistic exploration of what is, for her, a new technology. A woman then in her seventies, Varda finds that the digital camera liberates her physically. The apparatus is lightweight and possesses an extensive depth of field, eliminating the need for tripods, lenses, and crew; Varda enjoys increased mobility, therefore, and independence. Her free hand often standing in for her total physicality, she frequently trains the camera on herself by means of capturing this "second" hand as it picks or gleans its way through her surroundings. But when she sees her hand (and so her own self) cast on her camera's playback screen, what she encounters is unfamiliar—she is aging, her skin wrinkling, musculature weakening; she feels caged by the inevitabilities of time. Secondhand cinema not only describes a cinema that makes use of existing materials, but it is also understood as a practical, medium-specific version of "first-person" cinema. The term, in other words, articulates how digital autobiographical filmmaking leaves one hand free, and so is premised upon the self-sufficiency, mobility, and multiple occupations that lightweight equipment allows. A further dimension of the secondhand conceits that guide Varda's film is the subtle equation she makes between her own self and the discards that are gleaned by the subjects of her film. Aging, expiring, she is becoming alienated from the vessel or container of her identity; thus she is not only a gleaner, but also equated with that which is gleaned. The discourse on her aging body is articulated by approximating her ostensible limitations with the expired or surplus objects that litter the terrain of her documentary. Varda subtly situates herself and the category of elderly alongside the inanimate objects that are portrayed in the film. She is, in other words, expired; a cast-off, overlooked, marginalized, or otherwise left behind.

Secondhand cinema, understood here, is distinct from the tradition of found footage filmmaking on the one hand or compilation filmmaking on the other (divergent practices in their own right).[22] Further, there is a critical difference between a cinema that represents waste and one that is explicitly rendered from the husks that have been pared away in order to reveal the tailored, structured form that is a finished film. The term secondhand cinema is used here to theorize filmmaking practice that is based on random encounter, localism, interactivity between that which is proximate and the practitioner, and so exceeds being simply a filmic representation of waste or embodying a collage or compilation aesthetic. For Varda, making a film, a documentary specifically, is an approximation of gleaning because it literally uses only what is available, that which she finds in her immediate world and, through editing, transforms into an essay, an investigation, a narrative of self and others and the society that binds them. And what is available is what the filmmaker and her camera and their rather restricted means of financing, transport, and cinematic resources can access. Thus, as Varda's free hand, the punning "second" hand that does not hold the camera, literally (manually) encounters disposed-of objects, it becomes emblematic of her film's digital brand of autobiography and her aging, expendable self. Additionally, this free hand also takes on the dimension of limited accessibility, making use of that which is within reach of the filmmaker's hand. The secondhand, Varda's film suggests, is a cinema of limited resources, assembled out of what is close by, and includes not just what is in front of the camera, but how the two came together—the energy (generated by a human or a machine). An approximation of what Gilles Deleuze and Felix Guattari describe as the nomadic war machine, and as will be discussed in this book's concluding chapter, the secondhand is typically characterized by independent, self-sufficient cinematic practitioners whose energy sources and dissemination practices are as fluid and malleable as the images they gather.[23] The secondhand might be an anticipation of and model for a carbon-neutral cinema. Using available, natural light, the camera operator's own energy and ambulatory mobility, a sustainable film practice takes for its pro-filmic environment that which is within the vicinity of the free or liberated hand. The secondhand, then, is about proximity, focusing not only on the self as a subject but on the practitioner's immediate, available realm. This is, by extension, a local cinema and potentially low-energy; whether out of necessity or political conviction, a secondhand cinema is paradigmatically sustainable, and intentionally or otherwise scales back its own anthropogenic pollutants and consequent environmental erosion. Again, Varda's documentary is particularly prescient, for it anticipates on numerous levels how cultural production must acknowledge resource limitation as a way to both represent, render as a practice, and also engage with (and/or critique) dominant forms of eco-consciousness (in the media or marketplace, for example), and do so aesthetically and practically.

Specifically informed by strictures of limitation, Kristan Horton's photographic approximations of film stills taken from Stanley Kubrick's 1964 *Dr. Strangelove* are also exemplary of a secondhand cinema. Horton's project takes a still from each of the scenes that compose Kubrick's film, remodels it using detritus the artist scrounged within the confines of his own studio, and then reproduces the original with his own analog photographic camera. Horton's secondhand practice operates, like Varda's, by reaching out and grasping for those objects within his immediate realm, reconfiguring his personal surroundings into the model landscapes that so uncannily suggest the stills selected from Kubrick's film. Horton's is a secondhand cinema; in material terms, the objects it uses are composed of detritus, garbage, broken throwaways and random bits gleaned from the artist's own environment. It is also secondhand in terms of its practice, for it relies on a principle of "arm's reach" by which to construct each photograph's environment. Also, by photographing each still Horton reproduces the original text, transforming *Dr. Strangelove* into a recycled, post-consumer, secondhand version, and vision, of cinema. The project's implications, specifically regarding cinematic practice—digital and photo-mechanical—abound. Evoking a narrative of an "enforced" creative economy, one that is based on scarcity rather than excess, Horton constructs an enduring discourse on the image's materiality, as well as the possibilities inherent in conditions of limitation and rationing. Though composed of photographs, "*Dr. Strangelove, Dr. Strangelove*" is nothing if not cinematic. Because it is static, this cinema is, of course, carbon-neutral. And it is primitive, reducing as it does the camera's mobility to the point that it becomes physically fixed, positing that the film itself is unable rather than unwilling to move. The extremity to which Horton restricts his project's resources renders each photograph an uncanny vision of a proto-cinematic sensibility. Dialoguing with Kubrick's Cold War satire, Horton positions his project as an epilogue, and responds to the source film's cynical vision of nuclear catastrophe by suggesting that the images themselves are artifacts from a post-apocalyptic and post-Kubrick future. Horton's is a message from that same mine shaft where the film's eponymous mad scientist proposes select members of humanity might survive nuclear fallout. Thus, conceivably, scarcity of resources and equipment has limited the means of cinema but not the cinematic imagination. "*Dr. Strangelove, Dr. Strangelove*" is thus a science-fictional dystopia that casts Kubrick's film as the residue of a cultural practice that is no longer materially possible. Here is a carbon-free cinema rather than just carbon-neutral one; here is the post-cinema, beyond digitality, forced back to its earliest, most rudimentary photo-mechanical practice. It also renders Kubrick silent and soundless, thus further reducing the image down to its essence and taking carbon-neutral filmmaking to a radical place. Eliminating plastic water bottles from a film set is one way to green a production—as Green Screen continually endorses—but so is making it static and silent.[24] Horton's mocked-up approximations are equally haunted and frustrated by the memories and mythologies of the cinematic imagination, preserved in the original film stills that are situated alongside his own photographs. The essential implication of reading Horton's work as both a secondhand cinema and a glimpse of a lost civilization sheltered in Strangelove's mine-shaft—the infrastructure of an extraction-based culture—is how the relationship between cinema and resources is foregrounded. Radically deprived of material means, motion itself is the most glaring omission from Kubrick's source text, the "cine" that made *Dr. Strangelove* a narrative told in the real time of energy rather than the entropy of the static shot. But when experienced in a gallery space, the viewer follows the *Dr. Strangelove* narrative along by foot, still by still, circling the room, and thus he or she reinserts the motion that Horton has taken away.

While Horton's project telescopes the history of the mechanically repro-duced image, Varda's film documents the transformation from pre-industrial to post-industrial gleaning. Before industrialization, her film suggests, gleaning was, like the dominant mode of production and economy, agrarian; as such, the surpluses that field workers foraged from a harvest's leftovers were natural (organic) and thus unquestionably fit for consumption. As Susan Strasser points out, the shift from agrarian to industrial economies, and from rural to urban geographies, also transformed the surplus objects that were available to be gleaned. Instead of agrarian society's residual fruit and vegetables, industrializing urban centers exuded their detritus in the form of scraps of mechanically manufactured materials. Varda's rural gleaners were thus redefined as rag pickers. But at this early stage of urbanization, there was still no such thing as garbage or compost. These categories, Strasser argues, were produced by the transition to full-scale mass production and the conver-sion to a one-way, open flow, linear ecology. The shift to consumer culture was accompanied by the erosion of recycling behaviors that introduced a radical change in the perception of the material object. "For the first time in human history," Strasser writes, the disposal of detritus "became separated from production, consumption and reuse."[25] Mass production thus super-seded systems of "transference," wherein an object was transformed by the stages of its use as it traveled from manufacturer to primary consumer to picker, then was sold back to industry where its materials were recycled and reabsorbed into the system. As philosophies of obsolescence and disposability were introduced and then naturalized, the salvaged shard and broken bit lost their economic worth and so the rag picker was recast as the harvester of garbage, essentially disenfranchised from the industrial economy whose surpluses were deemed valueless and unworthy of recovery.

And there is now, of course, a local and geopolitical economy of recycling; receiving money for a found item such as a glass bottle reveals how the ecolog-ical is entwined with cultural and economic dimensions.[26] Attaching value to a discard—arbitrarily or randomly so—transforms it from waste into a found object; the Dumpster-diver assumes the role of the recycler or the gleaner. Situ-ating Horton's work next to Varda's *Gleaners* articulates a similar shift. Taken together these films map the secret life of detritus and suggest not only the essential instability of the category of garbage, but also how cultural produc-tion bears responsibility for manufacturing and then naturalizing what are the arbitrary distinctions between useful and useless. The secondhand cinema is therefore a way to articulate the transformative dimension of the image, as well as, potentially, a waste management system in and of itself, wherein the cinematic environment critiques and contributes to the sustainable possibilities implicit in making images ecologically by making them with less. There is of course a huge body of low or no budget filmmaking from which a growing number of formal initiatives such as the Planet in Focus International Film Festival in Toronto might draw to exemplify the possibility of making film (and a festival) sustainably. A secondhand cinema and a secondhand festival, then, would glimpse how film production and—very importantly—audience expectations might modify, willingly or otherwise, to meet the demands of ecological sustainability on a broad, socially expansive level.

Overexposure: Devaluing the Image

A cinema of limitation is a cinema of randomness and chance. While Varda happens upon gleaners and images of gleaning in what she maintains are fortuitous moments, Horton's senses are likewise finely attuned to finding *Dr. Strangelove* in his environment and by extension, his environment in *Dr. Strangelove*. Horton has described how the source film was randomly acquired when a friend passed the artist a VHS version, which would become the only viewing material he had in his studio, and in two and a half years Horton viewed the film over seven hundred times. The film completely saturated his perceptions, such that Horton attests that he could no longer distinguish the film from his universe and as his two worlds collided, the artist saw his everyday world in the film and the film in his daily world. Again, Horton's behavior bespeaks a primitivism and an imposed aesthetic of limitation and rationing not unlike the conditions imposed upon the Russian avant-garde. Viewing D. W. Griffith's *Intolerance* with repeated zeal, for example, led to the film being recut and its parts reordered, and forced Eisenstein and others to find potential in deprivation. Their education and formal training did not entail abundant exposure to a range of films, but rationed overexposure to a lone example. Exposing himself to a single film with relentless dedication and self-enforced deprivation, Horton's steady diet of *Dr. Strangelove* complicates the relations between viewer and viewed, questioning which one is truly overexposed: the film to the viewer or the viewer to the film.

Horton's title cleverly suggests that the defining technological feature of cinema is, of course, the capacity for repetition. Since the ascendency of digital video in the late 1990s, much continues to be said about the ontological difference between analog and digital images and specifically how the digital image's lack of indexicality alters the viewer's relationship to the pictured universe. While the analog imaging process is physical, inscriptive—light imprinted upon a support surface—the digital paradigm converts light into something without substance, binary coded data. David Binkley has written (and many have since reiterated) that while analog media retains what he calls "cultural information" in the physical "disposition of concrete objects," digital media retain it as "formal relationships in abstract structures."[27] This conversion principle is what makes digital so desirable a medium, because the world-as-information can be rewritten in exact replica without degeneration; celluloid or paper negatives, by contrast, experience some loss of quality each time they are copied. Digital files have nothing to lose, however—because they are nothing. Or are they? Is the structure really so abstract, as Binkley writes? What of the massively intricate, energy and resource dense interfaces required to access those immaterial infrastructure of the digital sprawl? Google Energy's 200-million-dollar investment in an offshore wind farm (Atlantic Wind Connection) in October of 2010 speaks to offsetting some of its massive carbon footprint rather than mere investment diversification. The ability to replicate information finds parallel in the culture of innovation that dominates technologies industries and forces consumers to upgrade computers (or other electronic devices) rather be saddled with illiterate software or incompatible hardware. Theorizing the perfect replication of the digital image must also involve consideration of the engineering and economic drives that produce ever-higher resolutions. Given that the equipment that facilitates digital culture (and its cinema) is on the verge of becoming hazardous waste material (otherwise known as obsolete) the moment it is released into the marketplace, the line of inquiry applied to digital and analog imaging technology needs to transcend ontology and indexicality and ask how the serial replacement of computing machinery alters the viewer's relationship to the world from whence images and information derives.

Jonathan Sterne points out that technologies industries operate according to a "halfway" principle, wherein computer scientists and software engineers are trained to regard designs as works in progress; the next model or version will solve the shortcomings of what came before.[28] But what if computer equipment and other electronics were well designed, and built to last? Or what if consumers used their machines—and cultural texts—however imperfect to their maximum capacity? Horton's project does just that, celebrating seeming inadequacies—the VCR and the analog video—as well as reveling in that which is lost when the moving image degrades. Seven hundred viewings of a single analog cassette lends the *Dr. Strangelove* photographs a grayscale that is murky at best and a lived-in aesthetic that testifies to repeated encounters between viewer and image, magnetic tape and video cassette recorder. Like the Model T Ford, the film camera and the film projector were perfect technologies, build to last and to endure over a lifetime. Celluloid film, however, was not intended to last. Rather, photo-mechanic support surfaces typically came with a shelf life and the film industry treated its product accordingly—expendable, transient, and ultimately disposable. Filmstrips were ephemeral objects shown repeatedly to numerous audiences until their commercial value was fully exploited, by which time the carrier surface was so deteriorated they were thrown out.[29] Celluloid's alteration by environmental exposure—oxygen for developed stock, light for raw celluloid as well as the stress of repeated projection—finds a discursive parallel in the transformation of actual content, each time a film is viewed—no matter its format. Writing at a moment in the mid-1970s when concerns over both ecological erosion and global energy security were particularly heightened, Susan Sontag argued that the photographic images we consume so recklessly, like any other plentiful and inexpensive consumer good, are not just reflections of the world, they *are* the world. "Images," she wrote, "are more real than anyone could have supposed. And just because they are an unlimited resource, one that cannot be exhausted by consumerist waste, there is all the more reason to apply the conservationist remedy."[30] Rationing our exposure to images, Sontag suggests, would uphold their inherent integrity and their indexical content so that they are still possessed of the power to affect. Maintaining an ethical relationship to the world, what with all its Others and its strangers, depends upon such an image ecology. That the life span of images is limited, their support surface fragile, bears the metaphoric suggestion that overexposure is toxic not just to the image's physical integrity but also to the viewer's psychosocial constitution. Kristan Horton's dedication to *Dr. Strangelove* both observes Sontag's rationing—for he does limit himself to one text—but also upends her calls for restraint. The artist thus parodies not only the parodic film itself, but reception studies, cultural studies, and other disciplines invested in critiquing the media's oversaturation of contemporary sensory landscapes. Horton's strict *Dr. Strangelove* regimen clearly articulates how the artist's overexposure absorbed the film's hyperbolic spirit, articulated here in its own ironic twist of an ironic text as an aesthetic of hyperactive minimalism. It is thus through his cinematic primitivism that Horton manages a critique of repetitive viewing, as well as of contemporary culture's digital domination. That is, instead of using contemporary, available, conventional means to download, burn, or otherwise reproduce a copy of Kubrick's film, Horton's method of reproduction is entirely, literally manual. Casting himself as a cinematic scrivener in a pre-Gutenberg galaxy, the artist foregrounds how cinephilic enthusiasm for a particular film is typically articulated not only by multiple viewings but also through reproduction and therefore individual possession.

Picking up Sontag's lead, Paolo Cherchi Usai describes a glutted image environment, but directly relates the cause to digital technology and the capacity to reproduce image texts exclusive of restraint or seeming consequence. Without making explicit his qualitative assessments of contemporary mainstream cinema, the archivist maintains that overproduction floods the movie marketplace and makes it impossible to separate out what is worthwhile. While Sontag equates photographing with a insatiable desire to consume and burn up the visible world, Cherchi Usai argues that the urge to preserve is equally consumptive as well as unsustainable, in that only a finite amount of films can actually be adequately archived— and that is only the celluloid-based moving image. The destruction of image carriers was once both as unavoidable as it was advantageous; a physically ruined or commercially tired filmstrip was simply replaced with something fresh and newly profitable. Digital images, however, are both disposable (in terms of their cost-effectiveness and overabundance) as well as durable (infinitely reproducible). The tension between these two attributes, that the disposable is durable, also defines the general terms of a global e-waste crisis. There is acute political danger in the ability to collect, archive, and store so many images, for quantity makes content less accessible, less desirable, and therefore less than visible.

The Disposable Documentary

In September 2010, China threatened Japan with suspending exports of "rare earth elements" after dispute over the arrest of the captain of a Chinese fishing trawler. Though readily available throughout the world, China controls 93 percent of the production of rare earth elements. These trace components have a host of uses, but are essential to the manufacture of everything from superconductors and guided missiles to iPods and hybrid car engines. Because Japan's high-tech industry is the world's largest consumer of rare earth elements, China's move threatened the very integrity of the Japanese economy, as well as that of any other industrial nation that imports Japanese technologies. But never mind sovereign economies; the availability of rare earth elements transcends borders and directly impacts the borderless universe of digital culture as we know it. While China's threat generated a flurry of media interest around these heretofore obscure entities, what could not have been more clear was just how "earthly," rather than ethereal, is technology. Gabrys exposes the myth of purity attached to digital devices when she describes how processing components such as the microchip creates any amount of chemical compounds that are released into the environment as pollutants. Digital data is underwritten not only by the physicality of its hardware; the images digital cameras capture and store are by association equally solid and corporeal—ontologically, economically, and environmentally. As Sontag so succinctly described the consistent and dangerous tendency to express political choice with the availability of technology, "the freedom to consume a plurality of images and goods is equated with freedom itself."[31] Goods as images, images as goods; of course what is really being consumed is the technology itself, whether a smart phone or a tablet device, especially when aggressively marketed as cutting at the edge or necessary to fully participate in a knowledge-based economy.

As was the case of analog video in the 1960s and 1970s, the lower price point of digital technology ushers in not only greater access to and private ownership of cinema, but also more independent production. Perhaps more than any other pre-established mode, the documentary has come to define, and be defined by in turn, the terms and conditions of digital culture. As Varda's film exemplifies, part of the appeal of the digital camera is its weight. Liberated from tripod and multiple lenses, the operator is self-sufficient, while the infrastructure necessary to store, manipulate, and disseminate the resultant cinematic images is contained within the space of a personal computer that is often as mobile as the camera itself. The process of crafting narrative cohesion from the accumulation of gleaned images is relatively manageable; that digital is particularly forgiving of errors contributes to the diminishing difference between amateur and professional filmmaker. Regarding the photograph, Sontag points out how the introduction of the camera into the mass market was accompanied by the promise that even the most unassuming user was capable of achieving a perfect image. Kodak's famous slogan—"You press the button, we do the rest"—finds its contemporary equivalent in the digital camera; the capacity to erase and thus repair an image defines the digital as a truly accommodating medium, only now the "we" that does "the rest" is nothing less than camera technology itself. The result of all this easy sophistication is a burgeoning population of film practitioners, giving voice to otherwise marginal groups and spheres of interest such as Zacharias Kunuk and Indigenous video makers, as Faye Ginsburg's work consistently points out. However, it also expands cinema to a point of excess, wherein the glut of cached and recirculated images is matched by the overproduction of image makers.

But though her mini-DV is a brand-new tool, Varda is a professional, if not an auteur. The digital video camera she uses lends itself to drawing attention to and redeeming the bodies and populations that biopolitical discourse would otherwise situate as "disposable" or "invisible." The digital documentary form, of which Varda's is one, is not only centered on the first-hand exploration of self, but is also characterized as a tool of protest which targets political conspiracy, scandal, inequality, and otherwise picks up the slack of conventional mainstream news media and makes visible its various oversights. Megan Boler points out how new media technologies and Internet forums in particular are shifting categories of author and audience such that those who consume web content are often the same as those who actively produce it. What Boler terms "digital dissent" describes the informally organized practice of harnessing standard communications platforms so as to leverage tactical responses to both dominant news outlets and the political hegemonies they speak for. While tacticians preserve some skepticism about the viability of such open-access channels to speak the "truth," user-generated websites continue to play a vital role promoting awareness of social justice, engaging in political discourse, and perhaps even exposing government misconduct.[32] "Wiki Leaks" is one such example, as was the use of digital video and camera phones to bring global attention to protests in Iran in 2009 and in Burma in 2007. Anders Ostergaard's 2009 documentary *Burma VJ* is a striking account of how digital images captured on camera phones of the 2007 protests were smuggled out of the country, shared with news media, and exposed the military's egregious anti-democratic platforms. Ostergaard's film exemplifies key questions about authorship and the appropriation of digital voices, as well as the invisibility and ubiquity of digital technology. Though Ronald Deibert warns that it is temping to read liberation in technologies such as camera phones, the marketing of a so-called culture of access veils the widespread use of that same technology to suppress democracy. As they reach out to penetrate new markets in places like the United Arab Emirates, for example, companies such as Research in Motion have capitulated to rather than resisted pressures of international governments to comply with encryption policies, reminding us that not only do network citizens take media ecosystems for granted, but that the technology industry is motivated by profit margins rather than promoting the freedom to communicate.[33]

While digital images and information are assumed to be available in ready, unregulated supply, so too does physical movement appear unburdened by the lightness of digital imaging equipment, for the HD camera un-tethers the camera operator, rendering him or her ever more ambulatory than what analog video managed. But the practitioner's freedom comes at someone else's deprivation of the same. Sontag has argued that once the photographic camera was liberated from the tripod and mass-produced into affordability, it was increasingly trained on the abject and the impoverished.[34] The camera became the voyeuristic tool of a bourgeois flâneur who turned his or her sights to discovering urban environments in all their polarities and extremes. The digital documentarian is the contemporary equivalent of Sontag's early modernist photographer-voyeur, self-appointed agent of ethnographic exposition and subsequent social change. The shift from industrial to post-industrial culture, and likewise from photo-mechanic, still-life images to digital moving pictures, extends the documentary maker's trawling grounds from the local to the global, from the concrete reality of the material world to the electronic geographies of cyberspace. The relative proximity of the privileged classes to squalor and suffering were the result of, among other conditions, industrial society's urbanization, which produced encounters between disparate social strata. The camera-toting middle class took pictures of what they saw, reifying in tangible document a reality that was otherwise concealed.[35] The key is access: the assumed openness of urban, global, and cyber environs combines with the commodification of digital imaging technology, as well as with the operator's mobility and the camera's versatility, to lend the digital practitioner what is assumed to be an unobstructed view of the Other and their hitherto hidden realities.

Unlike the photochemical images Sontag so eloquently discussed, the digital image is inherently cheap, and characterized by its various layers of expendability—instantly erased and replaced, shifted into the crypt of a memory card where it might forever remain without being seen. The expendability of the digital image is only a potential condition, however, not an inevitable fate. An essential dimension of discourse around disposability is how the same terms that are applied to the treatment of images or other consumer goods are particularly well suited for capturing the "expendable" human subjects and wasted lives which constitute invisible populations around the globe. Michel Foucault argued that modernity marked the paradigmatic shift from the classical model of biopower, wherein sovereigns exercised the divine right to "take a life or let live," to modern biopolitics, which flexes its power more productively by "'making' live and 'letting' die."[36] Biopolitics is therefore enabling; modern discourses of medicine, communications technology, and education are actively monitoring and controling human populations, but only so they can, if and when necessary, die. Death, though, is never caused; it is merely "allowed"—represented in the causalities of military conflict and industrial accidents, for example, or medical experimentation conducted in poor communities and developing nations. Bauman insists, more directly, that "human waste"—the excessive and superfluous populations that overcrowd the planet—is a direct result of consumer culture's principles of obsolescence and industrial capital.[37] But the biopolitical Other is a necessary construct, as Stuart Murray reminds us, because for us to live well, "they" must die. Biopolitics works according to a naturalized system of binary distinction that constantly reminds us who are the virtuous and who are the disposable.[38] But it is vital to recall that biopower comes from within rather than from above; it is invisible, in other words, as nebulous and totalizing as the borderless globe. Biopolitical discourse insists that matters of life and death, the fate and physicality of the body, living or dead, are at the heart of how modern and now postmodern reality is mapped out, from the way punishment is levied upon the subject to the social organization of cities.[39] Accordingly, such terms as "throwaway" and "expired" can and must be extended to include those hidden social strata who are the counterparts of the material goods that they themselves may, often enough, toil to produce for export or break apart for recycling. An extension of that vitally important link between the disposable object and the invisible populations of developing and developed nations, in particular, is the cinematic image, for it is within that discursive space that voice can be given and invisibility be exposed. Varda's film situates the expendable image as the aesthetic complement to the cast-off commodities and the marginalized citizens that are her subjects—the gleaners who are as socially expendable as their salvaged objects are materially so. Added to this nexus of expendability is the filmmaking process itself, with Varda's narration clearly analogizing between gleaning and filmmaking, rag-picking and the random accumulation of impressionistic images gathered from modernity's chaotic and unpredictable social and cultural landscapes.

Taking into account the essential ontology of disposability and digitality, Varda's medium casts her as an expendable subject on two levels. First, her own aging body is made accessible by the principle of secondhand: that is, her camera's capacity to "use one hand to film the other" makes it clear that her physicality has become unrecognizable, as withered and misshapen as the objects her subjects pick from the trash. Second, the ontology of the digital camera (embedded in layers of disposability) likewise and necessarily situates her within the realm of the expendable. So even if the subject is not explicitly "allowed to die" or otherwise rendered dispensable in Bauman's sense, the image as commodity object as well as the cheapness and expendability of digital pictures inscribes it with the unshakeable potential to become as such.

Varda's documentary and its digital specificity bears the same aesthetic and practical principles that Sontag locates within the proclivities of the modernist photographer's documentary impulse and tendency for social tourism. The flâneur is not attracted to acceptable realities but rather takes self-guided tours of those who live in dominant society's shadows, the unsightly and unseen. While the ethnographic gaze of the tourist's camera often upholds the distinctions between the virtuous and the expendable, and further naturalizes the logic of biopolitcal power, cameras also expose and remedy inequalities. Turned on ourselves, they also monitor our own lives and experiences, and turn us into our own strangers. Bridging the social documentary with the introspective one, Varda's equation between herself and her subjects makes an important intervention, incorporating herself, the citizens she documents, and the objects they collect within the disposable scope of her medium. In this way digital is the great equalizer, as it renders disposable all those who are picked out by the DV camera's frame. And because the camera is as likely to be trained on the privileged, introspective operator as on the hidden or invisible lives of those relegated to the margins, the ubiquitous digital camera extends to all the potentiality of being, like the image, objectified, commodified, and eventually discarded.

There is no better example of the collision between the expendable human body and the politics of postmodern image culture than the hurricane that throttled New Orleans in 2005. Henry Giroux identifies how integral the photographic and cinematic image, captured by media and citizens both, was in rendering visible—or veritably exploding—the otherwise offscreen racial and economic discrimination that was really the source responsible for letting die so many disposable American lives, in New Orleans and beyond.[40] Spike Lee's epic 2006 HBO documentary about the storm, *When the Levees Broke*, sources its emotional power from the digital images—photographs and video—captured by New Orleans residents as they directly confronted the terrific throes and lingering aftermath of the infamous hurricane known as Katrina. The film compresses and then explodes the ontologies of digital and analog media, environmental ideology, and the cultural practice of throwaway consumerism; the result is a conflation between the image-politics of overexposure and the biopolitics of expendability. Lee's project picks up and then extends many of the same principles that Varda investigates in her *The Gleaners and I*. Though Lee's documentary is neither introspective nor digitally captured, the film owes much of its effectiveness to the digital resources gathered from those who experienced the storm and its aftermath at first hand. Like Varda, Lee uses the documentary to expose or render visible a marginalized population: in this case, the people of New Orleans, whose impoverished conditions earned the focus of the world's intense but ultimately fleeting gaze. Lee's enterprise consists of re-exposing the grave injustice which the news media's excessive production of certain, well-chosen images effectively overexposed and thus diminished. Too much imagistic space, attention, and broadcast time, too much light, too many cameras, and the expenditure of too much energetic activity created a crisis and then naturalized it, rendering the situation familiar and therefore forgettable. That Lee chose a conventional approach to documentary exposition, basing the film on interviews conducted in a uniform studio setting, both grants legitimacy to the project and also counters the chaos that defines the news footage and digital clips that punctuate each of the four emotionally exhausting "acts." So while Lee's own original footage starkly contrasts the digital shards he employs, he similarly resuscitates the horrific glimpses that might otherwise have been suppressed, challenging the dictates of what Sontag in *Regarding the Pain of Others* calls the "repressive standards" of "good taste" that perpetuate the marginalization of New Orleans residents.[41] The use of sourced second-hand digital images opens up a number of implications inherent in the propensity for digital video to expose disposable populations as well as to over-expose them, enforcing differences constructed by biopolitical discourses and once again rendering them expendable. The film equates the expendable (digital) image and the expendable citizens of New Orleans, but by drawing attention to and then correcting perceptions of the crisis, insisting that it is not normalized as one more example of a larger set of social and economic conditions, Lee refuses to "let die" either the citizen or the image. What the representation of Hurricane Katrina ultimately reveals is the interconnection between the ephemeral value of contemporary culture's images and the fragility of our physical infrastructures. From consumer goods to architectures and images, the guiding principle of planned obsolescence places deconstruction ahead of decomposition; what is manufactured is intended to break, not unlike the precarious and ill-conceived levees that failed to hold New Orleans together. Lee's film argues that rebuilding New Orleans is necessary precisely because of the fact that the inadequate engineering procedures and shoddy materials that separated the city from the ocean did indeed live up to their (transient, temporary) expectations and were finally breached. That Lee constructs his documentary out of image shards and residual narratives is itself a gesture of reconstruction and rehabilitation. The disposability of New Orleans and its populations was enhanced by the unbalanced and overextended media attention it generated. Lee's film is an attempt not only to rescue and reclaim the Katrina narrative, but to grant it longevity and durability, its exposure deliberately measured in an attempt to ensure that it remains legible, visible, and relevant beyond its own immediate context rather than an isolated single-use event. Constructing the monumental rather than the momentary, rendering a document that shall not be disposable: such is Lee's structuring challenge.

Trouble the Water (2008) by Carl Deal and Tia Lessin is a powerful but decidedly more accessible representation of the Katrina crisis than Lee's miniseries. The film focuses on one family's experience and adds nuanced social layers to the aftermath and forced diaspora of New Orleans citizens; it also gained exposure in its own right when it was nominated for the Best Documentary Oscar in 2009. Like Lee, the filmmakers make extensive use of digitally captured amateur footage, lending further testimony to the ubiquity of the digital camera and its potential to empower citizens, turning them into default documentarians and their images into the visible evidence of social injustice—and, in this case, environmental racism. As such, *Trouble the Water* is as much about Hurricane Katrina's ravaging of New Orleans as it is about the democratizing effects of the digital movie camera. By implicitly foregrounding digital technology's relationship to obsolescence, economies of waste, and throwaway culture, the film questions the viability of technology to compel citizens to participate in or challenge the dominant media. In what might be the film's most decisive moment, just as the storm is coming to a head, the protagonist, Kimberly Rivers Roberts, is forced to shut off her apparatus, exclaiming that she is "out of juice"—that is, her battery power is ebbing low and, given the flood conditions, she has no means to recharge—and perhaps never again will. This scene keenly challenges the assumptions made by theorists and practitioners alike about digital media's unfailing potential to enable communication and to give voice by extension. But, as Kimberly's footage—or lack of it when her battery fails—reminds us, cameras depend on energy. What, then, happens to political discourse when the technological interfaces to which it is so intractably tied suddenly break down or otherwise fail? When trade in rare earth elements is suspended, for example? As a further dimension, the film also asks how democratic and inclusive digital imaging truly is when amateur images must first be filtered by professional practitioners and then transferred to the more resilient and legitimating support surface of celluloid before reaching a wide audience. While the affordability, accessibility, and user-friendly format of digital cinema are credited with rendering immediately visible moments of political crisis, disaster, and their underlying social inequality, Lee and Deal and Lessin demonstrate that story still matters. As Rivers Roberts gathers the raw footage of the storm she is clearly aware of the power her document could have, if she and it survive; but in order for her footage to be effective it had to be intercepted, brought to light professionally, and thus saved from obscurity—that zone of the expendable Other, who is still invisible despite the digital camera in her hand. Or perhaps the de-centered subject remains invisible despite her digital camera due to the glut of images produced by the same principle of digital accessibility. It is the dialectical paradox that haunts cinema and photography whatever the format. The conflation of technology and the image itself (what Virilio understands as the aesthetic of disappearance) speaks to how ever-refined recording devices gain increased access to what might otherwise be restricted realities and untouchable lives.

Image Archiving as Waste Management

Varda's, Lee's, and Deal and Lessin's respective investigations of the disposable subject find an antagonist and also a surprising complement in Justin Kan's Internet life-cast, Justin.tv. Using a small digital camera mounted onto his baseball cap (or on a tripod, while he is sleeping) twenty-four hours a day and seven days a week, Kan made available to the world the images of his daily routine by streaming them directly onto his website. Launched in March 2007, the life-casting gimmick caught the media's attention and gained some notoriety. While the project was ultimately short-lived, the website was restructured as a platform on which to post and watch live-streaming videos, wherein content, generated by users, is broadcast over the user's own channel and while it does not necessarily abide by the life-cast stricture, the format remains self-documenting. In July 2008, the site was reported to have added its one millionth registered user, and to have thus far accumulated 119 years of video, including both active and archived. But what belies the more obvious parameters of the project is the fact that it exemplifies how making a spectacle out of the overexposure of self is effectively self-defeating (and diminishing) rather than affirming. The conditions of his life's constant revelation transform Kan from individual to atmosphere; the narcissism at the heart of Kan's enterprise ironically diminishes rather than highlights him as a subject. Like Varda's subjective documentary, Kan's project illustrates the digital video camera's propensity for introspection, self-examination, and autobiography; the indulgence in first-person self-portraiture transforms his daily expenditures into a nonevent, the minimalism of which is nothing if not paradoxically opulent. Amateur, self-indulgent, and totally lacking in restraint, it fulfills the requirements of Dziga Vertov's ambiguous futurism, Andy Warhol's energetic sloth, and Dogme95's fundamentalist prescription for pure cinema, while at the same time scaling new heights of open-aperture gluttony. While Justin.tv might seem to fulfill Warhol's ideal vision of a cinema without an operator and the film free of cuts, a perfect vision, without interruption, mistakes, or an overexertion of energy on the part of either operator or audience, of course, Kan's subjective vision necessarily, but minimally, edits his life-cast in real time. Life-casting thus proves an instance of film-without-film, reducing editing and energy expenditure as well as the difference between the camera and the basic physiology of seeing and moving through the world at large, and likewise communicating with it. Justin.tv, for all its apparent mediocrity, is discursively useful, foregrounding as it does the future of digital video, surveillance technology, and, therefore, digital subjectivities, not to mention the overextension and overconsumption of carbon-neutrality and eco-consciousness. The project is not about Kan so much as it is about how mechanized vision absorbs the operator and via the process of technological evolution, renders the human filmmaker useless and ultimately expendable. Life-casting can therefore be regarded as a representation of the digital image's future as well as a prescient vision of what might be called the disposable cinema.

Digital technology's vast storage space makes it physically possible to retain infinite amounts of images, but the prospect of viewing the totality of our personal or cultural image archives is rendered less and less tenable as a consequence. Thus, digital's intervention into the natural process of analog cinema's inevitable decay is also, ironically, its death knell, undermining the integrity of the image's limited life span while also diminishing its value via an oversaturated and unmanageable viewing economy. While the amount of viewing hours available on film, for example, has risen from 40 minutes in 1895 (most of these preserved) to an estimated 3 billion hours in 2006 (and by 2025 one hundred billion hours), the human's temporal or physical capacity for viewing can only become increasingly limited by comparison.[42] Thus amending the omni-voyant camera envisioned in Vertov's *Man with a Movie Camera*, Cherchi Usai argues for the omni-voyant consumer, whose capacity to ingest cinematic images expands to duly accommodate what the all-seeing camera, its metaphorical counterpart, relentlessly records. Perhaps the anathema of the "serious" film archive is Justin.tv, which had by July 2008 logged 119 years of user-generated video. It was this excessive accumulation, perhaps, that prompted the site to adopt a housecleaning policy; in March 2010 Justin.tv announced that unless specifically flagged, past broadcasts would be saved as a clip and then deleted from the site's archive after seven days. Cinema, however, is notably characterized by the propensity to generate waste. Not only is the editing process premised on cutting away, but the images' support surface—both digital discs and celluloid stock—are fated to decay. As the inherent disposability of cinema's support surfaces is mitigated by technology's improved preservation possibilities, scholarly interest in ephemeral cinemas quickens. Commercial interests have also contributed to the rehabilitation of the archive and the resuscitation of what once would have been left to decay. Utilizing digital technology and a multiplicity of distribution channels, Hollywood studios turn their own warehouses of used goods into repositories of risk-free revenue, repackaging material long since shelved and reselling it to an ever-expanding international market. The film industry's commitment to preserving what it designates as "classics" was inaugurated by the television rebroadcast, wherein the recycling of cinema and the manufacturing of the classic film placed new value on the lost features decaying in the industry's storage spaces.[43] In order to market a programming schedule based on older films, cable television specialty channels such as Ted Turner's Turner Classic Movies proved especially adept at fostering nostalgia for Hollywood cinema's historical and cultural importance; the resultant success was manifested in an increased interest—on the part of the public and industry—in what is now considered classic fare. In the United States in 1988 the battle between those interested in preserving cinematic records intact and Hollywood studios motivated by maximizing the archive's profitability escalated when archivists loudly protested Turner's practice of colorizing black-and-white films slotted for rebroadcast. By tampering with original materials, Turner was accused of destroying historical documents; the attention resulted in changes to U.S. law to specifically address the protection of cinema's material integrity, as well as the establishment of a National Film Registry, a canon of historically significant films built through a nomination process of those with academic or curatorial expertise in cinema.[44] But as Barbara Klinger points out, the film industry has made significant financial investment in creating the proper environmentally controlled circumstances necessary to prolong the life of celluloid. So, while film preservation has an important "ecological dimension," it is largely underwritten by economic interests; keeping movies safe, then, involves both the commitment to "safeguard a resource" and the desire to render it profitable.[45] Klinger's ecological rhetoric is charged with both practical and political currency. On the one hand, "ecology" has a literal application, for it accurately describes the closed, tightly controlled environment necessary to protect celluloid from the eroding effects of time and oxygen. On the other hand, Klinger is also foregrounding celluloid film (fragile, decaying, or otherwise imperfect) as a resource commodity worth protecting, but only with regeneration purposes in mind. The discourse surrounding film preservation reflects the environmental politics that are the necessary and obvious extension of film history. Integral to the social and cultural conditions needed for the continued consumption of classic or vintage cinema is the maintenance of a market value that resides in a perceived sense of scarcity and limited availability and thus produces and perpetuates a sense of cultural and historical worth. But when films are divested of material packaging and streamed over Netflix—and for only $7.99 a month—the implication is that there is no physical or economic correlative.

As Zimmerman explains in her summary of the legal history that has shaped the film archive on levels practical, political, and theoretical, in the early 1990s the U.S. government held a series of hearings in effort to assess the state of film preservation in America. Archivists representing both major national libraries and small local collections emphasized how the interests of commercial Hollywood studios have overshadowed vast reaches of culturally relevant film material. At the time perhaps only 1 percent of amateur films and home movies had been archived, representing a significant loss to the country's historical record. Representatives from these noncommercial archives argued that the parameters of what constitutes cinema, and thus what is culturally valuable in the public imagination, needed to be reassessed so as to include experimental, industrial, educational, scientific, and training films, as well as travelogues and home movies, for these are the ones representing regional histories and, often enough, de-centered voices.[46] One such archive represented at the hearings was the Prelinger Library. Located in San Francisco, as well as on the Internet where its vast archives are housed, the library is a privately owned open-access collection of American ephemera, much of it cinematic or image-based. Owners Rick and Megan Prelinger have made it their task to maintain their collection as an organic, almost self-generating entity which fosters conditions of randomness, disorder, and juxtaposition.[47] The archive's basic premise works in opposition to the specificity and efficiency of conventional library classification systems and digital search engines. Acquiring, storing, and organizing cinematic and other textual resources, the Prelingers espouse environmental models in order to manage and share their expansive material and immaterial reserves. By choosing landscape as the concept that centralizes the philosophy of their commitments—thus linking text to landscape, image to geography—the Prelingers make the archive explicitly environmental. Landscape does not mean the untouched or the immaculate, and neither does it mean naturally occurring terrain or "land," but is instead composed of debris, the residues and traces of how it has been used, abused, and then left behind, its history told in the imperfections inscribed on its surfaces. So, because "landscape" is not pure and pristine, neither is the archive, which is composed of salvaged detritus, that which otherwise would have been left to the trash heap. The Prelingers operate according to a broad moral and aesthetic guideline that would rather preserve the actively decaying film rather than the rehabilitated, artificially mended one. Roland Barthes, discoursing on the photograph, describes the inherent paradox he sees in turning an ephemeral medium into modernity's primary historical marker. Instead of the stone and metal of our pre-industrial forbearers, industrial society has refined a method of using light and chemical processing (and now data encoding) to act as an external memory; photography—and cinema—are forms of cultural inscription so inherently fragile (this applies to both celluloid decay and the digital image's limited life span) they will fall short of remembering us to the future. Barthes argues that the domination of the photograph (the cinema is equally applicable) marks modern society's "refusal" of the monument: "By making Photography, which is mortal, the general and almost natural witness of 'what has been,' modern society has renounced the Monument."[48] Barthes's words are equally applicable to moving images, and with them in mind, the film archive takes on its own particular logic, wherein a complex technological infrastructure is devoted to upholding what is essentially a cultural ruin. As we've seen, what will survive into the future is this material support mechanism—the computers and discs, the vaults and canisters, the skeleton of the archive rather than the archive's contents.

Because their "monument" is fully available for public access, the Prelingers avoid perpetuating a sense of scarcity (and its attendant nostalgia) otherwise associated with archival objects and collectibles. Both proponents and skeptics of digitization, the Prelingers are aware that digital technology has the power to transform a restored Hollywood film into an instant classic, marketed as a rare artifact worthy of purchase in hardcopy or file form. But mass reproduction and dissemination can also flood the marketplace with such rarities, inadvertently undermining the conditions of scarcity that makes a cultural production (a text, a film, a piece of music) collectable and thus commodifiable. The suggestion is that media industries have co-opted film history itself, ultimately equating the preservation of a film with its purchase. The responsibility for archiving and also for maintaining a national or cultural history is shifted onto the individual consumer, whose sense of nostalgia encourages and justifies participation in the privatized economy that is home cinema and, by extension, the home archive. Heather Rogers similarly argues that the responsibility for environmental conservation is too often transferred onto the consumer and the taxpayer; it is through purchasing power that an individual is encouraged to remedy the environment, never questioning whether or not it is consumerism and consumption that are at the heart of the problem itself.[49] Gay Hawkins's call for a new ethics of waste highlights a similar point, wherein consumers assume the role of environmental custodians not out of informed choice, but in compliance with a moral imperative that self-regulates social and political conduct. But given free choice, removing the moral codes or economic values that turn some pieces of detritus into ephemera and others into what Hawkins terms "phobic objects" forces a new relationship with that which has already been consumed, either by us or others.[50] What maintains the "worth" of the Prelinger archive is, quite brilliantly, its worthlessness—its sheer openness, public availability, willing submission to private reproduction and manipulation, thus rendering the conditions of an imposed or manufactured scarcity something of an impossibility.

And so it is in the interest of industry to perpetuate rather than to conceal what is becoming a pervasive sense of environmental calamity. Resources are commodities to be bought and sold; scarcity and crisis are necessary categories, for they perpetuate a resource-based economy that is founded on the short-term principle of supply and demand, driving up the price of the limited or the nonrenewable. Industrial ecology, similarly, theorizes how the environment might continue to sustain the commercial interests of industry: maintaining the biosphere's health in order to extract from it further amounts of energy. Shifting industrial processes from a linear flow or "open loop," in which resources and capital investments move through the system and end up as useless waste, to the closed-loop system, where waste feeds new growth, implies a reversion to an earlier mode of industrialization. In order to foster such a transition, industry must manufacture enduring technologies and goods made from materials that can be reabsorbed into the system—or at least break down without much temporal delay or toxic residue. The principles of industrial ecology fit with more than a little accuracy the flows of cultural production in general and the film good in particular. As Jonathan Sterne argues, recourse from the open loop and its abundance of garbage is designing technologies that work well, and endure, rather than serve as anticipations of the next design phase.[51]

Just as decay is a necessary biological category, waste is an essential part of both cultural and technological development. But in terms of image goods, digital's potential for limitless storage denies the possibility to generate the surplus and debris that would otherwise be tossed away, creating a state of overproduction and under-availability. Kristan Horton's project articulates just such a seeming contradiction, wherein the detritus he employs is all private and self-generated, implying a scarcity of waste; trash as a resource available only to the active, enfranchised consumer. Waste, in other words, ought to be democratized, making it visible, so that it can be harnessed and reactivated rather than moralized into obscurity.[52] While the very practice of gleaning, Varda's film demonstrates, has lost its status as a socially acceptable behavior, it was only after the economic shift to mass production that such things as trash, compost, or leftovers were effectively "invented."[53] There is nothing tragic in gleaning, only in the fact that it is restricted and, as Varda's film points out, often criminalized and always stigmatized, obviating it as a viable economic option and for both the individual and industry alike. Were recycling valued as productive work, our relationship to the waste we make might undergo a radical transformation, spurring interaction rather than reaction, as it is openly integrated into the larger economy rather than alternative subeconomies.

File-sharing and downloading from such forums as the Prelinger Archive might seem "immaterial" approximations of gleaning, except that a file, document, or image, once sourced, does not necessarily or immediately disappear or expire but instead remains available for another gleaner to appropriate and reproduce, thus setting the conditions for accumulation and potential glut. If the Internet and other electronic archiving infrastructures are left unmanaged, the durability of the digital and its capacity for storage become its detriment. Jennifer Gabrys argues that the failure of digital archiving resides in the inability to reconcile two key differences: preservation, which is essentially the effort to halt the march of time, and innovation, premised on a relentless commitment to the future, transition, and unhindered reinvention. "Digital technology," she writes, "cannot slow down to fit the archivist's slow time. The dilemma of preservation collides with the dilemma of electronic waste."[54] In a notable example of these same contradictions, Microsoft engineer Gordon Bell, who led the initiative to connect the world's supercomputers and thus create what is now the Internet, has committed his life to a digital archive. A spectacle of biopolitical self-regulation, Mylifebits contains every last scrap, note, text or image he has collected or will encounter; this includes over 100,000 photographs, 150,000 web pages, and 120,000 e-mails, as well as videos, home movies, grade school report cards, and other materials which have been scanned and uploaded onto his system. What is more, the "SenseCam," now perpetually suspended from around Bell's neck, is programmed to take a photograph every thirty seconds, thus accumulating 2,000 random images over a waking day, all of which are, predictably, transferred onto his archive. Shifting his life to hard drive and cyberspace, Bell contends, is valuable not only for the purpose of augmenting human memory capacity, but also for its environmental and economic logic. Bell's system so far occupies two gigabytes of storage space, and each one, he triumphantly claims, costs a mere fifty cents. But as Gabrys and other critics insist, the environmental, social, and cultural costs that belie the inexpensive and seemingly innocuous piece of plastic that is that microchip are beyond estimation. The basic logic of this equation cheapens Mylifebits irredeemably, particularly as Bell insists that it is founded in part on an environmentally inspired goal—the elimination of what might be called our culture's paper dependency. But the real fallacy of the project lies in the temporal incompatibility of preservation and digitization. Bell, it seems, is faced with the large technological wrinkle that continually renders systems obsolete and their information reserves irretrievable. His project is threatened by its own terms—namely, his industry's commitment to development and reinvention which in turn hastens the obsolescence of its existing infrastructure. Surely technology could solve the problem of continual format migration, but to do so would not make economic sense for an industry premised on serial replication. Bell's system must be continually updated if his life's memories are to be accessed in the future; otherwise his archive, his life, will be rendered obsolete. Not unlike the reversing effects of Justin Kan's commitment to documenting his life through cinematic overexposure, what Bell might well be engaged in is an enterprise of self-annihilation—the reduction of the self rather then its affirmation. The self as microchip, rendered disposable and thrown away, is absorbed into the sprawl of accumulated residues where it might be gleaned by someone else and somehow put to use, thus reducing, or perhaps re-inscribing, a life's footprint upon the earth.

CONCLUSION

This book began with the image of an Inuk hunter and a movie camera, taken around 1922, which set some of the terms of my inquiry, namely locating the relationship between the cinematic image and natural resources. I turned to that image in response to Dudley Andrew's perceptive reading of *Nanook of the North* in his "Roots of the Nomadic" as a narrative about a filmmaker and a hunter's parallel search for energy: for calories and fuel supplied by the blubbery seal, and for the energy of the Inuk hunter himself, whose physical fortitude fuels the filmmaker's imagination and the cinematic "assemblage" as it survives off the land and Inuk traditional wisdom. This simple image, read against Andrew's essay, assumes an enormous depth and within its intersecting points of reference is the spirit of this book. With this image in mind, I will cast ahead at the what the future might hold for energy and moving images and, by doing so, glance back at the terrain these five chapters have covered in search of the natural resources that are inextricably bound up in the production, dissemination, and reception of the moving image.

If this book were to have been written at an earlier moment, any time before the digital revolution or the rise of green consciousness, it would have assumed a different form but would not have lacked content. This book is of this moment, and grapples with how such categories as the "carbon footprint," "paperless," the "end of" oil and the "end of" cinema inform the twenty-first century's cinematic imagination. In order to do this, this book has looked back in order to better look ahead as it asks whether a "green" or carbon-neutral cinema is anything new. What the image of the Inuk hunter and the movie camera reveals is that resources are embedded in all moving images. It is a constant, by virtue of the fact that movies are more than shadow puppets or spirited musings: they are an industrial construct. What is changing, however, is our awareness of the same and the ability to recognize and critique how "plugged in" moving images are to the energy economy and thus to the biophysical world. So there is a difference between a "resource conscious image" (such as Jennifer Baichwal or Ali Selim produce) and a "resource image" (such as Robert Flaherty's photographs of Nanook or the BP Spillcam); the carbon neutral film is overtly self-conscious of its *cinematic* relationship with the biophysical world in a way that the Spillcam is not. It depends on who is looking at (or making) the image, and the interpretive awareness the viewer (or practitioner) brings to the encounter with the image, whether that happens in a theater or on YouTube, via a stable silver screen or a mobile LCD. Being conscious of the relationship between natural resource use and the moving-image economy can turn all cinema into a resource image (in spite of itself) and therefore open up bold new critical terrain for all who engage with images, as we all do. Would we have asked these questions at an earlier juncture of cinematic history? Perhaps not, for as the digital revolution and the green revolution continue to converge and the more that information about the depth of our reliance on nature's power becomes available, the more difficult to *not* see how the energy economy and the image economy (and the information economy more broadly) are inextricably entwined. It is necessary to consider both, together and separately, for each current comes together—collides, really—in the fluctuating space of the cinematic image.

This book has traced that image of the hunter and the camera throughout its discussions of the cinematic footprint, including consistent engagement with the question of which format, analog versus digital, is more or less sustainable. The answer, if any, is that it depends on scale. A chemically processed "film" shot on an analog camera is going to have less material impact on the earth than a carbon-neutral big-budget feature, no matter how many offsets the latter purchases; similarly, driving to a movie theater to take in a movie once a week is perhaps less energy intense than sustaining a Netflix account, for while the bounty of images Netflix supplies might seem touchless, the requisite hardware is not, and neither is the necessary electricity to run that equipment or to generate the content in the first place. Economy and ecology are, after all, flip sides of the same coin; both are linked etymologically from the Greek *oikos*, meaning "household" or place to live—managing a household is economics, while managing nature's household is ecology, both of which imply custodianship of where one lives. Scaling back on production is thus the "greenest" route to pursue; simple yet perhaps one too radical to ever be realized, especially after an eco-epic to the scale of *Avatar* throws off the balance. But, as this book points out, the "greenest" cinema is not "green" at all—it is not self-consciously "environmental," it is just ecological because it is economical. And this is where the books ends up: up in the Arctic, where a "nomadic," sustainable, nonfiction cinema began in 1922 with Flaherty's cinematic forays, and where it continues to develop, and set standards for the rest of us to emulate as we attempt to minimize our culture's footprints.

At the time of writing, Canadian Prime Minister Stephan Harper has just wrapped up his yearly odyssey to Nunavut Territory in the High Arctic, also known as the Canadian Far North. According to Harper's rhetoricians, "North" is an idea and an ideal, and a vital part of the Canadian national identity, a claim that is but a thin disguise for Harper's real interest in that remote area: tapping into its vast and ultimately "secure" natural resources (including minerals, oil, natural gas, water, and fish) before some other Arctic nation (Denmark or the more aggressive Russia) stakes a grater claim. In Harper's blunt parlance, Canada's position on the north is "use it or lose it." In other words, entrench the technological, logistical, and military infrastructure necessary to explore and exploit, extract and then export, the remote tundra's historically mythologized treasure-trove of natural wealth—and do so well removed from those communities whose suspicions or protests might catch media or activist attentions. The area is an energy hot spot because of just that—heat. Arctic shrinkage is releasing vast tracks of potentially oil-rich seabed from millennia of deep freeze. The area has long been thought to hold significant reserves, which recent estimates claim to be 166 billion barrels of oil and gas lying in wait along the near-shore Arctic, with much more in areas closer to the North Pole.[1] As the planet warms and the polar icecap melts, the Northwest Passage becomes navigable and the heretofore inhospitable Arctic will, with vast amounts of probing, begin to relinquish its vast hydrocarbon riches—to Canada and then to its international trading partners, namely the energy-hungry China and United States, Canada's largest customer.[2]

"Operation Nanook" is Harper's name for the annual military operation that unites the Maritime Command and Coast Guard in disaster preparedness exercises (such as if there is a fuel leak in Arctic waters) and Arctic sovereignty patrols. During the 2010 trek, the prime minister announced not only increased military spending, including 16 billion Canadian dollars toward sixty-five new Stealth fighters, as well as a 500-million-dollar investment in remote sensing satellites to help monitor northern navigation routes, but also the opening of a "world class" scientific research center in Cambridge Bay, Nunavut, whose purpose and mandate are ambiguous at best.

Operation Nanook? It is enough to pique a film scholar's interest, or that of anyone else who has seen or even heard mention of Flaherty's 1922 *Nanook of the North*, the source of documentary cinema as we know it as well as enduring racialized perceptions of the childishly primitive or nobly

savage "Eskimo." It is a curious choice, for the name conjures up a host of
cultural if not cinematic associations. Nanook does mean "polar bear" in
Inuktitut—Flaherty named his protagonist thoughtfully—but the legacy of
Nanook the film ensures that its mythology overshadows whatever original
linguistic value Harper was striving for. And even without Flaherty's legacy
complicating the mix, Nanook remains an ironic title. The polar bear is the
emblem of global warming; how self-reflexive that it is also the name assigned
to the operation in charge of securing Canada's sovereignty over a region that
holds much of the industrial world's energy future in its icy grip. In spite
of his limited imagination Harper's evocation of the Flaherty classic works
wonders to confirm the intractable connections between cinema and global
warming, the moving image and the biophysical world, and proves again that
the only reason any nation or corporation ventures into the Arctic tundra
(from Flaherty's corporate sponsors to the Cairn Energy project underway
in Greenland) is for the purpose of extracting its resource wealth and taking
them south, from oil, to diamonds, to ethnographic images of a "vanishing"
race of ice-ridden primitives.

While the Arctic is the primal scene (and screen) for nonfiction filmmaking
techniques, strategies, and ethics (or lack thereof) as they are still practiced and
theorized it is also, more critically, where cinema's very future—as a practice,
a technology, and means of political and social expression—currently resides,
and thrives, both emblematically and literally. That Arctic cinema takes the
shape of an ecologically sound means of making and distributing digitally
captured videos (fictional, mostly non) which aim to preserve and promote
the history and future of a traditionally nomadic oral culture whose way of
life still offers a radical corrective to the dominant industrial culture within
and against which it resides. And it is here that I will conclude this book: on a
high note, in the High Arctic, with a look ahead at the world's energy economy
and at an ecological image economy as well. Underlying this latter realm are
such vital dimensions of sustainability as "small-scale," "community-based,"
"digitally-rendered," "local," "recycled," and "solar-powered," all of which
are achieved unconsciously and in spite of the disadvantages and obstacles
presented by the energy riches that are in all our interest—and uninterest.

On a small island west of Baffin Island in Nunavut is the tiny hamlet of
Igloolik, home of Zacharias Kunuk and Isuma Productions, the independent, mostly Inuit-run, community-based film, television, and Internet TV
production unit dedicated to enhancing Inuit language and culture, creating
local employment opportunities and promoting traditional Inuit knowledge
among Inuit and non-Inuit the world over. Kunuk is the primary filmmaker
and producer behind Isuma, and the director of *Atanarjuat: The Fast Runner*

(2001), the first feature-length fiction film written, directed, acted in, and produced by Inuit (and in Inuktitut). Or, more properly, *Atanarjuat* is a feature-length *video*, for director and producer Kunuk has never shot film, and this is just one example of Kunuk and Isuma's numerous videographic projects. Kunuk's work has turned video production into one of Igloolik's primary sources of revenue, employment, and means of maintaining Inuit cultural identity. The hamlet's population hovers around 1,500 but is home to no less than three video organizations: the Inuit Broadcasting Corporation, Isuma, and the Tarigsuk Video Center. Kunuk and Isuma continue to show that digital video and Internet-based channels of communication are critical to the survival of the Inuit, as a culture and community. What Kunuk's breadth of video shows is this: just as the Arctic takes the planet's climactic pulse, it is also the wellspring of a singular and entirely future-oriented brand of cinematic practice. After winning the prestigious Camera d'Or for best first feature at the 2001 Cannes Film Festival, *Atanarjuat*, a small-budget feature made for less than 2 million Canadian dollars (much of sourced from government arts and culture grants) marked a flurry of laudatory discourse among academics and scholars (anthropologists in particular) that continues to this day. The film remains the standard-bearer for Indigenous film and video and exemplar of the moving image's power to heal, educate, and strengthen those "traditional" groups relegated to the peripheries of the Fourth World where they struggle to deal with devastating colonial legacies. *Atanarjuat*—and Isuma more broadly—together extend beyond important discourses surrounding postcolonial struggles and identity politics, for they bring into sharp focus key questions just now beginning to electrify humanities and social science research, namely how digital technology, new media (the Internet in particular), and network culture might be a way to educate a global population about ecological concerns and stave off environmental perdition.

Atanarjuat tells a 1,000-year-old Inuit legend that has passed down orally among the people who live in what is now Igloolik. *Atanarjuat*'s ethnographic detailing is meticulous. The DVD production notes iterate that Kunuk and his crew went to pains to re-create what was intended to be an authentic Inuit representation of traditional pre-contact Inuit life. But perhaps the most compelling aspect of the film comes at the end, when credits roll against glimpses behind the scenes of the cast and crew in "nontraditional" clothing, carrying props, interacting with the "primitive" mise-en-scène, and generally acknowledging the presence of the camera. It is here that *Atanarjuat* is revealed as a new paradigm for filmmaking: digital video harnessed as a political, social, environmental practice. Isuma Production's sustainability resides in a commitment to low-impact practices: digitally rendered and disseminated, democratically organized, tapping into local infrastructure and resources, and likewise giving back to the community rather than extracting from it. Isuma Productions makes video an essential part of sustaining the Igloolik community—offering employment, job training, and drawing in revenue that stays within the community. In terms of economics and politics, it achieves a rare balance between the ancient and modern, pre-industrial and post-industrial, local and global and is foregrounded not only in the narrative of *Atanarjuat* but also in the formal practice of collective-based filmmaking.[3]

And *Atanarjuat* is something else as well—a particularly rich example of what in the "South" might be termed carbon-neutral. The film's production features reveal that Kunuk's is an exterior cinema—outdoors, without studio walls, and therefore de-territorialized, in the literal and metaphorical Deleuzian sense. Shooting took place over six months in and around Igloolik. Actors—all members of the community—lived on site, in the fashion of their ancestors, whom the film characterizes.[4] Equipment was transported on snowmobile and living on location further reduced gas consumption. Mobile shots (such as the glorious run across the ice) were facilitated by sleds. Labor, including actors and crew, were locally sourced. In terms of sets and props, shelters used are not permanent; igloos melt and dissolve back into the earth where they came from, while skin tents used during summer hunting are transportable and reusable. Props and costumes were crafted by members of the Igloolik community, and then put to use within the community after filming. Because so much of the traditional craftwork had to be researched and learned, the pre-production process was itself an exercise in reintroducing lost skills—building boats, sleds, shelters, making tools, sewing clothes. And of course the story itself was sourced locally, complied by writer Paul Appak Angilirq from extensive interviews with several Igloolik elders. There is no excess or residue; infrastructure employed either biodegrades or was absorbed into the community itself; there are no Styrofoam shards for future archeologists to unearth. And lighting, that dimension of mise-en-scène, also comes naturally—from the profuse summer sun. The intensity of the light lends a sense of artifice; this in turn renders it accessible, of this world, rather than mythic or exotic. Sunlight saturates most of the scenes and is likewise reflected back, laser-like, off the crisp white of snow and ice; the video-like quality of the images is palpable, almost uncannily so. Sunlight dominates; it is the film's formal and operative nucleus. The sun comes to the Arctic only half the year and thus determined the time and conditions of the shoot. Indeed, we are all beholden to the sun, the ultimate dictator of any and all aspects of hydrocarbon culture—including this video. Kunuk now uses a solar-powered generator on his shoots; the video camera is literally plugged into where this book—and cinema—began, with the sun.

Atanarjuat places great emphasis on the ingenuity, skill, and creativity the Inuit developed in order to master and then thrive in such a formidably harsh environment. The extensive and patient observational shots featuring daily routines and subsistence practices—food preparation, hunting, readying tents, igloos, and other shelters—are nothing if not ethnographic. There is, however, an obvious lack of contextualization, or commentary that nonfictional documents conventionally employ to bridge the cultural encounter between viewer and subject. But this is primarily a narrative film, not a document, and the intended cultural encounter is Inuit to Inuit—traditional to modern—and so there is common ground, however thin or slippery, which Kunuk takes for granted and so dispenses with offering instructive or interpretive guidance.

Inuit were nomadic hunters who followed the seasons and wildlife migration routes—of the caribou primarily—adapting themselves to weather and the ebb and flow of resource availability; misjudgment or a failure in timing could determine a group's life or death.[5] Of course pipelines, mining, and roads disrupt these rhythms, causing Inuit to lose track of animals when herds deviate around manmade incursions; helicopter noise is also a source of tremendous ecological upset in a part of the earth where silence reigns. Survival also depended upon staying nimble, mobile, lightweight; groups kept small, breaking apart when they grew too large. Material possessions, including tools, were also small; artistic expression came in the form of clothing decoration and tattooing, rather than cumbersome artifacts. All objects—and group members—had to have a well-defined use value; any thing or person extraneous or excessive impeded agility and was culled.[6] What is more, there was an obligation to share and provide support—even begrudgingly, as *Atanarjuat* displays. These cultural principles inform the film's narrative and find complement in the film's production, based as Isuma is on collectivity and sustainability, a sense of thrift, and of community.[7] What is more, Kunuk makes his audience work—and the learning curve is steep when a culture one encounters is as ingenious and ancient as Kunuk's. But because of its narrative depth and openness, it is interpretively fluid—ensuring that the ancient story is exotic and is not rooted in the past. Watching the film now, again, in 2010, at the end of a summer of extreme weather (Russian forest fires, floods in Pakistan, China mudslides) or—more immediately—an anomalous September heat wave, *Atanarjuat* reads less as a glimpse of a past than an image of the future. The emphasis on the sustainable living techniques positions it as a survival guide for a post-hydrocarbon industrial world. This view testifies to the urgent tenor of environmental concern, and in particular how social and political conditions color the imagination. All cultural texts are nothing if not ecologically charged and "say" something about the biophysical world.

Kunuk and Isuma together challenge and add complexity to the theoretical evocation of "nomadology," Gilles Deleuze and Felix Guattari's rich metaphor for the fluidity, mobility, and borderlessness units whose lines of flight disrupt the territorializing programs of empire and resist the rootedness that is dominant (hydrocarbon) culture. In terms of Kunuk's nimble and carbon-light production logistics as well as the communal, small-scale ecosystem (or "assemblage" in Deleuze's terms) that is Isuma, the "nomad" is a nomad: less a convenient metaphor or clever descriptor than a living example of how Inuit traditions and digital technology can together help the planet and all its citizens adapt to the new terms of a warming globe. In his essay "Roots of the Nomadic," Dudley Andrew locates the numerous points of connection between Flaherty's *Nanook of the North* and Deleuze and Guattari's "Treatise on Nomadology" in their *A Thousand Plateaus*. Andrew's essay is fantastically adept at reading the layers of "energy" that underwrite Flaherty's career, and his individual films, especially the Arctic portrait for which he is so famous. Scholars of the 1922 documentary have long paralleled the white filmmaker and the Inuk hunter—pointing out how the Akeley camera tracking the Eskimo has a counterpart in the spear-wielding "Eskimo" who tracks the mighty walrus; the pair function a mirrors and metaphors, the one to the other.[8] Andrew takes the reading a step further by locating Flaherty and what became the documentary form as inherently nomadic—both literally and metaphorically—for indeed surviving an Arctic film shoot required Flaherty to adapt to the lifestyle of Allakariallak (the hunter who played Nanook). Inuit collaboration affected narrative structure and production practicalities—devising drying racks out of driftwood, hauling water out of ice holes for developing wash, or burning celluloid for fuel during a perilous hunting trip. Beyond the mobile camera and laboratory, sled and dog team, the camera operator himself is a constituent in the "war machine" (the nomadic assemblage that is made up as it goes along, using what is at hand to fuel its movement, following flows rather than exploiting them). Andrew points out thatDeleuze would have recognized the seal and walrus Nanook hunts as a "mobile subaqueous source of oil"—a source of life and energy, shot through with competing registers of value—calories and clothing for Nanook; cultural and economic capital for Flaherty.[9] Nanook, according to Andrew, is the power, the energy source, behind the film. His assemblage (tools and sled, dogs and boats) as well as the very hunt for energy thus powers the project, the projector, the image itself.[10] The very terms of this power relationship are a metaphor for the energy that is embedded in cinema itself and all moving images. In other words, the hunt sequences that structure the film's narrative are exemplary iterations of the resource image; for the Inuk hunter, for whom the mammals are life source and for the filmmaker who staked his career on extracting, refining and selling off this same fantasy of the noble northern primitive.

At a moment when Hollywood cinema—and the Inuit—was erecting walls and moving indoors to the controlled atmosphere of the studio, Flaherty made a radical move by keeping his images open—his practice ambulatory—and going after real life rather than its verisimilitude.[11] Flaherty's pursuit of the *plein d'air* cast both him and his subject in the role of the nomad-hero—pure, possessed of truthfulness and authenticity, and captured in a moving image correspondingly virtuous. Cinema now, however, is firmly rooted, tethered to "sedentary" power sources (economic, financial, and electrical). Nanook's ingenuity, what in Andrew's Deleuzian terms is an instance of nomadic "assemblage," is also something of a microcosmic ecology of local, self-sustaining film production—making do with what is at hand, and making films to educate the wider community about a better, more "pure" mode of existence.

Though originally dispatched to the Far North as a prospector for a mining company, the moving image replaced mineral prospecting as Flaherty's source livelihood; on a literal level, images of the Arctic hunter translated into the cultural capital he needed to survive and thrive, as a filmmaker and a citizen of an industrialized society. But there was choice for Flaherty—apart from personal drive or affinity for filmmaking, the cinematic image did not hold the balance of his life—or that of his family or community. For Zacharias Kunuk, however—Flaherty's detractor and also, I argue, his cinematic inheritor—the moving image is a source of life. Igloolik's Isuma has harnessed videography as part of a mobile assemblage that consistently accommodates peripheral groups, forgotten and underfunded in remote areas of the planet, often belonging to the Third and Fourth Worlds. Isuma Productions provides employment and job training, and brings revenue into a community with an incredible 60 percent unemployment (the highest in Canada). More significantly, video-making promotes something that cannot be imported from the South or anywhere else: a sense of autonomy, spirituality, self-knowledge, and, with it, *the preservation of life itself* in a community where substance abuse is endemic and the suicide rate is the highest in Canada. The root cause of such overwhelming problems is the erosion of traditional Inuit culture, much of it occurring in the last fifty years, and is due to federally mandated assimilation programs such as the notorious residential school system. With the erosion of language comes the erosion of culture; Kunuk has stated that "when we stopped telling stories, we started killing ourselves."[12] Storytelling is a resource

for Inuit, a life necessity. Without oral traditions Inuit vitality dries up, cultural
identity dissipates, and suicide rates soar to the point of imperiling the Inuit
as a people. Video, in Kunuk's estimation, is the nourishing antidote to that
hunger for traditional stories and, with them, a sense of cultural identity.
As for the Walpiri in Australia, video (analog and now HD) and Internet
dissemination platforms are Kunuk's means for channeling and sharing what
has become a vital source of Inuit culture.[13] From that perspective, the energy
embedded in the image of the Inuk hunter and the movie camera has far less
to do with the animal's flesh and tusk (source of oil, food, clothing) than in
the telling of how that animal is caught; the source of life is the transmission of this skill from one generation to the next. Without that knowledge,
the Inuit cross what Bruce Sterling calls the "line of no return," the point at
which a self-sufficient society is irreversibly cut off from an artifact-oriented
means of production and is instead beholden to an external power structure
for orientation—consumers, in other words, end users in a long, unmappable
supply system, and with no recourse if something breaks down.[14] It is a line
non-Inuit have crossed, and the reason why we need Kunuk to teach us how
to live and make culture sustainably, self-sufficiently.

For Norman Cohn, camera operator, Isuma cofounder, and only non-Inuit
crew member, DV is the reincarnation of low-cost video which at the end
of the 1960s enabled people "from Harlem to the Arctic" to harness TV as
a vehicle promoting political and social change at a grassroots local level.[15]
But now TV has given way to the Internet as a community-building tool and
digital technology has brought video-making into the mainstream, normal-
izing its production qualities and thus shifting our aesthetic expectations.
But of course the "new" media that Isuma utilizes—relying as it does on the
Internet as a chief distribution and communication platform—is not really
new at all. Like remediation theory or the archeological approach to moving-
image technology (cinema as shadow puppets) and "new" media technology
(the computer as a nineteenth-century Romantic invention) Kunuk's film
also evokes an archeology of the image. The constant that Kunuk identifies
is, quite simply, the compulsion to record, to speak our environs, and map
the world so that we can survive in it: the need to tell stories is primary, the
technology merely a facilitator. That is at the spirit of the cinematic enterprise,
and it is one that digital video is accommodating; somehow we—as Netflix
subscribers and YouTube uploaders—have lost sight of that. Storytelling,
for Walter Benjamin, is a political act.[16] To tell a story rather than to write a
novel is defiant in the sense that the unpublished, unpublicized story does not
become a tangible, saleable object—a commodity to reproduce, distribute,
consume. In its most ideal form, the story would return to a strictly oral

transmission, passed from person to person, group to group, generation to generation. *Atanarjuat* is for Kunuk first and foremost a story; it exceeds the terms of the medium itself. That this story empowers the Inuit people and re-presents Inuit to Inuit trumps the vehicle that facilitates its telling. Kunuk's work and Isuma Productions embraces both digital technology and new media in order to preserve an ancient culture: not as an archive, but as living, breathing, and fully sustainable. The moving image—shot on video, circulated on DVD, or transmitted on broadband Internet—is a source of life. Critics of transnational cinema such as Elizabeth Ezra, Robert Davis, and Ella Shohat point out that the homogenization of culture is a real consequence of the intersection between moving-image technology and global economics, wherein dominant cinema increasingly saturates global markets and muscles out local fare. But there is also a redemptive factor to what seems a rapid and alarming conflation of distinct cultures and media into a single mainstream space. Kunuk demonstrates that a balance between cultural homogeneity and heterogeneity is possible and desirable.

Michelle Raheja points out that among the Inuit and other Indigenous groups, visual modes of expression and the performance of oral narrative allow for the communication of notions of time and space that transcend the possibility of written forms. Cinema—video, more precisely—is, in other words, the logical extension of orality—and for this reason has proven an ideal medium for expression if not empowerment.[17] Andrew describes a similar alignment between video in West Africa and the oral tradition of the griot, but extends this to account for the political possibility located in video's portability and affordability, which allows it to slip through the cracks of dominant culture's striated spaces. But, as Kunuk has explained, the Inuit for a long time resisted moving-image technology, afraid that the impact would erode rather than foster traditional identity. A hunter and a traditional stone carver, Kunuk was possessed with a compulsion to preserve what he saw around him. In 1981 Kunuk traveled to Montreal where he sold some of his sculptures and bought a video outfit—camera, VCR, monitor. It is a telling exchange of medium, though the principles of each are, as Bauman argues, full of continuity rather than difference. Indeed, Kunuk's compelling parallel between the flow of a video camera and that of Inuit oral traditions describes how, as in video and the story, nothing is written down. Rather, "everything is taught by what you see. Your father's fixing up the harpoon; you watch how he does it and you learn. . . . For the medium I work in now, it was exactly the same thing. You don't need pen and paper to document what you see. Oral history and new technology match."[18] Instead of "speaking" the environment into memory, Kunuk is shooting it with an imaging tool, and passing on his perception of it, using a universal language that will *perhaps* be legible in the future. Again, though analog and now digital video allows for a perfectly fluid transition from oral storytelling, what is important is not the medium but the story—the transmission of narrative, and within the narrative wisdom and traditions. The camera functions as an extension of the brain, body, and connective tissue as synapses track between eyes and tongue, the visual and the oral, what is sighted and spoken. In this sense, Kunuk's video is an instance of film-without-film, and a critical reminder, as this book points out at several junctures, that cinema is an idea and that media is never "new." While cinema is sometimes traced back to Chinese shadow puppets, Kunuk suggests that it extends back even further, to oral traditions. But the DV camera Kunuk uses is on the industrial side of Sterling's line—and Kunuk is an end-user as much as an Inuk hunter. What renders Kunuk a nomad in the metaphorical Deleuzian sense and not in the anthropological one is this very adaption to flux and change, going both with and against the dominant flows.Ultimately he balances the traditional with the contemporary, by appropriating whatever tools necessary to sustain the Isuma "assemblage"—a video camera, dog sled or skidoo, the Internet, random sources of funding, traditional handicraft sets, and the use of Inuk "amateur" actors.

Kunuk's 2010 *Qapirangajuq!* is, like all Isuma's videos, available for free download on the collective's website. It is a rare document by a man who, as Kunuk describes himself, has gone from the "Stone Age to digital technology in one lifetime." In the documentary Kunuk and his video camera create a forum for Inuit elders to share their intimate perceptions of climate change (and those of their ancestors), and by doing so implicitly reveals himself as the only person in the world who could make such intercultural communication possible. Simple in premise but complex in scope, the video, first broadcast on the Internet and at the ImagiNative Indigenous film festival in Toronto in October 2010, intends to pose a challenge to and start a dialog with non-Inuit climate change scientists who because of linguistic and cultural divides so often overlook elder wisdom, an invaluable wealth of information and insight. Such gaps can be bridged, as Kunuk's video camera proves. The camera does not speak here, but it translates, and it acts as a conduit for an oral history of one of the earth's most critical ecological zones. Underneath the dialogue forum and alternative history (and future) of climate change is an implicit lesson about cross-culture video practice that is invaluable for filmmakers, moviegoers,and other cinematic citizens, Inuit and non-Inuit alike.

But Kunuk's work does not come with a rhetoric of dire anxiety or anger that one might expect from an artist whose mandate it is to right colonial legacies and instill a sense of pride and strength of spirit in an ailing community; this equanimity is both distinguished and refreshing. The Inuit, he recognizes, have not quite stepped beyond Sterling's boundary, wherein the pre-industrial—and pre-contact—past is inaccessible. The Inuit and other Indigenous groups are getting close to losing touch with traditional ways—and so is the world in its entirely. As Michael Robert Evans notes, growing reliance on global positioning systems (GPS) in place of traditional naviga-tion skills is a perilous trend and one that is indicative of the boundary line between traditional and technological societies (as well as between analog and digital formats).[19] When GPS breaks down due to extreme cold or loss of battery power, the Arctic traveler, far from home, has little chance of finding his or her way and surviving in a frozen tundra where there are few obvious geographical markers to provide orientation. For Kunuk, this has ecological as well as spiritual dimensions. We non-Inuit have crossed the line of no return and must, Sterling argues, harness technology to our advantage—as a means of living within our means, sustainably, rather than as a mere consumer commodity—bought, sold, and disposed of at rates that imperil our civiliza-tion rather than enable its survival. Here, now, in environmental terms, the grass on the other side of the line of no return looks pretty green.

While the Internet enabled a live-broadcast of preliminary sections of *Qapirangajuq!* at the 2009 Copenhagen summit on climate change, *Atanar-juat*, likewise, drew the viewer into the realm of video and as well as into the zone of the pre-contact Arctic, both idealized as a space and time outside of geographic borders. But while *Atanarjuat* counters colonial legacies and the continued homogenization of Inuit culture, Isuma's current documen-tary work counters the homogenization of the global environment. The construction of *Qapirangajuq!* is openly shared as a living work-in-progress; raw portions are available on the Isuma website both for streaming or pay-what-you-can download. Kunuk and his collaborator Tim Mauro remained in Igloolik rather than accompanying their work to Copenhagen; their physical absence openly critiquing the vast amount of fossil fuels hypocriti-cally expended by the delegates traveling to the event. In keeping with nomad tradition, long-distance travel would be deemed an unnecessary and burden-some expenditure of time, money, and energy. The Internet allows the Inuit community to cohere despite vast distances and to remain mobile, nimble.[20]

Notably, the ice fields upon which sections of *Atanarjuat* were shot have since melted.[21] From news of the melting ice cap to the image of the displaced "Nanook" or polar bear—the poster child of the environmental movement—the Far North has become emblematic of what lies ahead for the entire planet. The guiding premise of Kunuk's work is that Inuit wisdom, if properly tapped, can have a marked impact on the survival not just of Inuit and the Arctic, but planet Earth. Kunuk's concerns surpass geographic borders and national citizenships, unifying the globe (ideally at least) in a shared, urgent concern. But as Mauro comments, the anxious tenor with which we conceive global warming is specific to Southerners.[22] Climate change invites fear outside of Inuit communities precisely because we have no recourse to deal with environmental crisis. As *Qapirangajuq!* makes implicit, this disordered panic is attributable to our culture's sense of anthropocentric time—both past and future—and our place within it. So, though climate change is accelerating in the Far North, the dialog among Inuit is notably calmer. Inuit culture in the Igloolik region is, after all, 4,000 years old; the people and the climate have encountered periods of change—and peril—before. Inuit elders understand that humans can and must adapt to change, but scientists and global citizens must listen to Inuit wisdom, for it is grounded in adaptation. The video camera and Internet forums can lock that knowledge resource, and share it with those willing to listen. Part of the challenge is that Southerners want the climate to remain static, like Flaherty's conception of the pure and primitive Eskimo. But the climate flows and is not pure. And the earth will survive, the Inuit elders seem to suggest, though we—its inhabitants—will inevitably disintegrate. But before that happens, Mauro insists that for the Inuit who know how to live off the land, an oil crisis would not be a crisis at all, but simply a challenge. For some it might even be a welcome invitation to snip the umbilical cords that plug the North to South (and South to North) and facilitate a return to traditional nomadic ways—sustainable ways—such as *Atanarjuat* showcases.

Though Kunuk's work has brought the attention of scholars and scientists to the Arctic, Inuit culture, the use of video, and what the Inuit can teach us about surviving in a post-hydrocarbon world, the dominant Southern gaze is fixed elsewhere: on Arctic resources. The loosely defined Arctic is being reclassified, both in terms of its borders and its climate. To be "Arctic," the temperature should not climb above 10 degrees Celsius. Now, though, summer temperatures regularly reach into the teens, and as the Arctic melts, the major players in the energy game salivate at the possibility of drilling the vast region for precious petroleum. Is the future of Nunavut to be as ugly and catastrophic as that of Gulf Coast Louisiana? Will Big Oil offer a better livelihood to those in Igloolik than the main sources of income—government support, the volatile fur trade, or an Inuit-led video production company specializing in sustainable living? There are then two competing resource images now visible in the Arctic: the "Indigenized" one showcasing the traditional sourcing of caloric, cultural, and cinematic energy, and the hydrocarbon one, exemplified by Canada's spectacle of military prowess under the heading of Operation Nanook. As the energy-hungry U.S. and China search for stable oil sources, the Arctic's warming comes at an auspicious moment. But while Canada props up the U.S. thirst for oil, it also acts as cheap labor for the moving-image industry. Faye Ginsburg notes in her rather patronizingly titled article "Move over Marshall McLuhan! Live from the Arctic!" that Canada has long been an avant-garde leader when it comes to media theory and practice. So it is within the mainstream as well, as tax incentives, attractive exchange rates, and ability to appear similar to many U.S. locations have turned both Toronto and Vancouver into notable production sites of choice for Los Angeles-based companies, and is a major source of revenue for both cities.[23] Indeed, Canada is not just Hollywood North, but Gulf Coast North. Less than one hundred years after sunny California boomed with oil and turned moving images into industry, the power and wealth sourced from all that sun is no longer sufficient to sustain that state's economy. And so cinema must, like the nomad of not too distant past, migrate, in search of new sources of energy; but unlike that nomad, this cinema, if it is at all "southern" in spirit, will lay a heavy, perhaps intractable, footprint.

NOTES

INTRODUCTION

1. Dudley Andrew, "The Roots of the Nomadic: Gilles Deleuze and the Cinema of West Africa," in *The Brain is the Screen: Deleuze and the Philosophy of Cinema*, ed. Gregory Flaxman, (Minneapolis: University of Minnesota Press, 2000), 222.

2. Walter Benjamin, "The Work of Art in the Age of Mechanical Reproduction," in *Illuminations*, trans. Harry Zorn, ed. Hannah Arendt (New York: Schocken, 1968), 219.

3. Elizabeth Kolbert, "Running on Fumes," *The New Yorker*, November 5, 2007, 90.

4. André Bazin, *What is Cinema? Vol. 1*, trans. Hugh Gray (Berkeley: University of California Press, 1967), 13.

5. UCLA Institute of the Environment, "Southern California Environmental Report Card 2006," available at http://www.ioe.ucla.edu/reportcard/article.asp?parentid=1361 (last accessed December 1, 2010), 5.

6. For an even more comprehensive, inclusive, and updated report, see Green Screen Toronto's "Green Practices Manual: Environmental Options for the Film-Based Industries." Available at http://www.greenscreentoronto.com/.

7. UCLA Institute of the Environment, "Sustainability in the Motion Picture Industry" (Sacramento: California Integrated Waste Management Board, 2006), 23.

8. Quoted on "Treehugger" website, available at http://www.treehugger.com/files/2006/11/sweet_land_the.php (accessed October 1, 2010).

9. UCLA Institute of the Environment, "Sustainability in the Motion Picture Industry," 36.

10. On the politics of turning the invisibility that is carbon into a commodity, see Mark Shapiro, "Conning the Climate, Inside the Carbon-Trading Shell Game," *Harpers*, February 2010.

11. UCLA Institute of the Environment, "Sustainability in the Motion Picture Industry," 50–51.

12. Michel DeCerteau, *The Practice of Everyday Life*, trans. Steven Rendell (Berkeley, University of California Press, 2002), 167.

13. Craig Saunders, "Carbon Offsets," *Green Living*, Autumn and Winter 2007, 53.

14. "Ecological footprint" was first coined by University of British Columbia environmental scientist William E. Rees in his "Ecological Footprints and Appropriated Carrying Capacity: What Urban Economics Leave Out," *Environment and Urbanization* 4: (1992), 121–30.

15. Jeff Rubin, *Why Your World is About to Get a Whole Lot Smaller* (Toronto: Random House Canada, 2009).

16. Wolfgang Schivelbusch, *Disenchanted Night: The Industrialization of Light in the Nineteenth Century*, trans. Angela Davies (Berkeley: University of California Press, 1988), 67.

CHAPTER 1 — ENERGY

1. Melissa Felder et al., "Green Practices Manual: Environmental Options for the Film-Based Industries," available at http://greenscreentoronto.com/green_practices/, accessed November 1, 2010. This comprehensive document will be used throughout this chapter and this book as a key reference point to what carbon neutral production might mean for cinema.

2. J. R. McNeill, *Something New Under the Sun: An Environmental History of the Twentieth Century World* (New York: W.W. Norton, 2001), 52.

3. For a refresher in or introduction to the basic and essential mechanics of how images are captured, see James Monaco's chapter 2, "Technology: Image and Sound," in his *How to Read a Film: Movies, Media and Beyond Fourth Edition* (Oxford: Oxford University Press 2009).

4. William J. Mitchell, *The Reconfigured Eye: Visual Truth in the Post-Photographic Era* (Cambridge, Mass.: The MIT Press, 1992), 4–5.

5. See ibid., chapter 6, "Virtual Cameras."

6. David Rodowick, *The Virtual Life of Film* (New York: Oxford University Press, 2007), 9.

7. Leo Enticknap, *Moving Image Technology: From Zoetrope to Digital* (Brighton: Wallflower, 2005), 203.

8. Mitchell, *The Reconfigured Eye*, 24.

9. Alfred Crosby, *Children of the Sun: A History of Humanity's Unappeasable Appetite for Energy*, (New York: W. W. Norton, 2006), 159.

10. Timothy Morton, *Ecology without Nature: Rethinking Environmental Aesthetics* (Cambridge, Mass.: Harvard University Press, 2007), 1.

11. Zygmunt Bauman, *Liquid Life* (Cambridge: Polity, 2005), 96.

12. Ibid.

13. Ibid.

14. André Bazin, *What is Cinema? Vol. 1*, trans. Hugh Grey (Berkeley: University of California Press, 1967), 21.

15. Paul Virilio, *The Art of the Motor*, trans. Julie Rose (Minneapolis: University of Minnesota Press, 1995), 67.

16. Ibid.,105.

17. Bazin, *What is Cinema?*, 10.

18. Paolo Cherchi Usai, *The Death of Cinema: History, Cultural Memory and the Digital Dark Age* (London: British Film Institute, 2001), 23.

19. Lev Manovich, *Language of New Media* (Cambridge, Mass.: The MIT Press, 2001), 47.

20. Dziga Vertov, *Kino-Eye: The Writings of Dziga Vertov*, ed. Annette Michelson, trans. Kevin O'Brian (Berkeley: University of California Press, 1983), 17.

21. Andre Habib, "Ruin, Archive, and the Time of Cinema: Peter Delpeut's Lyrical Nitrate," *SubStance* 110 (2006): 126.

22. Alan Weisman, *The World Without Us* (New York: Harper Collins, 2007), 247.

23. Ibid., 248.

24. Enticknap, *Moving Image Technology*, 231.

25. Jon Mooallem, "Raiders of the Lost R2: Excavating a Galaxy Far, Far Away," *Harpers*, March 2009.

26. Felder et al., "Green Practices Manual." Felder's guide outlines key sources of waste that result from large-scale productions (crews of one hundred or more). Because filmmaking is so energy-dense and interacts with numerous other industries (food service, transportation, construction), there is a host of negligent behaviors to cite, but a sore spot is the ubiquitous disposable drink container outlined on the guide's page 48.

27. Enticknap, *Moving Image Technology*, 1.

28. Mooallem, "Raiders of the Lost R2," 63.

29. Paolo Cherchi Usai, *Silent Cinema: An Introduction* (London: British Film Institute, 2000), 161.

30. David Bruce, *Sun Pictures: The Hill-Adamson Calotypes* (Greenwich, Conn.: New York Graphic Society, 1974), 5.

31. For descriptions of Talbot's career and methods throughout the chapter, see Larry J. Schaaf, *William Henry Fox Talbot: Photographs from the J. Paul Getty Museum*, ed. Weston Naef (Los Angeles: The J. Paul Getty Museum, 2002), 8.

32. Crosby, *Children of the Sun*, xv.

33. Ibid,, 61–63.

34. Enticknap, *Moving Image Technology*, 10.

35. Charles Musser, *Thomas Edison and His Kinetographic Motion Pictures* (New Brunswick, N.J.: Rutgers University Press, 1997), 14.

36. Enticknap, *Moving Image Technology*, 39.

37. Kristin Bordwell and David Thompson, *Film History: An Introduction* (New York: McGraw Hill, 2003), 42–43.

38. Zelda Cini and Bob Crane, *Hollywood: Land and Legend* (Westport, Conn.: Arlington House, 1980), 63.

39. For discussion of arc lighting see Richard Koszarski, *An Evening's Entertainment: The Age of the Silent Feature Picture 1915–1928. History of the American Cinema vol. 3*

(New York: Scribner, 1990). On arc lighting developments in dark studios, 150–54; 18–19 for discussion of lighting stage sets.

40. Wolfgang Schivelbusch, *Disenchanted Night: The Industrialization of Light in the Nineteenth Century*, trans. Angela Davies (Berkeley: University of California Press, 1988), 78.

41. Georges Bataille, *The Accursed Share, Vol. I: Consumption.*, trans. Robert Hurley (New York: Zone Books, 1988), 28–29.

42. Paul Roberts, *End Of Oil: On the Edge of a Perilous New World* (New York: Houghton Mifflin, 2005), 193.

43. Paul Virilio, *Aesthetics of Disappearance*, trans. Philip Beitchman (Paris: Semitext(e), 1991), 54.

44. Schivelbusch, *Disenchanted Night*, 7–8.

45. See John Alton's *Painting with Light* (Berkeley: University of California Press, 1995).

46. Manovich, *Language of New Media*, 25.

47. Thomas Elsaesser, "Early Film History and Multi-Media: An Archeology of Possible Futures?" *New Media, Old Media: A History and Theory Reader*, eds. Wendy Hui Kyong and Thomas Keenan (New York: Routledge, 2006). Similar continuity between cinema and Impressionism has been theorized by Jacques Aumont in *The Image* (London: British Film Institute, 1998) and Jonathan Crary, *Suspensions of Perception* (Cambridge, Mass.: The MIT Press, 1998).

48. Robert Hughes, *Shock of the New* (London: Thames and Hudson, 1991), 118.

49. Ibid., 124.

50. Ibid., 18.

51. Ibid.

52. Roland Barthes, *Camera Lucida: Reflections on Photography*, trans. Richard Howard (New York: Hill and Wang, 1981), 119.

53. Richard Humphries, *Futurism* (London: Tate Gallery, 1999), 20.

54. Christine Poggi, *Inventing Futurism: The Art and Politics of Artificial Optimism* (Princeton, N.J.: Princeton University Press, 2009), 110–11.

55. Umbro Appolonio, *Futurist Manifestos* (London: Thames and Hudson, 1973), 19.

56. Anson Rabinbach, *The Human Motor: Energy, Fatigue and the Origins of Modernity* (New York: Basic Books, 1990), 87.

57. Schivelbusch, *Disenchanted Night*, 221.

58. Bazin, *What is Cinema?*, 12.

59. Noël Burch, *Life to those Shadows*, ed. trans. Ben Brewster (Berkeley: University of California Press, 1990), 2–3.

60. See Gilles Deleuze and Felix Guattari's "1227: Treatise on Nomadology:—The War Machine," in their *A Thousand Plateaus: Capitalism and Schizophrenia*, trans. Brian Massumi (Minneapolis: University of Minnesota Press, 1987), 351–423.

61. See Dudley Andrew "Roots of the Nomadic." Nomadology, as Andrew points out, is increasingly relevant in the wake of independent video production and trans-

national distribution networks (digital video and open access cinema, by extension). The concept is taken up in discussion of Zacharias Kunuk's *The Fast Runner* in this book's conclusion.

62. Akira Mizuta Lippit, *Atomic Light (Shadow Optics)* (Minneapolis: University of Minnesota Press, 2005), 65.

63. Chris Marker, *La Jetée: Ciné-roman* (New York: Zone Books, 1992), 17–18.

64. Enticknap, *Moving Image Technology*, 6.

65. Bordwell and Thompson, *Film History: An Introduction*, 2–3.

66. Timothy Corrigan, "Immediate History: Videotape Interventions and Narrative Film," in *The Image in Dispute: Art and Cinema in the Age of Photography*, ed. Dudley Andrew (Austin: University of Texas Press, 1997), 309–331.

67. Timothy Corrigan, *A Cinema without Walls* (New Brunswick, N.J.: Rutgers University Press, 1993).

68. Virilio, *Aesthetics of Disappearance*, 107.

69. Ibid., 57.

70. Lars von Trier and Thomas Vinterberg, "Dogme 95 Vow of Chastity," in *Technology and Culture: The Film Reader*, ed. Andrew Utterson (New York: Routledge, 2005), 87.

71. Hamid Naficy, "Situating Accented Cinema," in *Transnational Cinema: The Film Reader*, eds. Elizabeth Ezra and Terry Rowden (New York: Routledge, 2006), 124.

72. Elizabeth Ezra, "What is Transnational Cinema?" in *Transnational Cinema*, eds. Elizabeth Ezra and Terry Rowden, 6.

73. Corrigan, "Immediate History," 319.

CHAPTER 2 — RESOURCE

1. David Harvey, *The New Imperialism* (New York: Oxford University Press, 2005), 25.

2. Paul Virilio, *War and Cinema: The Logistics of Perception*, trans. Patrick Camiller (London: Verso, 1989), 7.

3. Jay Leyda, *Kino: A History of the Russian and Soviet Film* (New York: Collier, 1973), 148.

4. Bruce F. Kawin and Gerald Mast, *A Short History of the Movies* (New York: Macmillan, 1992), 158.

5. Ibid., 160.

6. Kristin Deasy, "Backers of Baghdad Film Production Center Seek Iraqi Cinema Revival," Radio Free Europe, September 29, 2010, available at http://www.rferl.org/content/Iraq_Cinema_Revival_New_Film_Production_Center_Baghdad/2169628.html, accessed October 6, 2010.

7. Giles Slade, *Made to Break: Technology and Obsolescence in America* (Cambridge, Mass.: Harvard University Press, 2006), 278.

8. See David Rodowick, *Reading the Figural, or, Philosophy after the New Media* (Durham, N.C.: Duke University Press, 2001).

9. David Rodowick, *The Virtual Life of Film* (Cambridge, Mass: Harvard University Press, 2007), 9. See Rodowick's arguments throughout; his clear insights into grasping the material difference between digital and analog underlie his inquiry into how the radical transformation of how and where we interact with "cinema" might render the discipline of cinema studies an anachronism.

10. Megan Boler, ed., *Digital Media and Democracy: Tactics in Hard Times*, (Cambridge, Mass: MIT Press, 2008), 25.

11. Charles Musser, "Truth and Documentary in the Age of George W. Bush," lecture presented at Centre for American Studies Lecture Series. University of Toronto, November 10, 2006.

12. See Vance Packard, *The Waste Makers* (New York: Pocket Books, 1963).

13. Slade, *Made to Break*, 4.

14. Howard Besser, "Digital Preservation of Moving Image Material?" *The Moving Image*, Fall 2001. Available at http://besser.tsoa.nyu.edu/howard/Papers/amia-longevity.html, accessed March 1, 2007.

15. Ibid.

16. Daniel Rombes, *Cinema in the Digital Age* (Brighton: Wallflower Press, 2009), 24.

17. Susan Sontag discourses on this point, first introduced in *On Photography*, throughout her *Regarding the Pain of Others* (New York: Picador, 2003).

18. Chalmers Johnson, *The Sorrows of Empire: Militarism, Secrecy and the End of the Republic* (New York: Henry Holt, 2004), 22.

19. Ibid., 151–152.

20. Phillipe LeBillon, "Political Ecology of Resource Wars: Natural Resources and Armed Conflicts," *Political Geography* 20 (2001): 564.

21. See Cleo Paskal, *Global Warring* (Toronto: Key Porter Books, 2010).

22. LeBillon, "Political Ecology of Resource Wars." For discussion of the semiotics of resources see 564; for specific examples, including "natural" and "unnatural" resources, see 565.

23. Ibid., 565.

24. Paul Virilio, *Desert Screen: War at the Speed of Light*, trans. Michael Degener (London, Continuum, 2002), 44.

25. See Jean Baudrillard, *The Gulf War Did Not Take Place*, trans. Paul Patton (Bloomington: University of Indiana Press, 1995).

26. Henry Giroux, *Beyond the Spectacle of Terrorism: Global Uncertainty and the Challenge of the New Media* (Boulder, Colo.: Paradigm, 2006), 51.

27. Tom Bissell, "Hidden Mainstream," *Harper's*, December 2006, 75.

28. Virilio, *Desert Screen*, 131.

29. For a sobering discussion of how technological innovation is never more than a repurposing of what came before, see Jay David Bolter and Richard Grusin, *Remediation: Understanding New Media* (Cambridge, Mass: The MIT Press, 1999).

30. The energy costs of Google's vast data processing centers might be the real reason

behind the establishment of Google Energy, the search engine's subsidiary which in 2010 began significant financial investment in clean power initiatives, wind power most notably. The company's numerous centers are located around the globe strategically placed in proximity to inexpensive and abundant power sources. The complexes themselves and the energy they consume further testifies to the fact that the Internet is neither ethereal or green, but a massive power-hungry industry. See Ginger Strand, "Keyword: Evil," *Harper's*, March 2008.

31. Paul Virilio, *The Art of the Motor*, trans. Julie Rose (Minneapolis: University of Minnesota Press, 1995), 140.

32. Jonathan Sterne, "Out with the Trash: On the Future of New Media," in Charles Acland, ed., *Residual Media*, 17.

33. Walter Benjamin, "The Storyteller," in *Illuminations*, ed. Hannah Arendt, trans. Harry Zohn (New York: Schocken Books, 1968), 90.

34. Benjamin, "The Storyteller," 84.

35. Johnson, *The Sorrows of Empire*, 100.

36. Harvey, *The New Imperialism*, 24.

37. See "Introduction: Rhizome" in Gilles Deleuze and Felix Guattari, *A Thousand Plateaus: Capitalism and Schizophrenia*, trans. Brian Massumi (Minneapolis: University of Minnesota Press, 1987), 3–35.

38. Timothy Murray, *Digital Baroque: New Media Art and Cinematic Folds* (Minneapolis: University of Minnesota Press, 2008), 5–6.

39. Patricia Zimmerman, *States of Emergency: Documentaries, Wars, Democracies* (Minneapolis: University of Minnesota Press, 2000), 172.

40. Anna McCarthy, *Ambient Television: Visual Culture and Public Space* (Durham, N.C.: Duke University Press, 2001), 4.

41. Bill Nichols, "The Work of Culture in the Age of Cybernetic Systems," *Electronic Culture: Technology and Visual Representation*, ed. Timothy Druckrey (New York: Aperture, 1996), 123–43.

42. Nicholas, Mirozeff, *Watching Babylon: The War in Iraq and Global Visual Culture* (New York: Routledge, 2005), 67.

43. Mike Davis, *Buda's Wagon: A Brief History of the Car Bomb* (London: Verso, 2007), 5.

44. Ibid., 6.

CHAPTER 3 — EXTRACTION

1. Telephone interview with Jennifer Baichwal, conducted in September 2008.

2. Derek Bousé, "Computer Generated Images: Wildlife and Nature Films," in *Image Ethics in the Digital Age*, ed. Larry Gross, John Stuart Katz, and Jay Ruby (Minneapolis: University of Minnesota Press, 2003), 227.

3. See the concept discussed throughout Timothy Morton's *Ecology without Nature: Rethinking Environmental Aesthetics* (Cambridge, Mass.: Harvard University Press, 2007).

4. Kenneth Baker, "Form Versus Portent: Edward Burtynsky's Endangered Landscapes," in *Manufactured Landscapes: The Photographs of Edward Burtynsky*, ed. Lori Pauli (Ottawa: National Gallery of Canada, 2005), 45.

5. See Carolyn Merchant, "Reinventing Eden: Western Culture as Recovery Narrative," in *Uncommon Ground: Rethinking the Human Place in Nature*, ed. William Cronin (New York: W. W. Norton, 1996), 132–159.

6. Rebecca Solnit, *River of Shadows: Eadweard Muybridge and the Technological West*,
(New York: Penguin, 2003), 22–23.

7. Lewis Mumford, *The City in History: Its Origins, Its Transformations, and Its Prospects* (New York: Harcourt Brace Jovanovich, 1961), 451.

8. Barbara Novak, *Nature and Culture: American Landscape and Painting 1825–1875*
(New York: Oxford University Press, 1980), 167. For a full discussion of "technological sublime," see the originating source, Leo Marx, *The Machine in the Garden: Technology and the Pastoral Ideal in America* (New York: Oxford University Press, 1964).

9. For discussion of photographic processing and the direct impact on the natural world see Solnit, *River of Shadows*, 14; for Muybridge and the use of photography post-Civil War see 42.

10. Dean MacCannell, *Empty Meeting Grounds: The Tourist Papers* (New York: Routledge, 1992), 115.

11. Ibid.

12. Novak, *Nature and Culture*, 172.

13. Ibid.

14. Dziga Vertov, *Kino-Eye: The Writings of Dziga Vertov*, ed. Annette Michelson, trans. Kevin O'Brian (Berkeley: University of California Press, 1983), 19.

15. Ibid., 19.

16. Frederic Jameson, "Cognitive Mapping," in *Marxism and the Interpretation of Culture*, eds. Lawrence Grossberg and Cary Nelson (Urbana: University of Illinois Press, 1988), 349–350.

17. Gilles Deleuze and Felix Guattari, *A Thousand Plateaus*, trans. Brain Massumi (Minneapolis: University of Minnesota Press, 1983), 381.

18. Lori Pauli, "Seeing the Big Picture" in *Manufactured Landscapes: The Photographs of Edward Burtynsky*, ed. Lori Pauli (Ottawa: National Gallery of Canada, 2005), 13.

19. Solnit, *River of Shadows*, 43.

20. Timothy Corrigan, "Immediate History: Videotape Interventions in Narrative Film" in *The Image in Dispute: Art and Cinema in the Age of Photography*, ed. Dudley Andrew (Austin: University of Texas Press, 1997), 111 and Lev Manovich, *The Language of New Media* (Cambridge, Mass.: The MIT Press, 2001), 333.

21. For an overview of how the editing and processing of celluloid is inherently more deleterious than digital variants see the "Post-Production" section of Green Screen Toronto's 2009 Green Practices Manual. Chemicals used in the manufacture and processing of film are cited, as well as the significant amount of unwanted film

that is discarded after editing. Available at http://www.greenscreentoronto.com/
green_practices/1/?p=1&sf=title&sd=asc, accessed November 10, 2010.

22. John Bellamy Foster, *Ecology Against Capitalism* (New York: Monthly Review Press, 2002), 92.

23. Nicholas Rombes, *Cinema in the Digital Age* (Brighton: Wallflower Press, 2006), 23–24. As this is a commonplace line of inquiry, David Rodowick moves the question ahead and asks what the future will tell for cinema studies as digitization absorbs it—cinema—bit by byte. See *The Virtual Life of Film* (New York: Oxford University Press, 2007).

24. David Harvey, *The Condition of Postmodernity: An Inquiry into the Origins of Cultural Change* (Oxford: Blackwell, 1990). See in particular chapter 17, "Time-Space Compression and the Postmodern Condition," 285–367.

25. Dudley Andrew, *What Cinema Is!: Bazin's Quest and Its Charge* (West Sussex: Wiley-Blackwell, 2010), 58.

26. Lev Manovich, *The Language of New Media*, 144.

27. Ibid., 310.

28. Rombes, *Cinema in the Digital Age*, 38–40.

29. Meanwhile, the seismic shift in narrative and storytelling that digital technology has launched really belongs to the gaming industry—another vast area of exploration for media ecology.

30. Henri Lefebvre, *The Production of Space* (Cambridge, Mass.: Blackwell, 1974).

31. Mumford, *The City in History*, 451.

32. Ibid., 450.

33. Jay Edward Epstein, *The Big Picture: The New Logic of Money and Power in Hollywood* (New York: Random House, 2005), 7.

34. Richard Koszarki, *An Evening's Entertainment: The Age of the Silent Feature Picture 1915–1928. History of the American Cinema, Vol. 3* (New York: Scribner, 1990), 153.

35. For a thorough discussion of the politics and principles of cinema's global dissemination see Toby Miller, Nitin Govil, John McMurria, and Richard Maxwell, *Global Hollywood* (London: British Film Institute, 2001); for questions of how moviegoing as a practice is shaped by the global integration of commercial cinema see Charles Acland, *Screen Traffic: Movies, Multiplexes and Global Culture* (Durham, N.C.: Duke University Press, 2003).

36. Harvey, *The Condition of Postmodernity*, 159.

37. See the Prologue to Manovich's *Language of New Media*, which uses *Man with a Movie Camera* as a guide to understanding digital communications technology and its new linguistic and aesthetic conditions. Here, in "Vertov's Dataset," Manovich separates out the layers of Vertov's filmmaking practice, paralleling each to a principle of new media.

38. Bousé, "Computer Generated Images," 226–229.

39. Barbara Klinger, *Beyond the Multiplex: Cinema, New Technologies and the Home* (Berkeley: University of California Press, 2006), 9.

40. Michael Hardt and Antonio Negri, *Empire* (Cambridge, Mass.: Harvard University Press, 2001), 221.

41. Ibid.

42. Susan Sontag, *On Photography* (New York: Farrar, Strauss and Giroux, 1973), 179.

43. Hardt and Negri, *Empire*, 227.

44. Ibid., 226.

45. One wonders how Dekovic might respond to the massive televisual ruin that comes with the shift to HD and 3D television, the replacement of plasma units with the LCD, and the global transition from analog broadcasting to digital dissemination.

46. Lisa Parks, "Falling Apart: Electronics Salvaging and the Global Media Economy," in *Residual Media*, ed. Charles Acland (Minneapolis: University of Minnesota Press, 2003), 32–33.

47. Gay Hawkins, *The Ethics of Waste: How We Relate to Rubbish* (Oxford: Rowman and Littlefield, 2006), 24–25.

48. Sontag, *On Photography*, 80.

49. Klinger, *Beyond the Multiplex*, 66.

50. Haidee Wasson, *Museum Movies: The Museum of Modern Art and the Birth of Art Cinema* (Berkeley: University of California Press, 2005), 18.

51. Paolo Cherchi Usai, *Silent Cinema: An Introduction* (London: British Film Institute, 2000), 12.

52. Gay Hawkins, "Sad Chairs," in John Knechtel, ed., *Trash* (Cambridge, Mass.: MIT Press, 2006), 55–56.

53. Ibid.

54. Jonathan Sterne, "Out with the Trash: On the Futire of New Media," in Charles Acland, ed., *Residual Media*, 17.

55. Barry Allen, "The Ethical Artifact: On Trash," in John Knetchel, ed., *Trash*, 198.

56. Susan Strasser, *Waste and Want: A Social History of Trash* (New York: Henry Holt, 1999), 9.

57. With the ascendancy of video games comes an equivalent amount of critical theory. As a starting point into the brave new intersection between cinema and the business of gaming, see Robert Alan Brookey, *Hollywood Gamers: Digital Convergence in the Film and Video Game Industries* (Bloomington: University of Indiana Press, 2010).

CHAPTER 4 — EXCESS

1. Barry Salt, *Film History and Technology: History and Analysis* (London: Starword, 1992), 321.

2. Nicholas Rombes, *Cinema in the Digital Age* (Brighton: Wallflower Press, 2009), 38–40.

3. See Brian Henderson, "The Long Take," in Bill Nichols, ed., *Movies and Methods: An Anthology* (Berkeley: University of California Press, 1976), and Bordwell and Thompson, *Film Art: An Introduction* (New York: McGraw-Hill, 2004), 284–291.

4. Canonical theorists of cinema, including Bazin, Rudolph Arnheim, Lev Kuleshov, and Dziga Vertov, have been cited as having anticipated what we now call digital cinema either in terms of spatialization, editing techniques, or lack thereof. See, for example, John Andrew Berton's "Film Theory for the Digital World," *Leonardo*, vol. 3, 1990, 5–11.

5. André Bazin, *What is Cinema? Vol. One*, trans. Hugh Grey (Berkeley: University of California Press, 1967), 35–36.

6. Kristen Thompson, "The Concept of Cinematic Excess," in *Film Theory and Criticism*, eds. Leo Braudy and Marshall Cohen (New York: Oxford University Press, 2004), 518.

7. Ibid., 514.

8. Richard Taylor, *The Politics of the Soviet Cinema 1917–1929* (Cambridge: Cambridge University Press, 1967), 63.

9. Georges Bataille, *The Accursed Share: An Essay on General Economy, vol. 1*, Consumption, trans. Robert Hurley (New York: Zone Books, 1988), 23–25.

10. L. W. Jelinski et al., "Industrial Ecology: Concepts and Approaches," in *Proceedings of the National Academy of Science* vol. 89, February 1992, 793.

11. Ibid.

12. Susan Strasser, *Waste and Want: A Social History of Trash* (New York: Henry Holt, 1999), 291.

13. Bataille, *The Accursed Share*, 35–37.

14. Jonathan Sterne, "Out with the Trash: On the Future of New Media," in *Residual Media*, eg. Charles Acland (Minneapolis: University of Minnesota Press, 2007), 30.

15. See Thorsten Veblen's section "Conspicuous Consumption" in his *Theory of the Leisure Class: An Economic Study of Institutions* (New York: Viking Press, 1931), 91–110.

16. Kristen Whissel, *Picturing American Modernity: Traffic, Technology, and the Silent Cinema* (Durham, N.C.: Duke University Press, 2008), 124–125.

17. The contradictory impulse is discussed throughout Len Marx's seminal *Machine in the Garden: Technology and the Pastoral Ideal in America* (New York: Oxford University Press, 2000).

18. See Brian Henderson's discussions of style and aesthetics, for example, in "The Long Take," 313–24.

19. David Bordwell and Kristen Thompson, *Film History: An Introduction* (New York: McGraw-Hill, 2003), 284–285.

20. Private conversation with Charles Musser, Toronto, November 10, 2008.

21. For an array of perspectives on sound technology's impact on film history, see *Film Sound: Theory and Practice*, ed. Elizabeth Weis and John Belton (New York: Columbia University Press, 1985).

22. John Belton, "Glorious Technicolor, Breathtaking CinemaScope, and Stereophonic Sound," ed. Tino Balio, *Hollywood in the Age of Television* (Boston: Unwin Hyman, 1990), 185–211. Belton's essay provides a through overview of the resources that were invested in expanding the cinema physically—on and offscreen—in the 1950s and 1960s in America. Written at a moment when VRC technology was again threatening to undercut the film industry, Belton points out the recurrence of cinema's certain death and its ability to recuperate from such pronouncement.

23. Louis Giannetti and Scott Eyman, *Flashback: A Brief History of Film* (Englewood Cliffs, N.J.: Prentice Hall, 2001), 320.

24. See Peter Ward, *A History of Domestic Space* (Vancouver: University of British Columbia Press, 1999) and Gwendolyn Wright, *Building the Dream* (Cambridge, Mass.: The MIT press, 1988).

25. Richard.Taylor, *The Politics of the Soviet Cinema*, 29.

26. On entropy see Tony Rayns, "Death at Work: Evolution and Entropy in Factory Films" in *Andy Warhold: Film Factory*, ed., Michael O'Pray (London: British Film Institute, 1989), 160–66.

27. Paul Monaco, *The Sixties: 1960–1969, vol. 8, History of the American Cinema* (Berkeley: University of California Press, 2000). For truncated shot lengths see 87; on rapid editing and the work of Sam Peckinpah, see 101.

28. The most comprehensive example of this running discourse is Paul Virilio's *Aesthetic of Disappearance*, trans. Philip Beitchman (Paris: Semiotext(e), 1991).

29. Leo Enticknap, *Moving Image Technology: From Zoetrope to Digital* (Brighton: Wallflower, 2005), 38–39.

30. Eric Barnouw, *Documentary: A History of Non-Fiction Film* (Oxford: Oxford University Press, 1974), 286–287.

31. Bataille, *The Accursed Share*, 119.

32. Deyan Sudjic, *The Edifice Complex* (New York: Penguin, 2005), 358.

33. Bataille, *The Accursed Share*, 132.

34. Carol Willis, *Form Follows Finance: Skyscrapers and Skylines in New York and Chicago* (New York: Princeton Achitectural Press, 1995), 90.

35. Neal Bascomb, *Higher: A Historic Race to the Sky and the Making of a City* (New York: Doubleday, 2003), 8.

36. Bataille, *The Accursed Share*, 33.

37. Ibid., 28–29.

38. Danni Zuvela, "Talking About Seeing, A Conversation with James Benning," *Senses of Cinema*, www.sensesofcinema.com/2004/33/james_benning/, last accessed November 6, 2008.

39. See Michael Ned Holtde's review of Ruhr, "Digital Watch," in *Art Forum*, January 6, 2010, available at http://artforum.com/film/id=24610, last accessed March 12, 2011.

40. For a view of Ruhr as an ebbing industrial center, see *Winners and Losers* (2006), a documentary by Ulrike Franke and Michael Loeke. The narrative depicts how the mighty Kaiserstuhl coke factory in the Ruhr Valley, closed down in 2000, was in 2003

resurrected by four hundred Chinese laborers who descended on the abandoned facility. The factory was dismantled and shipped to China where it was reassembled and put into production.

41. Holtde, "Digital Watch."

42. David Harvey, *The Condition of Postmodernity: An Inquiry into the Conditions of Cultural Change* (Cambridge: Blackwell, 1990), 240.

43. In an interview with Michael Guillen, "Darkest Americana: Ruhr," in Twitch Film, March 2, 2010. Available at http://twitchfilm.net/interviews/2010/03/darkest-americana-elsewhere-ruhr-a-few-questions-for-james-benning.php, accessed November 2, 2010.

44. Rayns, "Death at Work," 164.

45. See Eric Barnouw's chapter five, in *Documentary*, "Sharp Focus," which contains a detailed discussion of observational cinema in America, Europe, and elsewhere in the 1960s and 1970s.

46. Monaco, *The Sixties*, 209.

47. Anson Rabinbach, *The Human Motor: Energy, Fatigue and the Origins of Modernity* (New York: Basic Books, 1990), 90.

48. Bazin, *What is Cinema?* 36.

49. Dziga Vertov, *Kino-Eye: The Writings of Dziga Vertov*, ed. Annette Michelson, trans. Kevin O'Brian (Berkeley: University of California Press, 1983, 17.

50. Thomas Levin, "Rhetoric of the Temporal Index: Surveillant Narration and the Cinema of "Real Time," in *CTRL[SPACE]: Rhetorics of Surveillance from Bentham to Big Brother*, eds. Thomas Y. Levin, et al. (Karlsruhe, Germany: ZKM Center for Art and Media and Cambridge, Mass.: The MIT Press, 2002), 593.

51. Lev Manovich, *Language of New Media*, 134.

52. Greg Kennedy, *An Ontology of Trash: The Disposable and Its Problematic Nature* (Albany: State University of New York Press, 2007), 83–85.

53. David Rodowick, *The Virtual Life of Film* (New York: Oxford University Press, 2007), 173.

54. Jay David Bolter and Richard Grusin, *Remediation: Understanding New Media* (Cambridge, Mass.: The MIT Press, 1999), 5.

55. Timothy Murray, *Digital Baroque: New Media Art and Cinematic Folds* (Minneapolis: University of Minnesota Press, 2008), 6.

56. See Tom Standage, *The Victorian Internet: the Remarkable Story of the Telegraph and the Nineteenth Century's On-line Producers* (New York: Berkeley Books, 1998).

57. Ronald Deibert and Rafal Rohozinski, "Beyond Denial: Introducing Next-Generation Information Access Controls," in Ronald Deibert et al., eds., *Access Controlled: The Shaping of Power, Rights, and Rule in Cyberspace* (Cambridge, Mass.: The MIT Press, 2010), 3–4.

58. Paul Virilio, *Vision Machine*, trans. Julie Rose (Bloomington: Indiana University Press, 1994), 75.

59. See Nicholas Rombes's brief discussion, *Cinema in the Digital Age*, 38.

60. Paolo Cherchi Usai, *The Death of Cinema: History Cultural Memory and the Digital Dark Age* (London: British Film Institute, 2001), 93–94.

61. Patricia Zimmerman, "The Home Movie Movement: Excavations, Artifacts, Minings," in Karen L. Ishizuka and Patricia Zimmerman, eds., *Mining Home Movies: Excavations in Histories and Memories* (Berkeley: University of California Press, 2008), 18–19.

62. Enticknap, *Moving Image Technology*, 178.

63. Hille Koselka, "Cam Era—The Contemporary Urban Panopticon," *Surveillance & Society* 1 (3) 2003: 304, accessed April 10, 2008, http://www.surveillance-and-society.org,

64. Ibid., 304.

65. Ibid., 306.

66. Markey's comments were widely reported. One such example is available at http://www.energyboom.com/policy/live-webcam-feed-underwater-oil-spill-go-tonight, last accessed October 26, 2010.

67. Mary Douglas, *Purity and Danger* (London: Routledge and Keagan Paul, 1966), 35.

CHAPTER 5 — WASTE

1. Gay Hawkins, *The Ethics of Waste: How We Relate to Rubbish* (Lanham, Md.: Rowman and Littlefield, 2006), 4–5.

2. Mary Douglas, *Purity and Danger: An Analysis of Concepts of Pollution and Taboo* (New York: Routledge, 1966), 2.

3. Susan Strasser, *Waste and Want: A Social History of Trash* (New York: Henry Holt, 1999), 9.

4. Jennifer Gabrys, "Media in the Dump," in *Trash*, ed. John Knechtel (Cambridge, Mass.: The MIT Press, 2006), 163.

5. For figures and policy see Giles Slade's thorough account of the geopolitics of e-waste management in his chapter 6, "Cell Phones and E Waste," *Made to Break: Technology and Obsolescence in America* (Cambridge Mass.: Harvard University Press, 2006).

6. See the concept used throughout Jennifer Gabrys, "Media in the Dump," 156–65.

7. Jonathan Sterne, "Out with the Trash," in *Residual Media*, ed. Charles Acland (Minneapolis: University of Minnesota Press, 2007), 19–20.

8. Susan Sontag, *On Photography*, 180; Sontag responds to her earlier call for restraint in *Regarding the Pain of Others* (New York: Farrar, Straus & Giroux, 2003), 104–06.

9. Zygmunt Bauman, *Wasted Lives: Modernity and its Outcasts* (Cambridge: Polity, 2004). 22.

10. Lisa Rochon, "Streets of Trash," in *Trash*, ed. John Knetchel, 25.

11. Heather Rogers, "Message in a Bottle," in *Trash*, ed. John Knetchel, 114–15.

12. Hervé Fischer, *Decline of the Hollywood Empire*, trans. Rhonda Mullins (Vancouver: Talon, 2004), 61.

13. Robert E. Davis, "The Instantaneous Worldwide Release: Coming Soon to Everyone, Everywhere," in *Transnational Cinema, The Film Reader*, eds. Elizabeth Ezra and Terry Rowden (New York: Routledge, 2006), 76–77.

14. Charles Acland, *Screen Traffic: Movies, Multiplexes, and Global Culture* (Durham, N.C.: Duke University Press, 2003), 151.

15. Barbara Klinger, *Beyond the Multiplex: New Technologies and the Home* (Berkeley: University of California Press, 2006), 63.

16. Timothy Corrigan, *Cinema Without Walls: Movies and Culture After Vietnam* (New Brunswick, N.J.: Rutgers University Press, 1991), 5–6.

17. Heather Rogers, *Gone Tomorrow: The Hidden Life of Garbage* (New York: The New Press, 2005), 118.

18. Davis, "The Instantaneous Worldwide Release," 76.

19. Will Straw, "Embedded Memories," in *Residual Media*, ed. Charles Acland (Minneapolis: University of Minnesota Press, 2007), 3.

20. M. M. Bakhtin, "The Problems of Speech Genres," in *Speech Genres and Other Late Essays*, trans. Vern W. McGee, eds. Caryl Emerson and Michael Holquist (Austin: University of Texas Press, 1986) 75.

21. Ibid., 89.

22. For detailed discussion of the history of compilation films, see Jay Leyda, *Films Beget Films* (London: George Allen and Unwin, 1964); concerns of found footage are discussed in depth in William C. Wees, *Recycled Images: The Art and Politics of Found Footage Films* (New York: Anthology Film Archives,1993).

23. This fluid and well-traveled concept, defined by its inherent resistance to definition, unfolds throughout Gilles Deleuze and Felix Guattari's "1227: Treatise on Nomadology:—The War Machine," in their *A Thousand Plateaus: Capitalism and Schizophrenia*, trans. Brian Massumi (Minneapolis: University of Minnesota Press, 1987), 351–423.

24. See Melissa Felder et al., "Green Practices Manual: Environmental Options for the Film-Based Industries," Green Screen Toronto, 2009, available at http://greenscreen-toronto.com/green_practices/, accessed November 1, 2010. Felder targets the waste generated by disposable water bottles at several points in the manual. A large-scale production crew of 100 can save 10,000 dollars and 60,000 disposable bottles over two months just by converting to re-useable vessels.

25. Strasser, *Waste and Want*, 109.

26. For the cultural and economic dimensions of recycling see Susan Strasser, *Waste and Want*; Gay Hawkins's chapter 5, "Empty Bottles," in *Ethics of Waste*; as well as William Rathje and Cullen Murphy, *Rubbish: The Archeology of Garbage* (New York: Harper Collins, 1992).

27. David Binkley, "Refiguring Culture," in *Future Visison: New Technologies of the Screen*, eds. Patricia Hayward and Teresa Wollen (London: British Film Institute, 1993), 96.

28. Jonathan Sterne, "Out with the Trash," 29.

29. Paolo Cherchi Usai, *The Death of Cinema: History, Cultural Memory and the Digital Dark Age* (London: British Film Institute, 2001), 67.

30. Sontag, *On Photography*, 180.

31. Ibid., 179.

32. Megan Boler, "Introduction," in *Digital Media and Democracy: Tactics in Hard Times* ed. Megan Boler (Cambridge, Mass.: The MIT Press, 2008), 7.

33. Ronald J. Deibert, "Cyberspace Confidential," *Globe and Mail*, August 6, 2010.

34. Sontag, *On Photography*, 55.

35. Ibid.

36. Michel Foucault, *Society Must be Defended: Lectures at the Collège de France, 1975–1976*, trans. David Macey (New York: Picador, 2003), 241.

37. Bauman, *Wasted Lives*, 6.

38. Stuart J. Murray, "Thanatopolitcs: Reading in Agamben a Rejoiner to Biopolitcal Life," *Communication and Critical/Cultural Studies* 5:2 (June 2008), 204–05.

39. Michael Hardt and Antonio Negri, *Empire* (Cambridge Mass.: Harvard University Press, 2000), 23.

40. See Henry Giroux, *Stormy Weather: Katrina and the Politics of Disposability* (Boulder and London: Paradigm, 2006).

41. Sontag, *Regarding the Pain of Others*, 63.

42. Cherchi Usai, *The Death of Cinema*, 111.

43. Klinger, *Beyond the Multiplex*, 91.

44. Patricia Zimmerman, "Introduction: The Home Movie Movement: Excavations, Artifacts, Minings," in Patricia Zimmerman and Karen L. Ishizuka, eds. *Mining Home Movies: Excavations in Histories and Memories* (Berkeley: University of California Press, 2008), 11.

45. Ibid., 117.

46. Zimmerman, *Mining Home Movies*, 11.

47. Gideon Lewis-Kraus, "A World in Three Aisles: Browsing the Post-Digital Library,"
Harper's, May 2007.

48. Roland Barthes, *Camera Lucida*, trans. Richard Howard (New York, Hill and Wang, 1981), 146.

49. Heather Rogers, *Gone Tomorrow*, 144.

50. Hawkins, *Ethics of Waste*, 14.

51. Sterne, "Out with the Trash," 30.

52. Gay Hawkins makes this point throughout her *Ethics of Waste*.

53. Strasser, *Waste and Want*, 109.

54. Gabrys, "Media in the Dump," 162.

CONCLUSION

1. Demos Telios, "The Great Arctic Oil Rush," *Fortune Magazine*, August 8, 2007, available at

http://money.cnn.com/2007/08/07/news/international/arctic_oil.fortune/index. htm?postversion=2007080810, accessed August 20, 2010.

2. A 2009 study from the U.S. Geological Survey declares that the Arctic contains 13 percent of the world's remaining undiscovered oil and 30 percent of its natural gas (as reported in the *Globe and Mail*, May 28, 2009).

3. See Faye Ginsburg, "Atanarjuat Off-Screen: From 'Media Reservations' to the World Stage," *American Anthropologist* vol. 105 no. 4 (2003), 827–31.

4. Interview with Zacharias Kunuk conducted on October 16 and 17, 2010.

5. See Sam Hall, *Fourth World: The Heritage of the Arctic and Its Destruction* (New York: Vintage, 1988).

6. Michael Robert Evans, *The Fast Runner: Filming the Legend of Atanarjuat* (Lincoln: University of Nebraska Press, 2008), 120.

7. For critical insight into how *Nanook of the North* was also a collaborative effort, see Faye Ginsburg, "Screen Memories: Resignifying the Traditional in Indigenous Media," in *Media Worlds: Anthropology on New Terrain*, eds. Faye Ginsburg, Lias Abu-Lughold, and Brian Larkin (Berkeley: University of California Press, 2002), 39–57. Clearly Flaherty recognized that the harsh environment of the Arctic necessitated making use of the local resources, customs, and labor. Ginsburg argues that Kunuk and others have ironically picked up Flaherty's collaborative model. Or it is less ironic than practical—the climate, Inuit intuition, as well as the collaborative nature of filmmaking itself render cooperation unavoidable.

8. See William Rothman, "Filmmaker as Hunter: Robert Flaherty's Nanook of the North," in *Documenting the Documentary: Close Readings in Documentary Film*, eds. Barrie Keith Grant and Janet Sloniowski (Detroit: Wayne State University Press), 1998.

9. Dudley Andrew, "Roots of the Nomadic: Gilles Deleuaze and the Cinema of West Africa," in *The Brain Is the Screen: Deleuze and the Philosophy of Cinema*, ed. Gregory Flaxman (Minneapolis: University of Minnesota Press, 2000), 222.

10. Ibid.

11. Eric Barnouw, *Documentary: A History of the Non-Fiction Film* (Oxford: Oxford University Press, 1998), 41.

12. Joyanne Sidimus, "Zacharius Kunuk speaks with Joyanne Sidimus," available at http://www.isuma.tv/hi/en/journals-knud-rasmussen-sense-memory-and-high-definition-inuit-storytelling/zacharias-kunuk-speaks, accessed November 5, 2010.

13. Faye Ginsburg compares Igloolik Isuma with this Australian Aboriginal video production unit in remote Alice Springs in her "Screen Memories." Michelle Raheja notes too that Isuma picks up on Indigenous video practices in Africa, Latin America, and the Pacific Rim, in "Reading Nanook's Smile: Visual Sovereignty, Indigenous Revisions of Ethnography, and Atanarjuat (The Fast Runner)," *American Quarterly* 59:4 (2007), 1167.

14. See Bruce Sterling, *The Shape of Things* (Cambridge, Mass.: The MIT Press, 2005).

15. Norman Cohn, "Community-Based Filmmaking," in *Atanarjuat: The Fast Runner* (Toronto: Coach House Press and Isuma Publishing, 2002), 27.

16. Andrew, "Roots of the Nomadic," 237.

17. Raheja, "Reading Nanook's Smile,"1163.

18. Sidimus, "Zacharius Kunuk speaks with Joyanne Sidimus."

19. Evans, *The Fast Runner*, 125.

20. Raheja, "Reading Nanook's Smile," 1183, note 29. Inuit uses of the Internet: preservation and bolstering of community, language; augments their culture rather than threatens it. Media is a logical extension of traditional ways.

21. Evans, *The Fast Runner*, 126.

22. Radio interview with Ian Mauro on "Take 5," December 3, 2009. Available at http://www.isuma.tv/hi/en/inuit-knowledge-and-climate-change/ian-mauro-radio-interview-take-5, last accessed March 12, 2011.

23. See Mike Gasher, *Hollywood North: The Feature Film Industry in British Columbia* (Vancouver: University of British Columbia Press, 2002).

BIBLIOGRAPHY

Acland, Charles. *Screen Traffic: Movies, Multiplexes, and Global Culture.* Durham, N.C.: Duke University Press, 2003.

Allen, Barry. "The Ethical Artifact: On Trash." In *Trash.* Edited by John Knetchel. Cambridge, Mass.: The MIT Press, 2006. 196–213.

Alton, John. *Painting with Light.* Berkeley: University of California Press, 1995.

Andrew, Dudley. *What Cinema Is!: Bazin's Quest and Its Charge.* West Sussex: Wiley-Blackwell, 2010.

———. "Roots of the Nomadic: Gilles Deleuaze and the Cinema of West Africa." In *The Brain Is the Screen: Deleuze and the Philosophy of Cinema.* Edited by Gregory Flaxman. Minneapolis: University of Minnesota Press, 2000. 215–249.

Angilirq, Paul Apak. *Atanarjuat: The Fast Runner.* Toronto: Coach House Press and Isuma, 2002.

Appollonio, Umbro. *Futurist Manifestos.* Translated by Robert Brain. New York: Viking, 1973.

Aumont Jacques. *The Image.* London: British Film Institute, 1998.

Baker, Kenneth. "Form versus Portent: Edward Burtynsky's Endangered Landscapes." In *Manufactured Landscapes: The Photographs of Edward Burtynsky.* Edited by Lori Pauli. Ottawa: National Gallery of Canada; New Haven: Yale University Press, 2005. 40–45.

Bakhtin, M. M. *Speech Genres and Other Late Essays.* Translated by Vern W. McGee, edited by Caryl Emerson and Michael Holquist. Austin: University of Texas Press, 1986.

Barnouw, Eric. *Documentary: A History of Non-Fiction Film.* Oxford: Oxford University Press, 1974.

Barthes, Roland. *Camera Lucida: Reflections on Photography.* Translated by Richard Howard. New York: Hill and Wang, 1981.

Bascomb, Neal. *Higher: A Historic Race to the Sky and the Making of a City.* New York: Doubleday, 2003.

Bataille, Georges. *The Accursed Share. Vol. 1, Consumption.* Translated by Robert Hurley. New York: Zone Books, 1988.

———. *Visions of Excess: Selected Writings, 1927–1939.* Edited and translated by Allan Stoekl. Minneapolis: University of Minnesota Press, 1985.

Baudrillard, Jean. *The Gulf War Did Not Take Place.* Translated by Paul Patton. Bloomington: Indiana University Press, 1995.

Bauman, Zygmunt. *Liquid Life.* Cambridge: Polity, 2005.

———. *Wasted Lives: Modernity and Its Outcasts.* Cambridge: Polity, 2004.

Bazin, André. *What Is Cinema?* Vol. 1. Translated by Hugh Grey. Berkeley: University of
California Press, 1967.

Belton, John. "Glorious Technicolor, Breathtaking CinemaScope, and Stereophonic
Sound." In *Hollywood in the Age of Television.* Edited by Tino Balio. Boston: Unwin
Hyman, 1990. 185–211.

Benjamin, Walter. *Illuminations.* Edited by Hannah Arendt. Translated by Harry Zohn.
New York: Schocken Books, 1968.

Belton, John and Elizabeth Weis, editors. *Film Sound: Theory and Practice.* New York:
Columbia University Press, 1985.

Berton, John Andrew. "Film Theory for the Digital World: Connecting Old Masters to
the New Digital Cinema." *Leonardo: A Journal of the International Society for the Arts,
Science and Technology.* Supplemental Issue, vol. 3 (1990): 5–11.

Besser, Howard. "Digital Preservation of Moving Image Material?" *The Moving Image*
1:2 (2001): 236–240.

Binkley, David. "Refiguring Culture." In *Future Vision: New Technologies of the Screen.*
Edited by Philip Hayward and Tana Wollen. London: British Film Institute, 1993.
90–122.

Boler, Megan, ed. *Digital Media and Democracy: Tactics in Hard Times.* Cambridge,
Mass.: The MIT Press, 2008.

Bolter, Jay David, and Richard Grusin. *Remediation: Understanding New Media.*
Cambridge, Mass.: The MIT Press, 1999.

Bordwell, David, and Kristen Thompson. *Film Art: An Introduction.* New York: McGraw-
Hill, 2004.

———. *Film History: An Introduction.* New York: McGraw-Hill, 2003.

Bousé, Derek. "Computer Generated Images: Wildlife and Nature Films." In *Image
Ethics in the Digital Age.* Edited by Larry Gross, John Stuart Katz, and Jay Ruby.
Minneapolis: University of Minnesota Press, 2003. 217–238.

Brookey, Robert Alan. *Hollywood Gamers: Digital Convergence in the Film and Video
Game Industries.* Bloomington: Indiana University Press, 2010.

Bruce, David. *Sun Pictures: The Hill-Adamson Calotypes.* Greenwich, Conn.: New York
Graphic Society, 1974.

Burch, Noël. *Life to those Shadows.* Edited and Translated by Ben Brewster. Berkeley:
University of California Press, 1990.

Cini, Zelda, and Bob Crane. *Hollywood: Land and Legend.* Westport, Conn.: Arlington
House, 1980.

Corrigan, Timothy. *A Cinema without Walls: Movies and Culture After Vietnam.* New
Brunswick, N.J.: Rutgers University Press, 1993.

———. "Immediate History: Videotape Interventions and Narrative Film." In *The Image
in Dispute: Art and Cinema in the Age of Photography.* Edited by Dudley Andrew.
Austin: University of Texas Press, 1997. 309–331.

Crary, Jonathan. *Suspensions of Perception.* Cambridge, Mass.: The MIT Press, 1998.

Crosby, Alfred. *Children of the Sun: A History of Humanity's Unappeasable Appetite for Energy.* New York: W. W. Norton, 2006.

Davis, Mike. *Buda's Wagon: A Brief History of the Car Bomb.* London: Verso, 2007.

―――. *Ecology of Fear: Los Angeles and the Imagination of Disaster.* New York: Henry Holt, 1998.

Davis, Robert E. "The Instantaneous Worldwide Release: Coming Soon to Everyone, Everywhere." In *Transnational Cinema, The Film Reader.* Edited by Elizabeth Ezra and Terry Rowden. New York: Routledge, 2006. 73–80.

De Certeau, Michel. *The Practice of Everyday Life.* Translated by Steven Rendell. Berkeley: University of California Press, 2002.

Deibert, Ronald J., and Rafal Rohozinski. "Beyond Denial: Introducing Next-Generation Information Access Controls." In *Access Controlled: The Shaping of Power, Rights, and Rule in Cyberspace.* Edited by Ronald Deibert, John Palfrey, Rahal Rohozinski, and Jonathan Zittrain. Cambridge, Mass.: The MIT Press, 2010. 1–14.

Deleuze, Gilles, and Felix Guattari. *A Thousand Plateaus: Capitalism and Schizophrenia.* Translated by Brian Massumi. Minneapolis and London: University of Minnesota Press, 1987.

Douglas, Mary. *Purity and Danger.* London: Routledge, 1966.

Elsaesser, Thomas. "Early Film History and Multi-Media: An Archeology of Possible Futures?" In *New Media, Old Media: A History and Theory Reader.* Edited by Wendy Hui Kyong and Thomas Keenan. New York: Routledge, 2006. 13–26.

Enticknap, Leo. *Moving Image Technology: From Zoetrope to Digital.* London: Wallflower, 2005.

Epstein, Edward Jay. *The Big Picture: The New Logic of Money and Power in Hollywood.* New York: Random House, 2005.

Evans, Michael Robert. *The Fast Runner: Filming the Legend of Atanarjuat.* Lincoln: University of Nebraska Press, 2008.

Ezra, Elizabeth and Terry Rowden. "What Is Transnational Cinema?" In *Transnational Cinema: The Film Reader.* Edited by Elizabeth Ezra and Terry Rowden. New York: Routledge, 2006. 1–13.

Felder, Melissa, and Associates. "Green Practices Manual: Environmental Options for the Film-Based Industries." Available at http://greenscreentoronto.com/green_practices/. Accessed November 1, 2010.

Fischer, Hervé. *Decline of the Hollywood Empire.* Translated by Rhonda Mullins. Vancouver: Talon, 2004.

Foster, John Bellamy. *Ecology Against Capitalism.* New York: Monthly Review Press, 2002.

Foucault, Michel. *Society Must Be Defended: Lectures at the Collège de France, 1975–1976.* Translated by David Macey. New York: Picador, 2003.

Gabrys, Jennifer. "Media in the Dump." In *Trash.* Edited by John Knechtel. Cambridge, Mass.: The MIT Press, 2006. 156–165.

Gasher, Mike. *Hollywood North: The Feature Film Industry in British Columbia.* Vancouver: University of British Columbia Press, 2002.

Giannetti, Louis, and Scott Eyman. *Flashback: A Brief History of Film.* Englewood Cliffs, N.J.: Prentice Hall, 2001.

Ginsburg, Faye. "*Atanarjuat* Off-Screen: From Media Reservations to the World Stage." *American Anthropologist* 105 (2003): 827–831.

———. "Screen Memories: Resignifying the Traditional in Indigenous Media." In *Media Worlds: Anthropology on New Terrain.* Edited by Faye Ginsburg, Lisa Abu-Lughold, and Brian Larkin. Berkeley: University of California Press, 2002. 39–57.

Giroux, Henry. *Beyond the Spectacle of Terrorism: Global Uncertainty and the Challenge of the New Media.* Boulder, Colo.: Paradigm, 2006.

———. *Stormy Weather: Katrina and the Politics of Disposability.* Boulder, Colo.: Paradigm, 2006.

Govil, Nitin, John McMurria, Richard Maxwell, and Toby Miller, eds. *Global Hollywood.* London: British Film Institute, 2001.

Hall, Sam. *Fourth World: The Heritage of the Arctic and Its Destruction.* New York: Vintage, 1988.

Hawkins, Gay. *The Ethics of Waste: How We Relate to Rubbish.* Lanham, Md.: Rowman and Littlefield, 2006.

———. "Sad Chairs." In *Trash.* Edited by John Knechtel. Cambridge, Mass.: The MIT Press, 2006. 50–60.

Hardt, Michael, and Antonio Negri. *Empire.* Cambridge, Mass.: Harvard University Press, 2001.

Habib, Andre. "Ruin, Archive, and the Time of Cinema: Peter Delpeut's *Lyrical Nitrate*." *SubStance* 110 (2006): 120–139.

Harvey, David. *The Condition of Postmodernity: An Inquiry into the Origins of Cultural Change.* Oxford: Blackwell, 1990.

———. *The New Imperialism.* New York: Oxford University Press, 2005.

Henderson, Brian. "The Long Take." In *Movies and Methods: An Anthology.* Vol. 1. Edited by Bill Nichols. Berkeley: University of California Press, 1976. 313–324.

Herzog, Werner. *Herzog on Herzog.* Edited by Paul Cronin. London: Faber and Faber, 2002.

Horton, Kristan. *Dr. Strangelove, Dr. Strangelove.* Toronto: Art Gallery of York University, 2007.

Hughes, Robert. *Shock of the New.* London: Thames and Hudson, 1991.

Humphries, Richard. *Futurism.* London: Tate Gallery, 1999.

Jameson, Fredric. "Cognitive Mapping." In *Marxism and the Interpretation of Culture.* Edited by Lawrence Grossberg and Cary Nelson. Urbana: University of Illinois Press, 1988. 331–350.

Jelinski, L. W., T. E. Graedel, R. A. Laudise, D. W. McCall, and C.K.N. Patel. "Industrial Ecology: Concepts and Approaches." *Proceedings of the National Academy of Science* 89 (February 1992): 793–797.

Johnson, Chalmers. *The Sorrows of Empire: Militarism, Secrecy, and the End of the Republic.* New York: Henry Holt, 2004.

Kawin, Bruce F., and Gerald Mast. *A Short History of the Movies.* New York: Macmillan, 1992.

Kennedy, Greg. *An Ontology of Trash: The Disposable and Its Problematic Nature.* Albany:

State University of New York Press, 2007.

Klinger, Barbara. *Beyond the Multiplex: Cinema, New Technologies and the Home.* Berkeley: University of California Press, 2006.

Koselka, Hille. "Cam Era—The Contemporary Urban Panopticon." *Surveillance & Society 1:3 (2003): 292–313.*

Koszarski, Richard. *An Evening's Entertainment: The Age of the Silent Feature Picture 1915–1928. History of the American Cinema, Vol. 3.* New York: Scribner, 1990.

LeBillon, Phillipe. "Political Ecology of Resource Wars: Natural Resources and Armed Conflicts." *Political Geography* 20 (2001): 561–584.

Levin, Thomas. "Rhetoric of the Temporal Index: Surveillant Narration and the Cinema of 'Real Time.'" In *CTRL[SPACE]: Rhetorics of Surveillance from Bentham to Big Brother.* Edited by Thomas Y. Levin. Karlsruhe, Germany: ZKM Center for Art and Media; Cambridge, Mass.: The MIT Press, 2002. 578–593.

Leyda, Jay. *Kino: A History of the Russian and Soviet Film.* New York: Collier, 1973.

Lippit, Akira Mizuta. *Atomic Light (Shadow Optics).* Minneapolis: University of Minnesota Press, 2005.

MacCannell, Dean. *Empty Meeting Grounds: The Tourist Papers.* New York: Routledge, 1992.

Manovich, Lev. *Language of New Media.* Cambridge, Mass.: The MIT Press, 2001.

Marker, Chris. *La Jetée: Ciné-roman.* New York: Zone Books, 1992.

Marx, Leo. *The Machine in the Garden: Technology and the Pastoral Ideal in America.* New York: Oxford University Press, 1964.

McCarthy, Anna. *Ambient Television: Visual Culture and Public Space.* Durham, N.C.: Duke University Press, 2001.

McNeill, J. R. *Something New Under the Sun: An Environmental History of the Twentieth Century World.* New York: W.W. Norton, 2001.

Merchant, Carolyn. "Reinventing Eden: Western Culture as Recovery Narrative." In *Uncommon Ground: Rethinking the Human Place in Nature.* Edited by William Cronin. New York: W. W. Norton, 1996. 132–159.

Mirozeff, Nicholas. *Watching Babylon: The War in Iraq and Global Visual Culture.* New York: Routledge, 2005.

Mitchell, William J. *The Reconfigured Eye: Visual Truth in the Post-Photographic Era.* Cambridge, Mass.: The MIT Press, 1992.

Monaco, James. *How to Read a Film: Movies, Media, and Beyond Fourth Edition.* Oxford: Oxford University Press, 2009.

Monaco, Paul. *The Sixties: 1960–1969.* Berkeley: University of California Press, 2001.

Mumford, Lewis. *The City in History: Its Origins, Its Transformations, and Its Prospects.* New York: Harcourt Brace Jovanovich, 1961.

Murray, Timothy. *Digital Baroque: New Media Art and Cinematic Folds.* Minneapolis: University of Minnesota Press, 2008.

Murray, Stuart J. "Thanatopolitcs: Reading in Agamben a Rejoiner to Biopolitcal Life." *Communication and Critical/Cultural Studies* 5:2 (2008): 203–207.

Musser, Charles. *Thomas Edison and His Kinetographic Motion Pictures.* New Brunswick, N.J.: Rutgers University Press, 1995.

Naficy, Hamid. "Situating Accented Cinema." In *Transnational Cinema: The Film Reader.* Edited by Elizabeth Ezra and Terry Rowden. New York: Routledge, 2006. 111–130.

Nichols, Bill. "The Work of Culture in the Age of Cybernetic Systems." In *Electronic Culture: Technology and Visual Representation.* Edited by Timothy Druckrey. New York: Aperture, 1996. 123–43.

Novak, Barbara. *Nature and Culture: American Landscape and Painting 1825–1875.* New York and Oxford: Oxford University Press, 1980.

Ondaatje, Michael. *The Conversations: The Art of Editing Film.* New York: Random House, 2004.

O'Pray, Michael, ed. *Andy Warhol: Film Factory.* London: British Film Institute, 1989.

Packard, Vance. *The Waste Makers.* New York: Pocket Books, 1963.

Parks, Lisa. "Falling Apart: Electronics Salvaging and the Global Media Economy." In *Residual Media.* Edited by Charles Acland. Minneapolis: University of Minnesota Press, 2003. 32–47.

Paskal, Cleo. *Global Warring.* Toronto: Key Porter Books, 2010.

Pauli, Lori. "Seeing the Big Picture." In *Manufactured Landscapes: The Photographs of Edward Burtynsky.* Edited by Lori Pauli. Ottawa: National Gallery of Canada; New Haven: Yale University Press, 2005. 10–33.

Poggi, Christine. *Inventing Futurism: The Art and Politics of Artificial Optimism.* Princeton, N.J.: Princeton University Press, 2009.

Rabinbach, Anson. *The Human Motor: Energy, Fatigue, and the Origins of Modernity.* New York: Basic Books, 1990.

Raheja, Michelle. "Reading Nanook's Smile: Visual Sovereignty, Indigenous Revisions of Ethnography, and *Atanarjuat (The Fast Runner)."* *American Quarterly* 59:4 (2007): 1159–1185.

Rathje, William, and Cullen Murphy. *Rubbish: The Archeology of Garbage.* New York: HarperCollins, 1992.

Rayns, Tony. "Death at Work: Evolution and Entropy in Factory Films." In *Andy Warhol: Film Factory.* Edited by Michael O'Pray. London: British Film Institute, 1989. 160–166.

Rees, William E. "Ecological Footprints and Appropriated Carrying Capacity: What Urban Economics Leave Out." *Environment and Urbanization* 4:2 (1992): 121–130.

Roberts, Paul. *End Of Oil: On the Edge of a Perilous New World.* New York: Houghton Mifflin, 2005.

Rochon, Lisa. "Streets of Trash." In *Trash.* Edited by John Knetchel. Cambridge, Mass.: The MIT Press, 2006. 16–31.

Rodowick, David. *Reading the Figural, or, Philosophy after the New Media.* Durham, N.C.: Duke University Press, 2001.

———. *The Virtual Life of Film.* Oxford: Oxford University Press, 2007.

Rogers, Heather. *Gone Tomorrow: The Hidden Life of Garbage.* New York: The New Press, 2005.

————. "Message in a Bottle." In *Trash.* Edited by John Knetchel. Cambridge, Mass.: The MIT Press, 2006. 112–131.

Rombes, Daniel. *Cinema in the Digital Age.* London: Wallflower Press, 2009.

Rothman, William. "Filmmaker as Hunter: Robert Flaherty's *Nanook of the North.*" In *Documenting the Documentary: Close Readings in Documentary Film.* Edited by Barrie Keith Grant and Janet Sloniowski. Detroit: Wayne State University Press, 1998. 23–39.

Rubin, Jeff. *Why Your World Is About to Get a Whole Lot Smaller.* Toronto: Random House Canada, 2009.

Salt, Barry. *Film History and Technology: History and Analysis.* London: Starword, 1992.

Saunders, Craig. "Carbon Offsets." *Green Living* (Autumn and Winter 2007): 53–55.

Schaaf, Larry J. *William Henry Fox Talbot: Photographs from the J. Paul Getty Museum.* Edited by Weston Naef. Los Angeles: The J. Paul Getty Museum, 2002.

Schivelbusch, Wolfgang. *Disenchanted Night: The Industrialization of Light in the Nineteenth Century.* Translated by Angela Davies. Berkeley: University of California Press, 1988.

Slade, Giles. *Made to Break: Technology and Obsolescence in America.* Cambridge, Mass.: Harvard University Press, 2006.

Solnit, Rebecca. *River of Shadows: Eadweard Muybridge and the Technological West.* New York: Penguin, 2003.

Sontag, Susan. *On Photography.* New York: Farrar, Strauss and Giroux, 1973.

————. *Regarding the Pain of Others.* New York: Picador, 2003.

Standage, Tom. *The Victorian Internet: the Remarkable Story of the Telegraph and the Nineteenth Century's On-line Producers.* New York: Berkeley Books, 1998.

Sterling, Bruce. *The Shape of Things.* Cambridge, Mass.: The MIT Press, 2005.

Sterne, Jonathan. "Out with the Trash: On the Future of New Media." In *Residual Media.* Edited by Charles Acland. Minneapolis: University of Minnesota Press, 2007. 16–31.

Strand, Ginger. "Keyword: Evil." *Harper's* (March 2008): 33–34.

Strasser, Susan. *Waste and Want: A Social History of Trash.* New York: Henry Holt, 1999.

Straw, Will. "Embedded Memories." In *Residual Media.* Edited by Charles Acland. Minneapolis: University of Minnesota Press, 2007. 3–15.

Sudjic, Deyan. *The Edifice Complex.* New York: Penguin, 2005.

Taves, Brian. "The B Film: Hollywood's Other Half." In *Grand Design: Hollywood as a Modern Business Enterprise 1930–39. History of the American Cinema, Vol. 5.* Edited by Tino Balio. New York: Scribner, 1993. 313–350.

Taylor, Richard. *The Politics of the Soviet Cinema 1917–1929.* Cambridge: Cambridge University Press, 1967.

Thompson, Kristen. "The Concept of Cinematic Excess." In *Film Theory and Criticism.* Edited by Leo Braudy and Marshall Cohen. New York: Oxford University Press, 2004. 513–524.

UCLA Institute of the Environment. "Southern California Environmental Report Card 2006." Los Angeles: University of California, 2006.

UCLA Institute for the Environment. *Sustainability in the Motion Picture Industry.* Sacramento: California Integrated Waste Management Board, 2006.

Usai, Paolo Cherch. *The Death of Cinema: History, Cultural Memory and the Digital Dark Age.* London: British Film Institute, 2001.

———. *Silent Cinema: An Introduction.* London: British Film Institute, 2000.

Veblen, Thorstein. *Portable Veblen.* Edited by Max Lerner. New York: Viking, 1950.

Vertov, Dziga. *Kino-Eye: The Writings of Dziga Vertov.* Edited by Annette Michelson. Translated by Kevin O'Brian. Berkeley: University of California Press, 1983.

Virilio, Paul. *Aesthetics of Disappearance.* Translated by Philip Beitchman. Paris: Semitext(e), 1991.

———. *The Art of the Motor.* Translated by Julie Rose. Minneapolis: University of Minnesota Press, 1995.

———. *Desert Screen: War at the Speed of Light.* Translated by Michael Degener. London: Continuum, 2002.

———. *Vision Machine.* Translated by Julie Rose. Bloomington: Indiana University Press, 1994.

———. *War and Cinema: The Logistics of Perception.* Translated by Patrick Camiller. London: Verso, 1989.

Von Trier, Lars, and Thomas Vinterberg. "Dogme 95 Voe of Chastity." In *Technology and Culture: The Film Reader.* Edited by Andrew Utterson. New York: Routledge, 2005. 87–88.

Ward, Peter. *A History of Domestic Space.* Vancouver: University of British Columbia Press, 1999.

Wasson, Haidee. *Museum Movies: The Museum of Modern Art and the Birth of Art Cinema.* Berkeley: University of California Press, 2005.

Wees, William C. *Recycled Images: The Art and Politics of Found Footage Films.* New York: Anthology Film Archives, 1993.

Weisman, Alan. *The World Without Us.* New York: HarperCollins, 2007.

Whissel, Kristen. *Picturing American Modernity: Traffic, Technology, and the Silent Cinema.* Durham, N.C.: Duke University Press, 2008.

Willis, Carol. *Form Follows Finance: Skyscrapers and Skylines in New York and Chicago.* New York: Princeton Architectural Press, 1995.

Wright, Gwendolyn. *Building the Dream.* Cambridge, Mass.: The MIT Press, 1988.

Zimmerman, Patricia, and Karen L. Ishizuka, eds. *Mining Home Movies: Excavations in Histories and Memories.* Berkeley: University of California Press, 2008.

———. *States of Emergency: Documentaries, Wars, Democracies.* Minneapolis: University of Minnesota Press, 2000.

INDEX

access: culture of, 51, 61, 68, 82, 123;
democratized, 51; to material
abundance, 14; to online video, 64
Acland, Charles, 23, 59, 160
Adams, Ansel, 93
Afghanistan, 56, 65, 67, 79, 82
Alberta tar sands, 16, 65
Allakariallak, 1
Allen, Dede, 132, 135
Alpert, John, 62
Alton, John, 35, 111
Andrew, Dudley, 1, 41, 51, 106, 108, 189,
196
Andrizzi, Mauro, 83, 84
Anthropocene era, 20, 30
anthropocentricism, 21
archiving: environmental, 184; image,
181–188; responsibility for, 185
Arctic: contestation over sovereignty,
85; filmmaking in, 192, 193; securing
resources in, 16, 191
Arendt, Hannah, 81
The Arrival of a Train at La Ciotat
(Lumières, 1895), 43
Atanarjuat: The Fast Runner (Zacharias
Kunuk, 2001), 14, 193, 194, 195, 199, 201,
202
Australian Minescapes (Edward
Burtynsky, 2006), 103
Avatar (James Cameron, 2009), 26, 27,
112, 113, 160

Baghdad ER (television), 62
Baichwal, Jennifer, 13, 14, 88, 89, 92, 95,
96, 97, 98, 99, 100, 101, 102, 104, 105, 107,
115, 138, 140, 141, 190

Baker, Kenneth, 91
Bakhtin, Mikhail, 164, 165
Balla, Giacomo, 37, 38
Barthes, Roland, 36, 123, 124, 184, 185
Bataille, Georges, 14, 33, 125, 126, 135, 137,
140, 151, 156
Baudrillard, Jean, 67
Bauman, Zygmunt, 21, 22, 28, 79, 158, 159,
163, 199
Bazin, André, 4, 13, 19, 22, 23, 24, 36, 39,
40, 44, 48, 49, 122, 123, 139, 147
Bell, Gordon, 187
Belton, John, 130
Benjamin, Walter, 2, 74, 75, 118, 161, 197
Benning, James, 14
Binkley, David, 171
biomass, 30
biopolitics, 96, 155, 176, 177; of
disposability, 14
biosphere, domination, 30
Blackboards (Samira Makhmalbaf, 2000),
13, 53
Black Maria, 31, 32, 33, 34, 111
Boler, Megan, 61, 175
Bolter, Jay David, 146
Bordwell, David, 128
Bourke-White, Margaret, 95
Bousé, Derek, 113
British Petroleum (BP) oil spill, 16, 21, 28,
65, 67, 79, 80, 89, 101, 106, 107, 141, 151,
152, 153, 190
Burch, Noël, 40, 43
Burtynsky, Edward, 13, 14, 88, 89, 91, 92,
93, 94, 95, 98, 99, 100, 101, 102, 103, 104,
105, 106, 107, 115, 116, 117, 118, 140, 156
Bush, George W., 65

California Integrated Waste Management
    Board (CIWMB), 5
Calvino, Italo, 20
camera: autonomous, 48; compact, 134;
    control of, 62; control of light in, 31;
    digital, 28, 47, 49, 50, 174; disappearance
    of, 48, 49; disposability of, 49, 146;
    encroachment of, 102–109; as extractive
    instrument, 91; fueled by sight, 149;
    hand-held, 50, 79; ideology of, 91; large
    format, 102, 104, 106, 107; as mechanical
    eye, 23; mobility, 11; nocturnal
    recording by, 39, 40; open-aperture,
    122, 129, 130–134, 137; as recycling
    implement, 91; remote-controlled, 79;
    surveillance, 150, 151
Cameron, James, 26, 27, 113
capitalism: digital, 74; ideology of, 41;
    instability in, 116; internalization
    of new spaces by, 114; relationship
    between old and new, 116
carbon: absorption, 28; credits, 17;
    dating, 24; economy, 6; emissions, 27,
    51; footprint, 23, 88, 171; fossilized, 29;
    offsets, 6, 17; released, 17; sourced in
    sunlight, 30; trading, 6
carbon dioxide, 17
carbon neutral: achievement of, 17;
    cinema, 7, 9, 24, 25, 51; idealism of, 8, 9
CarbonNeutral Company, 6
Cézanne, Paul, 36, 45
Cherchi Usai, Paolo, 23, 46, 150, 173, 182
Chile, 59
China, 89; displacement of laborers in,
    101, 102; industrialization in, 96, 107;
    rare earth elements in, 173; recycling in,
    116; Three Gorges Dam project, 90, 102,
    103, 106, 108
chronophotography, 35
cinema: alternative, 3; art, 50; artificial
    geography in, 110, 111; autonomous,
    10; carbon-neutral, 2, 7, 24, 25, 51, 167,
    194, 195; composted, 157; conservation
    of, 7; democratization of, 50;
    digitization of, 3, 74; direct, 62, 129,
    142; documentary, 11; dominant, 3, 41;
    early, 34; early Soviet, 56, 57, 58, 64,
    96–100; ecological dimensions of, 8, 11,
    147; as ecological practice, 6, 7; energy
    economy and, 4, 128, 129; engagement
    with Internet, 15; environmental
    determination of, 3, 8, 88; first-person,
    166; footprint, 190; fossilization

of, 45; green, 190; home-viewing
    technology, 161; industrialization of,
    33, 128, 129; as industry of light, 111,
    112; interiorization of, 109–115; of
    limitation, 40, 170; mobility and, 53,
    84, 127; myth of total, 22; narrative, 56;
    politicization of, 50; post-cinematic, 18;
    postcolonial, 15, 50; primitive and neo-,
    43, 45, 132; proto-solar, 34; relationship
    to recycling, 164, 183; residue from,
    25; as resource, 7; secondhand, 14,
    163–170; sound, 123, 125, 128, 129, 142;
    sunless, 41, 49; sustainable, 10, 24, 53;
    transnational, 112; verité, 62; in war,
    54; and waste, 14, 182; *See also* film(s);
    images, moving
cinematic: chastity, 50; culture, 28;
    economy, 41; excess, 124, 125, 126;
    footprint, 190; history, 48; "hunger,"
    50; imagination, 35, 189; packaging,
    159, 160; primitivism, 43, 44; pyramid,
    14, 135–138; realism, 122; scarcity, 62;
    technology, 38, 49
climate change, 6
CNN, 64, 65, 78, 79, 82, 83
Cohn, Norman, 197
coltan, 59
communication: breakdown of, 53;
    digital mode of, 4; digital platforms,
    130; instant, 148; mobile, 53; open-
    access systems of, 148; paperless, 74;
    standard platforms, 175; technology, 74
computers, 28; acquisition of, 148;
    digital, 35; life expectancy of, 156, 157;
    technology, 157
consciousness: digital, 11, 12; ecological,
    7; economy, 10, 113, 167; energy, 11;
    environmental, 12; resource, 8, 58, 65,
    72, 127
Constructivism, 99
consumers: as collectivity, 7; control of
    content by, 148; of film and television,
    7; as producers, 7; of resources, 7; and
    throwaway culture, 178
consumption: conspicuous, 34, 126, 156;
    ideology of, 61; of images, 114, 160;
    limiting, 12; private film libraries and,
    160; production and, 7; resource, 12, 90;
    of technology, 174; unsustainable, 127;
    waste and, 88; in waste-maker society,
    63
Corbet, Charles, 5
Corrigan, Timothy, 47, 48, 51, 103, 160, 161

Crosby, Alfred, 30

culture/cultural: of access, 51, 61, 68, 82, 123, 175; assumptions, 91; cinematic, 28; consumer, 14, 82, 86, 164, 169; digital, 63, 146, 173, 174; of excess, 51, 61, 68, 82, 123; hydrocarbon, 26, 89, 98, 100, 104, 105, 122; indigenous, 3; industrial, 1, 13, 14, 17, 22, 29, 30, 31, 54, 67, 98, 100, 108, 114, 156; industry, 8, 88; network, 112, 193; nomadic, 41, 53; post-industrial, 13, 73, 108, 155; production, 41, 60, 100, 102, 103, 158, 159, 163, 167; theory, 10; throwaway, 119; Victorian, 92; of waste, 161; Western, 92

cyberspace: control of, 148; as dumping ground, 164, 165; as militarized zone, 148

al-Daradji, Mohamed, 56

Davis, Mike, 76, 85, 86, 87

Davis, Robert, 199

The Day After Tomorrow (Roland Emmerlich, 2004), 6

Deal, Carl, 14, 180, 181

de Certeau, Michel, 7

Deibert, Ronald, 148, 149, 175

Dekovic, Ivo, 116, 117

Deleuze, Gilles, 41, 43, 80, 84, 102, 167, 196

Demme, Jonathan, 78

Democratic Republic of Congo, 59

dialogism, 164, 165

digital: art, 80; baroque, 14, 147; camera, 28, 47, 49, 50; capitalism, 74; cinema, 12, 74; consciousness, 11; culture, 63, 146, 173, 174; delivery systems, 51; dissent, 61, 175; documentaries, 54; "dumping grounds," 59; excess, 82; immateriality, 17, 74; innovation, 13, 117; media, 60, 74; memory, 103, 108; personal video recorders, 27; phone images, 175; realities, 157; revolution, 11, 12, 190; video, 3, 55, 61

digital technology, 10, 11, 49, 61; continuous shooting in, 107; culture of access and, 61; electronic waste epidemic and, 11; environmental awareness and, 11; format migration in, 11, 63; glut of images and, 63, 173; immateriality of, 12, 17, 74; intersection with oil security, 13; problems of, 11; social withdrawal and, 7; storage capacities, 63, 82, 107, 182; sustainability and, 11

digital video, 3, 55, 61; accessibility of, 47; amateur images in, 70, 86; democratization of, 61; as dissent strategy, 84, 86; formats, 51; lightweight equipment, 62; long-take capacity, 62; pervasiveness of, 86; political possibilities of, 62; quick-release capacity, 70; synchronization, 46, 47; use by marginal groups, 47. See also films, digital

disposability, 49

Dr. Strangelove (Stanley Kubrick, 1964), 167, 168, 172

documentaries, 11, 134; antiwar, 61, 62; digital, 4, 54; disposable, 173–181; environmental, 3, 88, 89; independent, 70, 122; making visible in, 100; politicization of, 4; social, 178; subjective, 181; war, 62, 75

Dogme95 collective, 50, 51, 181; "Vow of Chastity," 50

Douglas, Mary, 153, 155, 156, 159

Dream of Light (Victor Erice, 1992), 38, 39, 40

Drew, Robert, 141, 142

DVDs, 9, 86, 105, 143, 144, 157, 160, 161, 199

Earth (Alistair Fothergill, 2007), 4

ecological: awareness, 10, 18; crises, 106, 107, 130; decline, 74; disaster, 76; footprint, 147; imaginary, 21; neutrality, 17

ecology: defining, 190; digitization and, 81; of fear, 76; of the image, 7, 158, 165; industrial, 186; natural, 29; open/closed systems in, 125; political, 66, 67; politics of, 89; preservation of environment and, 183; residual, 157, 158; sustainable, 125; of war, 67

economy: agrarian, 169; carbon, 6; civil war, 56; creative, 168; energy, 1, 4, 9, 12; fossil fuel, 18; free market, 155; general, 125; image, 88; industrial, 43, 169; moving-image, 190; of obsolescence, 12; political, 66; war, 60, 70, 72

Edison, Thomas, 31, 32, 35, 127

editing, 132; choices, 129, 142; digital, 134; end of, 141–149; formal dimensions of, 144; in the moment of shooting, 129, 134, 142; open aperture and, 132, 133; waste and, 159

Eisenstein, Sergei, 57, 123, 124, 125, 126, 128, 144, 170

electricity: centralization of supply, 9; power generation, 32; reliance on, 9

electrification: dependence on centralized sources, 33; drive for, 32; of humanity, 37

Elsaesser, Thomas, 35

Emerging Pictures, 51

Emmerlich, Roland, 6, 8

Empire (Andy Warhol, 1964), 14, 131, 132, 133, 135, 137, 138, 151

Empire State Building, 135–138

energy, 17–52; alternate, 9; caloric, 1; captured, 24; compressed, 18; consciousness, 11; consumption, 5, 66; crisis, 10; density, 31; economy, 1, 4, 9, 12; of electric light, 38; emitted, 24; excess of, 125, 137; fossil fuel, 18, 56; generation, 4; industrial, 38; intensity, 15; kinematic, 149, 150; photovoltaic, 34; production, 4, 17; radiant, 20; renewable, 143; required in cinematic process, 33, 142, 143, 147; revolution, 11; rising prices of, 9; solar, 17, 19, 30, 33, 34, 36, 137; supplies, 9, 33; and war, 73

Enticknap, Leo, 26, 105, 134, 443

environment: altruism and, 21; artificial, 110, 112; awareness of, 8; cross-border, 112, 113; decay of, 13; effect of film industry on, 4; effect of photography on, 93; industry, 111; intersection with art, 97; organization through waste elimination, 156; relationship to images, 11, 89

environmental: analytics, 10; awareness, 11; cinema, 88; collapse, 77; consciousness, 12; crises, 73; degradation, 6, 11, 85, 105; erosion, 92, 113; ideology, 53; materiality, 74; perceptions, 76; politics, 8, 55, 74, 105, 127; pollution, 4; refugees, 66; revolution, 12; rhetoric, 34, 55, 158; stability, 55; symbiosis, 24; toxicity, 59; warfare, 76

environmentalism: filmmaking and, 7; non-anthropocentric, 21; politics of, 89

Erice, Victor, 38, 39

Evans, Michael Robert, 201

excess, 14, 121–154; accumulation of, 125, 126; as aesthetic term, 123, 129; cinematic, 123, 124, 125, 126; culture of, 61, 68, 82, 123; digital, 82; display of, 138;

economic, 14; of energy, 137; expended, 14; impoverishment and, 151; industrial, 14; measure of, 123–130; shot length and, 122; as surplus of energy, 125; value of, 123; viral cinema and, 61

extraction, 88–120; connection to sites of, 100; dependency on, 90; filmmaking as process of, 98; residue of, 115; sites of, 115

Ezra, Elizabeth, 199

film and television industry: Canadian, 17; dominant, 6, 7; energy consumption in, 5, 15; environmental achievements of, 5; environmental footprint of, 4, 5; expansion of, 130, 131; greenhouse gases and, 5; power of, 34; redefinition of, 130–134

filmmaking: amateur, 150; availability of light and, 39; big-budget, 34; biophysical world and, 7, 8; compilation, 166; in crisis conditions, 53; democratization of, 131; early Soviet, 56, 57, 58, 64, 96–100; environmentalism and, 7; environmentally benign, 51; found footage, 166; as gleaning, 166; independent, 134; as industry, 9; low-budget, 128; mobility and, 33; observational, 129, 142; outsourcing of, 71; post-cinematic, 46; as process of extraction, 98; resource-neutral, 13; studio, 33; sustainable, 6, 7; technology, 88; without film, 56

film(s): agitation, 124; archiving, 118; as artifact, 45; average shot length, 128, 129; carbon-neutral, 5, 17; consumption and, 160; Edison and, 31; editing, 97, 98; ephemeral life of, 24–28; experimental, 11, 13; history, 1; independent, 51; industry, 1; as language, 40, 41; light source in, 35; nature, 113; private libraries, 160; production, 10; self-reflexive, 90; short, 31; silent, 33; stocks, 118; theory, 10, 22; use of close-ups, 99; without film, 45, 46

films, analog, 68, 89; archiving of, 118; conflicts with digital, 90; continuities with digital, 106; decay of, 182; difference from digital, 18, 19, 51; disappearance of, 24; ecological dimensions of 12; long take in, 122; materiality and, 60; point-and-shoot practice, 127; preservation of, 14, 24, 105, 183; price comparison to digital, 174; proponents of, 139; recording rate, 70; regeneration of, 183; replication of, 63; resource war and, 55, 56; retention capabilities of 171; surface deterioration of, 171, 172; sustainability, 190; sustainability differences with digital, 105; technical capabilities of, 69; threat to health from, 104, 105; use of stationary camera in, 69, 72. *See also* cinema; image, moving

films, digital, 89; accuracy of, 19; ascendance of, 50; conflicts with analog, 90; computer-generated spaces in, 14; continuities with analog, 106; delivery systems of, 51; democratization of, 14; difference from analog, 51; ecological dimensions 12; ephemerality of, 14; indexicality and, 170; interfaces required for, 171; light and, 19; lightweight flexibility in, 103; materiality and, 60; memory in, 103; multicamera strategies in, 69, 72; obsolescence and, 63; recording rate, 70; replicating, 63; resource war and, 55, 56; retention rates of, 64; sustainability, 190; sustainability differences with analog, 105; technical capabilities of, 69; use of toxins in production of, 105. *See also* cinema; digital video

Flaherty, Robert, 1, 2, 14, 190, 191, 192, 196, 197, 202

Ford, Henry, 112

fossil fuel, 28–35; economy, 18; energy, 18, 56; moving-image technology and, 23; security, 66

Foucault, Michel, 96, 155, 176

Friedrich, Caspar David, 91

Futurism, 37, 38

Gabrys, Jennifer, 157, 158, 173, 187

garbage: evolution of, 157; exposure of, 155; image value of, 115–120; instability of category of, 169; potential use-value of, 118; preservation, 119; representation of, 14; resentment of, 118; wrapping and, 159. *See also* waste

geography: artificial, 110, 111; construction of, 109; creating, 96–102; creative, 97, 98; disappearance of, 113; mobility and, 112; rural/urban, 169

Geyrhalter, Nikolaus, 100, 101

Ghana, 59

Ginsburg, Faye, 174, 203

Giroux, Henry, 67, 68, 84, 178

The Gleaners and I (Agnès Varda, 2000), 14, 163, 169, 178

gleaning, 14, 164, 186, 187; agrarian, 169; as metaphor, 165; pre- to post-industrial, 169

globalization, 7, 100

global warming, 2, 3, 76; profitability in, 6

Godard, Jean-Luc, 50

Google Energy, 171

Gore, Al, 3, 4

Gorin, Jean-Pierre, 24, 25

greenhouse gas emissions, 5, 6, 17

Green Screen, 17, 58, 168; Green Practices Manual, 34

Griffith, D. W., 57, 108, 170

Grusin, Richard, 146

Guattari, Felix, 41, 80, 84, 167, 196

Gulf War syndrome, 78

Gursky, Andreas, 117

Haneke, Michael, 41, 42, 43, 45, 49, 50

Hardt, Michael, 114, 116

Harper, Stephan, 191, 192

Harvey, David, 105, 106, 140

Hawkins, Gay, 117, 118, 155, 185, 186

Haystacks (Monet painting, 1891), 35

HDNetworks, 51

Heath, Stephen, 123, 124

Herzog, Werner, 13, 55, 68, 69, 72, 77, 79, 82, 83

heteroglossia, 164

Hitchcock, Alfred, 121

Holdte, Michael Ned, 140

Holocene era, 20, 30

Homeland Security, 75

Horton, Kristan, 167, 169, 170, 172, 186

Hughes, Robert, 36

humanism, 21

Hurricane Katrina, 14, 178, 179, 180, 181

hurricanes, 76

ideology: anthropocentric, 21; of the camera, 91; capitalist, 41; of consumption, 61; dominant, 41, 61; environmental, 53, 178; of the ephemeral, 22; of excess, 58; of expendability, 14; hydrocarbon, 12; of landscape, 99; of obsolescence, 63; throwaway, 158; of war, 54; Western, 21

image: abundance of, 70; archiving,
    181–188; closed-circuit, 150, 151;
    derivation of, 99; devaluation of,
    170–173; ecologizing, 74; ecology of, 7,
    165, 172; glut of, 63; incursive, 102–109;
    live-feed, 82; materiality of, 168;
    mechanically reproduced, 28, 30, 169;
    meteorological, 75–80; overexposure
    of, 170–173; ownership of, 48; private
    consumption, 114; rationed, 56–64;
    as resource, 2, 64–68, 81–83, 127, 190;
    sunless, 40–49; trajectory, 91–102
images, cinematic: analog difference
    from digital, 18, 19 13, 24; history of,
    30; impact of war on, 55; as material
    resource, 13; as mummification of time
    (Bazin), 24; resource-based, 29. See also
    films, analog
images, digital: accessibility of, 19, 26; bit-
    rot and, 63; capture of, 20; continuous
    format migration, 26, 63; conversion
    by digital processor, 19; disposable,
    63; ecological difference from analog,
    18, glut of, 146; proliferation of,
    110; readability, 26; renewability in,
    116; replication of, 116, 171; support
    systems for, 19; time-sensitivity of, 119;
    unmanageable volume of, 151; viral, 86.
    See also films, digital
images, fossil, 13, 17, 18, 28–35, 45
images, moving: atomization of,
    161; auditory, 2; as carbon-heavy
    industry, 17; conflation with
    resources, 71; consumers of, 7;
    creating, 25; as cultural necessity,
    10; deep focus in, 122, 123; delivery
    of, 81; democratization of, 2; digital
    production, 54; environment and, 5,
    8, 11; ephemeral nature of, 24–28, 14;
    film-within-film, 96; gluttony of, 14;
    mass production, 31; material life of, 12,
    157; militarization of, 54, 67; mobility
    of, 58; natural resources and, 1, 13 189;
    oil supply and, 2, 3; open-aperture
    aesthetic in, 130–134; overconsumption
    of, 28; political associations and, 124,
    125; preservation of, 24–28; private
    consumption of, 162; residues of,
    157; unwanted, 14; use of electronic
    manipulation in, 47; value of, 85 See
    also cinema; films, analog; films, digital
images, photographic, 30, 35, 45, 88;
    impermanence of, 117; industrial, 95;

overexposure to, 158; proliferation of,
    119; relationship to environment, 89,
    93. See also photography
images, resource, 2, 54, 64–68, 81–85; as
    discursive category, 55; oil politics in,
    54
imagination, 100; cinematic, 35, 44, 189;
    colonial, 21; database, 113; hydrocarbon,
    12, 127; ideal form of cinema in, 44;
    industrial, 37; mechanistic, 126, 127
An Inconvenient Truth (Davis
    Guggenheim, 2006), 3, 4, 6
industrial: civilization, 18; culture, 1,
    14, 17, 22, 29, 30, 31, 54, 98, 100, 108,
    114, 156; development, 92; ecology,
    186; excess, 14; expansion, 89, 125;
    image making, 118; landscape, 94, 95;
    overconsumption, 22; residue, 88
industrialization: of cinema, 128, 129;
    digital technology and, 4; landscape
    photography and, 92; momentum of,
    92; processes of, 89; nature and, 92;
    unidirectionality of, 125; of vision, 39
industry: as consumer of resources, 7;
    culture of, 8, 13, 88; electrification of, 9;
    environment and, 111; environmental
    footprint of, 5; exposition of, 99; film,
    1; filmmaking as, 9; humanization of,
    101, 102; planned obsolescence in, 60, 63
information: conveyance of, 73, 157;
    expendability of, 74, 75; planned
    obsolescence of, 74; production, 73;
    reception of, 81; as resource, 73–75;
    storage of, 75; value of, 74, 75
infrastructure: of analog/digital images,
    19; carbon-neutral, 17; danger from
    decline in, 20; durability of, 27; erosion
    of, 20; of hydrocarbon culture, 26;
    industrial, 85, 100; of oil distribution,
    64; subterranean, 109
Internet: access, 79; broadcasting, 65;
    cinema and, 15, 149; delivery of images,
    51, 64; empowerment of decentered
    groups by, 148; political security and,
    148, 149; video distribution on, 3
Intolerance (D. W. Griffith, 1916), 57
Inuit Broadcasting Corporation, 193, 194
Iraq, 53, 56, 60, 61, 62, 65, 67, 70, 71, 75,
    79, 83, 85
Iraqi Short Films (Mauro Andrizzi, 2009),
    83
Israel, 78

Isuma Productions, 3, 130, 192, 193, 194, 196

Ivan the Terrible (Sergei Eisenstein, 1944), 124

The Jacket (John Maybury, 2005), 78
Jackson, William Henry, 91, 92
Jameson, Fredric, 100
Japan, high-tech industry in, 173
Jarhead (Sam Mendes, 2005), 78, 81
La Jetée (Chris Marker, 1962), 13, 24, 25, 26, 41, 44, 45, 46, 49, 110
Johnson, Chalmers, 65, 75
Justin.tv, 181, 182

Kan, Justin, 181, 182, 188
Keaggy, Bill, 118
kino-eye, 24, 98, 144, 150
Kino-Eye (Dziga Vertov, 1924), 100, 101
Klinger, Barbara, 114, 131, 161, 183
Kubrick, Stanley, 167
Kuleshov, Lev, 13, 57, 97, 98
Kunuk, Zacharias, 14, 51, 52, 130, 174, 192, 193, 194, 195, 196, 197, 199, 200, 202
Kurds, 53

landscape, 13; anthropogenic, 89; artificial, 89; commodification of, 115; constructed, 138; disposable, 115–120; formulation of, 90, 91; human perspective and, 99; idealized, 113; ideology of, 99; industrial, 94, 95; manufactured, 90, 98; natural, 14, 138; nature turned into, 91; photography, 92, 93, 94, 102, 113; technological interaction with, 98; urban, 87
language: cinematic, 124; erosion of, 197; maintenance of, 53, 54; new media, 113; secondhand, 164
Laporte, Dominique, 155
Lebanon, 78
LeBillon, Phillipe, 66
Lee, Spike, 14, 178, 179, 180, 181
Lefebvre, Henri, 109
Lessin, Tia, 14, 180, 181
Lessons of Darkness (Werner Herzog, 1992), 13, 55, 68, 69, 70, 77, 79, 83, 84, 87
Levin, Thomas, 145
light: Arctic, 32, 33, 39; artificial, 9, 33, 39, 40, 42; availability of, 35, 40, 45; cinema as industry of, 111, 112; digital, 50–52; in East/West Coast studios, 110, 111, 112; electric, 38; fossilization of, 13;

45; Hollywood studio developments in, 32; incandescent, 127; industrialized systems, 41; into latent images, 19; natural, 11, 18, 32, 34, 45; painting and, 35, 36; photo processing and, 31; in post-apocalyptic world, 42, 43; relationship to cinema technology, 28, 34–35; solar, 18, 24; sourcing of, 18; study of, 38; sunlight, 28, 29, 30
Lippit, Akira Mizuta, 43
Little Dieter Needs to Fly (Werner Herzog, 1997), 72
long take, 108, 138; aesthetic dimensions, 127; in analog film, 122; analysis of, 127; and battery limitations, 121; in British Petroleum (BP) oil spill, 152; decrease in use of, 132, 133; digital video capacity for, 62; in early cinema, 128; execution of, 121; measurement of, 121; prevalence of, 14; problems with, 62; theorizing, 150; unedited, 145; Warhol and, 14
Lucas, George, 26
Lumière brothers, 35, 43

MacCannell, Dean, 93
Makhmalbaf, Samira, 13, 53
Malraux, André, 161
The Manchurian Candidate (Jonathan Demme, 2004), 78
Manovich, Lev, 23, 35, 106, 107, 108, 113, 145
Manufactured Landscapes (Jennifer Baichwal, 2006), 13, 88, 89, 90, 92, 94, 95, 96, 101, 104, 107, 108, 110
Man with a Movie Camera (Dziga Vertov, 1929), 23, 39, 40, 96, 97, 98, 99, 113, 119, 143, 149
Marey, Jules-Étienne, 31, 35, 38, 143
Marker, Chris, 13, 24, 25, 26, 27, 41, 44, 45, 46, 48, 49, 50, 52, 110
Markey, Ed, 152, 153
Marx, Leo, 93, 127
Mauro, Tim, 201, 202
Maybury, John, 78
Maysles, Albert, 141
Maysles, David, 141
McCarthy, Anna, 81
media: digital, 60, 74; digital war coverage, 54; innovation, 23; interactive arts, 108; light-based, 40, 42; new, 23, 106, 113, 145, 156, 193; old, 23; saturation, 82; technology, 175
Méliès, Georges, 48

Mendes, Sam, 78
meteorology, 75–80
Mettler, Peter, 89, 107
MGM Studios, 111
military: -industrial complex, 66;
    motorization of, 54; privatization of, 71
mimesis, 36
minimalism, 172
Mirzoeff, Nicholas, 81
Mitchell, William J., 18, 20
modernity: artificial light and, 9; artistic
    domain, 36; doubt and, 36; electricity
    and, 9; infinity and, 21; industrial
    imagination in, 37; liquid, 22, 28;
    landscape and, 94
Monaco, Paul, 132, 142
Monbiot, George, 65
Monet, Claude, 35, 36
montage: disappearance of, 142; meaning
    and, 123; modernist, 145; principles, 143;
    spatial, 113; temporal, 113; universalizing
    equality of, 113; virtuosity, 133
Moore, Gordon, 157
Morton, Timothy, 21
Moscow State Film School, 57, 97
motion: captured, 37; of electric light, 38;
    illusion of, 44
Motion Picture Patents Company
    (MPPC), 32
Mumford, Lewis, 92, 109, 110, 159
Murdoch, Rupert, 2, 27, 114
Murray, Stuart, 177
Murray, Timothy, 80, 108, 147
Museum of Modern Art film library, 118
Musser, Charles, 61
Muybridge, Eadweard, 31, 35, 92, 93, 94,
    110
My Best Fiend (Werner Herzog, 1999), 72

Naficy, Hamid, 50
Nanook of the North (Robert Flaherty,
    1922), 14, 189, 196
Napoleon (Abel Gance, 1927), 34
narrative, 11; of biosphere modification,
    30; creative economy and, 168; digital
    cinema's transformation of, 108;
    dominant systems of, 51; of industrial
    capital, 140; new media, 145; reality-
    driven, 108; recovery, 92
National Film Registry, 183
national parks, 93, 94
nature: cinematic technology and,

89; industrial culture's perceptions
    of, 91, 92; films, 113; harnessing, 22;
    human interaction with, 88; image's
    reproduction of, 29; subordination of,
    54, 127
Negri, Antonio, 114, 116
Netflix, 9, 81, 114, 163, 184
News Corporation, 27, 114–115
Nichols, Bill, 81
nomad(ic): culture, 41, 196; "war
    machine," 41, 167
Nunavut Territory, 191

obsolescence, planned, 60, 63
oil: danger in procurement of, 16, 79;
    density, 30; distribution infrastructure,
    64; effect of end of, 2; fires, 68, 83;
    imperial expansion and, 66; movement
    of, 65; production, 78; scarcity of, 16;
    securing sources of, 65; security, 76,
    80; war over, 13, 54, 84. See also British
    Petroleum (BP) oil spill
O'Neill, Matthew, 62
online video, and open access, 64
Operation Nanook, 191
Ostergaard, Anders, 175
Our Daily Bread (Nikolaus Geyrhalter,
    2006), 100–102

Packard, Vance, 63
Pan-American Exposition (Buffalo,
    1901), 126, 127
Parks, Lisa, 59, 116, 117
Paskal, Cleo, 66
Pauli, Lori, 102
Peckinpah, Sam, 133
Penn, Arthur, 132
photodynamism, 38
photography: analog, 89;
    anthropocentric assumptions in, 29;
    calotype, 29; cultural production of,
    29; daguerreotype, 29; environmental
    abuse and, 93; government surveys
    and, 93; image trajectory and, 91–102;
    industrial landscape, 95; landscape,
    92, 93, 94, 102, 113; as light, 31; negative
    processing in, 29; nineteenth-century,
    13, 14, 91, 92, 93, 102; physical effects
    on environment, 93. See also images,
    photographic
Planet in Focus Film and Video Festival,
    10, 170

political: activism, 55, 56; culture, 66;
    discourse, 10, 144, 175; ecology, 66, 67;
    economy, 66; organization, 2
politics: aestheticized, 2; of disposability,
    62; of ecology, 3, 89; environmental, 8,
    55, 74, 105, 127; of environmentalism,
    89; identity, 193; material, 59, 60;
    resource, 1, 59; social, 161; of speed, 73
pollution: air, 5; environmental, 4;
    e-waste, 60; generation of, 4; toxicity
    of, 22
portapaks, 47, 134
post-humanism, 24
Post-Impressionism, 36
post-traumatic stress disorder, 78
power: displays of as moving image, 54;
    geopolitical, 66; hydroelectric, 127; of
    information, 73; mechanized forms of,
    37; natural mechanisms of, 42; state, 155
Prelinger, Megan and Rick, 15, 184, 185
Prelinger Library, 184, 186, 187
primitivism, 9, 41, 42, 170, 172; cinematic,
    43, 44
production: cultural, 41, 60, 100, 102, 103,
    158, 159, 163, 167; emissions generated
    by, 6; energy, 4, 17; film, 10; hazardous
    waste, 5, 6; information, 73; mass, 2;
    materiality and, 124; movie, 32; oil, 78;
    sustainable levels of, 10

Qapirangajuq! (Zacharias Kunuk, 2010),
    200, 201

Raheja, Michelle, 199
Rasheed, Oday, 56, 58
realism, 37; cinematic, 22, 122;
    dependence on artifice, 123; dividing
    with abstraction, 39; pure, 22
recycling, 58; cinema, 183; communities,
    157; crude practices of, 116; danger
    in, 156, 157, 164; economy of, 169; of
    film sets, 6; harmful effects of, 115;
    relationship to cinema, 164
reflexivity, 40, 46, 72
representation: cinematic, 13; crises of,
    39; digitally-rendered, 108; institutional
    mode of, 41; illumination and, 40;
    linguistic, 60; mechanization of, 39;
    modes of, 18, 106; naturalization of, 45;
    of nature, 92; pictorial, 36; primitive
    mode of, 41
Research in Motion, 175

residue/residual: in carbon-neutral
    practice, 25; of cinema, 17;
    cinematic footprints, 8; ecology, 157;
    infrastructural, 26; nontransient, 22; of
    sites of extraction, 115; of unmediated
    vision, 150
resource image, 2, 64–68, 81–83, 127, 190
resource(s), 53–87; abuse, 11; access to,
    121; artificial, 66; availability of, 2, 67;
    cinema as, 7; consciousness, 8, 58, 65,
    72; constructed, 60; consumption, 12,
    84, 90, 122; conversion into technology,
    121; dependence of film and
    television industry on, 5; depletion,
    6; deprivation, 13; destruction in
    war, 77; extracted, 60, 125; human,
    59; image as, 67, 71; information as,
    73–75; limitation, 167; manufactured,
    60, 67; material, 13, 55; patterns of
    consumption, 4, 7, 8; political economy
    of, 66; politics, 59; procurement, 55;
    rationing of, 60; scarcity of, 45, 57;
    transformation into moving images, 12;
    unnatural, 66
ReUse People (nonprofit organization), 6
Rivers Roberts, Kimberly, 180
Rochon, Lisa, 159
Rodowick, David, 19, 60, 80, 146
Rogers, Heather, 159, 185
Rombes, Daniel, 63, 105, 108
Rubin, Jeff, 9
Ruhr (James Benning, 2009), 14, 138–141
Russell, David O., 78
Russian Ark (Alexander Sokurov, 2002),
    14, 121, 128, 143, 144, 146, 147

Saba and the Rhino's Secret (Saba
    Douglas-Hamilton, 2006), 8, 9
Saddam Hussein, 58
Salt, Barry, 121, 129, 132
Sans Soleil (Chris Marker, 1982), 13, 24,
    25, 45, 46, 48
Schivelbusch, Wolfgang, 40
Scranton, Deborah, 13, 55, 68, 70, 71, 81,
    82
Second Cinema, 15
security: fossil fuel, 66; invasion, 148, 149;
    meteorological threat to, 75–80; oil, 13,
    76, 80
Selig Polyscope Company, 32
Selim, Ali, 5, 190
Shohat, Ella, 199

Slade, Giles, 59, 60, 156, 157

social: action, 109; activism, 47; alienation, 117; change, 176; class, 3; conduct, 42; equality, 55; institutions, 53; justice, 47, 175; politics, 161; rituals, 153; withdrawal, 7

society: eco-conscious, 100; effect of end of oil on, 2; extraction-based, 109; post-industrial, 149; surveillance in, 149; waste-maker, 63

Sokurov, Alexander, 14, 121, 128, 143, 146, 148

Solnit, Rebecca, 92, 94

Sontag, Susan, 7, 63, 96, 115, 158, 163, 172, 173, 174, 175, 176, 177, 179

"Southern California Environmental Report Card" (UCLA), 4

space: cinematic, 114; compression of, 140; indulgence in, 122; industrialized 113; interiorized cinematic, 109–115; produced through social action, 109

speed: ideologies of, 87; as surfeit of mobility, 86

Stanford, Leland, 94

Stapledon, Olaf, 20

Sterling, Bruce, 197, 200, 201

Sterne, Jonathan, 119, 126, 157, 171, 186

Still Life (Jia Zhang-ke, 2006), 14, 90, 101, 102, 103, 106, 108, 109

storage: of digital images, 63, 82, 107; hard media of, 63

storytelling, 197, 198; art of, 21; capacity for, 74; cinematic means of, 127

Strasser, Susan, 119, 125, 156, 169

Street Light (Giacomo Balla, 1909), 37, 38

Stuth, Thomas, 117

"Sustainability in the Motion Picture Industry" (UCLA), 5

Svilova, Elizaveta, 135

Sweet Land (Ali Selim, 2005), 5, 6

Syriana (Stephan Gaghan, 2005), 34

Talbot, William Fox, 29

tantalum, 59

Tarigsuk Video Center, 193

technology: analog, 89; cinematic, 15, 23, 28, 38, 49, 88, 89; climate-friendly, 6; communication, 74; computer, 157; consumption of, 174; digital, 18, 23, 49, 61; disposable, 63, 73; halfway principle in, 171; home-viewing, 161; image-based, 67; image-making, 97, 118; media, 156, 175; military, 54;

obsolescence and, 63; residual life of, 59; rupture with past, 23; sound, 129; videotape, 47, 48

terrorism, urban, 85

theory: critical flicker fusion, 44; cultural, 10; disappearance of, 133; economic, 156; of economic excess, 14; film, 10, 22; of general economy, 125, 140; media, 18; of mining, 109; of the mummy complex, 13; new media, 106; structuralist film, 123

Thompson, Kristin, 123, 125, 128

Three Kings (David O. Russell, 1999), 78

time: compression of, 140; embalming of, 23; geological, 30; indulgence in, 122; limits of, 23; mapping, 25; militarized, 76; photo exposure, 29; preservation of, 25; shrinking scope of, 105

Time of the Wolf (Michael Haneke, 2003), 41, 42

transience, 21, 22

Trouble the Water (Deal and Lessin, 2008), 14, 180

Turco, Richard, 5

Turner, Ted, 183

Twentieth Century Fox, 27

UCLA Institute of the Environment, 4

Underexposure (Oday Rasheed, 2005), 58

UN Intergovernmental Panel on Climate Change (IPCC), 3, 163

urbanization, 96, 176

Valéry, Paul, 2

Varda, Agnès, 14, 163, 164, 166, 167, 169, 170, 175, 177, 178, 181, 186, 187

VCRs, 48, 51, 160, 161

Veblen, Thorstein, 126, 156

Vertov, Dziga, 23, 24, 39, 48, 49, 57, 86, 96, 97, 98, 100, 113, 132, 142, 143, 144, 149

video: analog, 134; file sharing, 148; streaming, 148, 162; user-generated, 182. *See also* digital video

Virilio, Paul, 24, 48, 49, 54, 55, 67, 72, 73, 77, 82, 84, 133, 149, 181

vision: as excess, 149–154; industrialization of, 39; persistence of, 44; physical residue of, 150

von Trier, Lars, 50, 51

War and Cinema (Paul Virilio), 54

warfare: ambient, 76, 82; automobile as weapon in, 85, 86; casualties in, 78;

cinematic scarcity and, 61; cultural tolerance for, 84; digitally imaged, 54, 60, 61, 84, 86; documentaries, 62; ecologized, 75–80; economy of, 60, 70, 72; energy, 73; environmental, 55, 76; image rations and, 56–64; industrialized, 67, 74; mobility and, 85; as perceptual liquidity, 21, 28, 79; political ecology of, 67; post-industrial, 73, 77; resource, 59, 67, 85, 87; visual combustion of, 83–87; waste in, 87

Warhol, Andy, 14, 129, 131, 132, 133, 134, 136, 138, 141, 146, 150, 151, 181

Warner Bros. Studio, 6, 129

War Tapes (Deborah Scranton, 2006), 13, 55, 68, 71, 82, 83

waste, 155–188; archiving as management of, 181–188; conspicuous, 126, 156; consumption and, 88; creation of, 158; culture of, 161; cycles of, 55; denaturalization of, 153; disposal, 155; editing and, 159; electronic, 14, 26, 60, 74, 126, 156, 157; ethics of, 185; excessive production of, 156; gleaning, 164; hazardous, 5, 6; human, 96, 176; industrially converted, 125; long take and, 14; packaging and, 158–163; in post-industrial culture, 95; productive forms of, 125; recycling, 115, 116; reducing production of, 88; social position and, 155; solid, 157; toxicity of, 22; transformed nature of, 119; in war, 87; wealth located in, 126. *See also* garbage

Watkins, Carleton, 91, 92, 93

Weisman, Alan, 20, 27

Weston, Charles, 94

When the Levees Broke (Spike Lee, 2006), 14, 178, 179

Whissel, Kristin, 126

The Wild Bunch (Sam Peckinpah, 1969), 133

Wiseman, Frederick, 141

Worely, Steve, 152

Workman, Chuck, 131

YouTube, 54, 64, 82, 122, 153

Zhang-ke, Jia, 14, 90, 101, 102, 103, 106, 108

Zimmerman, Patricia, 80, 150, 184

Zuse, Konrad, 35

ABOUT THE AUTHOR

NADIA BOZAK holds a PhD in Comparative Literature from the University of Toronto. She is also a published novelist.

CPSIA information can be obtained at www.ICGtesting.com
Printed in the USA
BVOW040552111011

273274BV00002B/1/P